AF539434

PEOPLES AND ENVIRONMENT IN INDIA

PEOPLES AND ENVIRONMENT IN INDIA

Editor

K.K. Misra

Department of Anthropology
Central University of Hyderabad
Hyderabad (A.P.)

M.L.K. Murty

Centre for Regional Studies
Central University of Hyderabad
Hyderabad

2001

DISCOVERY PUBLISHING HOUSE

NEW DELHI–110 002

First Published-2001

ISBN 81-7141-586-5

Published by
DISCOVERY PUBLISHING HOUSE
4831/24, Ansari Road, Prahlad Street,
Darya Ganj, New Delhi-110002 (India)
Phone: 3279245 • Fax: 91-11-3253475

Printed at :
ARORA OFFSET PRESS
DELHI-110092

ACKNOWLEDGEMENT

This volume had an unusually long period of gestation for many unforeseen reasons. We record our deep sense of gratitude to the esteemed contributors to this volume for their patience and forbearance during this period of gestation. We are grateful to our colleagues at the University of Hyderabad for their direct or indirect help in shaping this volume. Our sincere thanks are due to Mr Tilak Wasan, Proprietor, M/s Discovery Publishing House, New Delhi, for his enthusiasm in publishing this volume.

K.K.M
M.L.K.M

Contents

Contributors

Dr Ajay K. Awasthi teaches at the School of Environmental Biology, A.P.S. University, Rewa, Madhya Pradesh.

Dr Baba Mishra is Senior Lecturer, Government College, Bhawanipatna, Orissa.

Dr Surendra Kumar Mishra is Research Officer, CINI, Calcutta, West Bengal.

Dr Kamal K. Misra is Reader, Department of Anthropology, Central University of Hyderabad, Hyderabad, Andhra Pradesh.

Dr Pradeep Mohanty is Senior Research Fellow, Department of Archaeology, Deccan College, Pune, Maharashtra.

Professor M. L. K. Murty is the Head of the Centre for Regional Studies and Director of Centre for Folk Culture Studies, Central University of Hyderabad, Hyderabad, Andhra Pradesh.

Dr S. B. Ota is Superintending Archaeologist, Eastern Region, Calcutta, West Bengal.

Dr Shanti Pappu is an archaeologist from the Department of Archaeology, Deccan College, Pune, Maharashtra.

Dr R. R. Prasad is Director, Centre for Social Development, National Institute of Rural Development, Rajendranagar, Hyderabad, Andhra Pradesh.

Dr D. Hanumantha Rao is Deputy Director, National Institute of Nutrition, Hyderabad, Andhra Pradesh.

Professor N. Sudhakar Rao is Professor of Sociology, Assam University, Silchar, Assam.

Dr P. Venkata Rao is Reader, Department of Anthropology, Central University of Hyderabad, Hyderabad, Andhra Pradesh.

Dr V. N. V. K. Sastry is Joint Secretary, Gurukulam (APTWREIS), Government of Andhra Pradesh, T.S. Bhavan, Masab Tank, Hyderabad, Andhra Pradesh.

Dr Gopal S. Singh is Director, Centre for Sustainable Environment and Heritage (SHE), R.K.Puram, New Delhi.

Dr Rajiv K. Sinha is associated with Indira Gandhi Centre for Environmental Studies, University of Jaipur, Rajasthan.

Ms Shweta Sinha is Research Scholar, Indira Gandhi Centre for Environmental Studies, University of Jaipur, Rajasthan.

Adhikary, Ashim Kumar (1991), The Tribal World View: Changing Perspective. In B.Saraswati (ed) *Tribal Thought and Culture*, New Delhi: Concept Publishing Co.

1

Environment, Culture and Development in India: A Thematic Introduction

M.L.K.Murty and *K.K.Misra*

INTRODUCTION

Ever since its emergence about three million years ago, the humankind has adapted and is adapting to varied environmental zones in the tropical and temperate regions of the world. Adaptability, which is a fundamental property of the living beings, is the mechanism of self-regulation and perpetuation, which in the case of human species is achieved through culture. Therefore, culture is defined as man's extrasomatic adaptation—it is an adaptive system which integrates a society with its environment and other socio-cultural systems (Binford 1972; Leone 1977 etc.). Environment, it is important to note, has two components, i.e. the physical and the social. The former comprises of the natural resources and resource zones, while the latter consists of social groups that share the environment with different adaptive strategies (e.g. hunting-foraging, swidden agriculture, agro-pastoralism etc.).

Culture, which is the key variable in mediating between the social groups and their respective environments, is explicated as a system. Cultural system, in other words, is an adaptive system with three major elements (viewed as subsystems), which are technological, sociological, and ideological. A systemic approach to the study of cultures, either of the past or the present, endeavours at an interpretation of the historicity of cultures (cultural history), the adaptive mechanisms (cultural processes), and cultural change (the causative factors that trigger a change from one mode to the other) in a spatial-temporal framework.

In the Indian subcontinent, the archaeological record indicates an occupational history in varied physiographic zones right from the prehistoric period (the Palaeolithic, Mesolithic and Neolithic-Chalcolithic cultures). In the contemporary times, numerous traditional/Indigenous/native communities (termed as Scheduled Tribes) having their own lifestyles and cultures, adapted to different environments. Historical sources reveal that such traditional social groups were in continuous interaction with the 'state' level societies from the early historic times; and they played a vital role, especially from the medieval period, in the affairs of the respective 'states' (such as supplying armies, production and distribution, revenue collection and sustenance of state's frontiers). In the historical period, the habitats of these traditional social groups were articulated with the kings' realm, and the former acknowledged the latter's sovereignty, though they were not total subjugates (Misra, in this volume; Murty 1993, 1994; Roy 1972; Sinha 1987 etc.). Ever since the colonial times, the traditional societies have been undergoing considerable stress as a result of regulations limiting their access to the conventional resource bases in their original habitats (Gadgil and Guha 1992; Guha 1983; Rangarajan 1996 etc.). Even during the post-colonial period, despite the implementation of several programmes for their development and to bring them into the mainstream, the indigenous social groups remain alienated (Misra 1995). In such a kind of scenario, this volume aims to present insights, contextualising Indian examples, into the interrelationships of the environment vis-à-vis culture (from the prehistoric past to the modern times) and situate (the role of) 'development' as an euphemism for appropriation (i.e. commercial exploitation) of the environments, which are the habitats of many traditional societies, by the 'state'. Therefore, the chapters in this volume encompass environment, culture and development in their varied dimensions.

Environment and Palaeo-ecology

The prehistoric record in different parts of the subcontinent shows that varied ecosystems, such as, hilly and forested, riverine and coastal zones etc. were inhabited by the humans from the Stone Age times. What is important is that the Stone Age occurrences, more often than not, are contiguous with the habitats of the ethnographic present. This indicates that the (palaeo) environments, which supported prehistoric populations, though are degraded today, provide optimal resources for the sustenance of the traditional societies. Such evidences drive home the point that the occupational history and man-land associations have a continuum from the past to the present. With the induction of early farming village economies (the Neolithic-Chalcolithic cultures) into these areas from about third millennium BC, the forested ecotones (the pristine hunting-gathering and swidden agricultural ecosystems) were manipulated for settled village life, farming, and pastoralism. This resulted not only in the alteration of physiographic zones, but also gave rise to a contact situation in which the traditional forest based cultures and agro-pastoral groups were drawn into the fold of each other, and in the formation of new cultural landscapes. This process continued with increasing intensity in the historic period. Thus the human adaptability to the changing physical and social environment is imprinted in the life worlds of the contemporary traditional social groups. Three chapters in this volume corroborate the man-environment relationships during the prehistoric period and trace their continuity from the past till the present.

Pappu's paper (Chapter 2) in this volume examines the ways in which environment can be used in Palaeolithic archaeology, drawing on a study conducted in the Kortallayar basin of Tamil Nadu in South India. This paper lucidly examines how environment, encompassing both natural elements (physical geography, climate, biota etc.) and cultural elements (archaeological sites and present cultural geography), influences the formation of sites, hominid settlements and subsistence strategies. Pappu observes that some sites display evidences of preliminary core trimming, considerable artifact diversity and higher proportion of debitage to tools. Since debitage does not commensurate with the number of finished tools, Pappu suggests that the period is characterized by considerable movement of tools across the landscape. In some other sites she finds high artifact density, which indicates periodic aggregation of several groups. As some sites show reoccupation, most probably there was moderate degree of mobility with territoriality. In some sites the sterile layers of clayey-silt are indicative of palaeo-pond situation during the late-Pleistocene period. Presence of specialized tools like blades, points and Levallois flakes indicates a subsistence strategy aimed at risk reduction, energy conservation, and capturing an unreliable game that needed to be exploited in a short time span.

Distribution of tool types as revealed in Pappu's paper suggests that while generalized subsistence strategies were common to the sites close to the source of raw material, lowland sites were marked by relatively specialized strategies, possibly due to the distribution of large and small game. Seasonal mobility of the people was evidently clear with movement towards hills during the wet seasons, and returning back to the sites near ponds/rivers in dry seasons. Reoccupation of the sites over a long period suggests a stable resource base in Kortallayar basin during the late-Pleistocene period.

The interface between ecology and prehistoric culture has been vividly brought forth in another paper in this volume by Mohanty and Mishra (Chapter 3), supported by their findings from the Kalahandi district of Orissa. Data from their fieldwork between 1966 and 1999 in the district reveal co-occurrence of heavy implements and microliths, suggesting their functional relationships with the environment (*cf.* Murty in this volume). Occurrence of heavy duty tools like uni- and bi-facial choppers, core scrappers, celts and ring-stones in the dense forest of Kalahandi region reveals Mesolithic adaptations to the tropical deciduous woodlands. Going by the edge-angle analysis of these tools, it is possible to infer their use for forest clearance, wood working, and food procurement and processing.

In yet another paper, Murty (Chapter 4) corroborates the nature of ecological adaptations in the Eastern Ghats from the prehistoric times to the present. The Eastern Ghats or more appropriately called the 'Eastern Hills' (Spate *etal.* 1992) is a group of disjointed hill ranges, extending from South Orissa to Tamil Nadu through Andhra Pradesh, in the interior of the southeast coast of the Bay of Bengal. Murty has evaluated the archaeological evidences to suggest that many different physiographic zones in the Eastern Ghats were extensively inhabited by the prehistoric populations from the Palaeolithic to the Neolithic-Chalcolithic periods. Given the varied nature of environmental opportunities in the region, it is but natural that the social groups living there have evolved an array of adaptive strategies, encompassing hunting-gathering, fishing-hunting-gathering, swidden agriculture, agro-pastoralism etc. This chapter unfolds the continuity of different adaptive strategies by the people over a period of time, based on archaeological findings as well as by reconstructing the past from the ethnographic present.

The Lower Palaeolithic period in the Eastern Ghats, ranging approximately between 400,000 years and 69,000 years (on the basis of relative dating), is characterized by the Acheulian technocomplex with handaxes and clevers, choppers, scrapers on core and flake, utilized and simple flakes, core dressing flakes, cores and debitage. Similarly, the Middle Palaeolithic period, ranging approximately from 32000 BC to 23000 BC, is associated with a flake tool technocomplex, dominated by scrapers and points on flakes. But what seems remarkable is the amorphous nature of this flake tool technocomplex, despite being made on rocks of the cryptocrystalline family. This is suggestive of the fact that it is more an accessory for the manufacture of a variety of wood and bone implements for hunting, trapping, snaring and analogus activities. The Upper Palaeolithic in the Eastern Ghats, which ranged approximately between 23460 BC and 8090 BC, is marked by two lithic co-traditions: (a) the blade-tool technocomplex and (b) the blade-and-burin technocomplex. While the former is dispersed in upland/open woodland/grassland ecotones, the latter is characteristic of the occupations in the riverine/scrub woodland/ thorny thicket zones, thus comprehending the geographical vastness of the Eastern Ghats. The blade-and-burin lithic co-tradition, considering the rich artifactual yield at these occupations, suggests demographic concentration and sedentarism. This co-tradition is also marked by a tendency towards microlithisation of artifacts, which is the hallmark of the succeeding Mesolithic period.

The Mesolithic period in the Eastern Ghats consists of a microlithic technocomplex, amorphous tools and heavy-duty implements. The heavy-duty component in the Mesolithic of Godavari valley and southern Eastern Ghats functionally suggests its use in the clearance of forests for settlements, and possibly for incipient cultivation. Murty's findings further reinforce the suggestions made by Mohanty and Mishra in case of prehistoric Kalahandi (Chapter 3 in this volume), regarding the functional importance of heavy implements in dense forested habitats. Presence of bits of charcoal in the Mesolithic sites is indicative of the use of fire for landscape management and hunting, which continues even today among the swidden cultivators in this region. Based on archaeological evidences, it could be suggested that the subsistence pattern during the Palaeolithic and Mesolithic periods was to a very large extent geared to group hunting, chasing and stalking the game, use of a variety of traps, use of bows and arrows, fire-aided hunting, and opportunistic scavanging.

The Neolithic-Chalcolithic period in this region, ranging from ca. 3000 BC to 1000 BC, was characterized by sedentary villages with permanent and semi-permanent structures, ground and polished tools made on hard rocks, long and thin blade artifacts made on cryptocrystalline rocks, hand-made and wheel-thrown potteries, and millet farming, combined with herdsman husbandry (predominantly cattle and sheep/goat to some extent). It is quite evident in all the preceding discussions that the prehistoric populations in India had devised appropriate adaptive strategies for different ecotones to ensure their livelihood.

Human Survival and Biodiversity

It is established that from the prehistoric times till the modern, hominids have been constantly interacting with their respective local environments. But the nature of this interaction has registered a dramatic change over a period of time. With the beginning of the Neolitihic period, marked by domestication of plants and animals, the interaction of human groups with their environment began to take varied forms. Technological development was coupled with demographic expansion of the human populations from historic to modern times, resulting in increasing intensity of natural resource exploitation. Degradation of tropical forest ecosystems, which was hitherto preserving rich genetic diversity of plants, animals and micro-organisms, became the cause of shrinking biodiversity. This phenomenon was a major issue at the Rio Earth Summit in Brazil in 1992.

After the Rio Summit, a dangerous trend of 'eco-imperialism' has unfortunately sneaked into the world politics, despite having a rather late realization to preserve the biodiversity for posterity. Sinha and Sinha (Chapter 5) in this volume observe that the whole world has been divided into two blocks on the issue of biodiversity preservation. One of them is the block of 'biological powers' of the North with rich biotechnology and poor biodiversity. The other is the block of the developing countries of the world with rich biodiversity in their valuable tropical rainforests, but poor in biotechnology compared to the North. The North wants the South to agree to some of the biodiversity-rich forests as common property for protection on behalf of the humanity in general, which is not acceptable to the South.

This kind of imposition of the North very much goes against the UN Convention on Biological Diversity, to which majority of the nations, both from the North and the South, are signatories. Article 8 of the Convention states: 'Each contracting party shall, as far as possible and as appropriate . . . (j) Subject to its national legislation, respect, preserve and maintain knowledge, innovations and practices of indigenous and local communities embodying traditional lifestyles relevant for the conservation and sustainable use of biological diversity and promote their wider application with the approval and involvement of the holders of such knowledge, innovations and practices and encourage equitable sharing of the benefits arising from the utilization of such knowledge, innovations, and practices . . . .' Therefore, Sinha and Sinha aptly observe that sharing of knowledge for greater human welfare is always desirable, but due recognition needs to be given to those who have been at the vanguard of not only preserving the biodiversity, but also possess rich and classified knowledge about food and herbal medicine. The traditonal knowledge systems, which are informal and site-specific such as that held by the indigenous peoples, or as those codified in the Ayurveda or *Charak Samhita* or other traditional texts (Kothari 1994), need to be given their due place by keeping these away from the purview of patenting. In fact, the Provisions of the Panchayats (Extension to the Scheduled Areas) Act 1996 in India make it rather explicit by stating: 'the Legislature of a State shall not make any law under (Part IX) of the Constitution, which is inconsistent with any of the following features, namely — (a) a State legislation on the Panchayats that may be made shall be in consonance with the customary law, social and religious practices and traditional management practices of community resources . . . (d) every Gram Sabha shall be competent to safeguard and preserve the traditions and customs of the people, their cultural identity, community resources and the customary mode of dispute resolution'. Given this background, Sinha and Sinha hope for a more meaningful interaction between the possessors of the traditional knowledge about rich genetic resources, such as the indigenous peoples and the scientists. There is an optimism that while the former could provide their knowledge of biodiversity, the latter could experiment upon the efficacy of this knowledge, and their mutual efforts could go a long way in the welfare of the larger humanity.

Minor Forest Produce and Forest Communities

India has about 68 million tribal people (referred to here as indigenous peoples) constituting about 8.08 per cent of the total Indian population, according to the Census of 1991. Most of them have been forest dwellers for millennia. Their material as well as emotional relationship with the forest is an undeniable truth. They have devised a culture of sustainable forest management with balanced human and ecological needs and ensured intra- and inter-generational equity (Minority Rights International 1999: 19). But the current spree of mindless deforestation by the mafia has left them homeless and without resources to support. Although the tribals are the direct victims of deforestation, the state is also a looser as a consequence of this. Prasad in his paper in this volume (Chapter 7) observes that the forestry sector in India with 23 per cent of coverage of the total geographical area provides an employment of 2.3 million man-years. Out of this, nearly 1.6 million man-years are generated by Minor Forest Produce (MFP). The potentiality of MFP in employment generation has been perpetually undermined by the planners, and is eventually given a back seat in the planning process. Prasad suggests a number of factors that need immediate attention of the administration in order to bring MFP-related tribal economies to fruition in India.

Prasad raises the most contentious issue of the ownership of MFP and pleads that despite all their labour and skill, the tribals are treated as mere collectors of MFP and not its owners. Forest policies in modern India have retained most of the strategic colonial characters, empowering the state to own everything that is there in the forest by de-recognising centuries of interaction between the tribals and the forest. He suggests, therefore, that MFP should be exempted from the payment of royalty, purchase tax and sales tax levied by the state. This could be accomplished, he believes, by the establishment of tribal MFP co-operatives and by de-nationalising MFP. His optimism is that MFP can contribute positively to revive the present state of shattered tribal economy, if primary processing and value addition is planned at the source, the forest itself. Among other measures, Prasad emphasizes on the involvement of Panchayati Raj institutions, in the light of the provisions of the 73rd Amendment of the Indian Constitution, in regeneration and management of MFP trade in the tribal regions of India.

As a specific example of tribal dependence on MFP, Ota and Mishra in their paper in this volume (Chapter 8) bring to the fore the importance of mohua (*Madhuca indica*) in the socio-cultural and economic life of the tribes of central India. Both the flowers and seeds of mohua are of high economic importance to the tribals. Despite variations in the soil conditions and the climate in which mohua tree grows, it has high annual yield capacity. The tribes use mohua both for domestic consumption as well as for the market outside. The fresh succulent mohua flowers are an important item of their food. The mohua flowers are sun-dried and stored for consumption in the lean seasons. Dried mohua flowers are used for the preparation of alcoholic beverages by the tribes throughout the year. Its tender green fruits are cooked as curries. The ripe fruits are eaten raw. Oil is extracted from the kernel of the mohua seed, and in lean seasons soup is prepared from the kernels by crushing them into powders. Mohua flowers, fruits and kernels fetch good money in the market. From cultural point of view, the tribes like the Kuttia Kondh of Orissa formulate their annual life cycle in terms of mohua seasons. They follow strict taboos, so that mature and productive mohua trees are not cut. Mohua is so much integrated into the tribal culture that the anthropologists name the cultures of some tribes in this region as 'mohua cultures'. Although mohua constitutes the lifeline of the tribes in this region, social forestry projects hardly consider it worthwhile to plant a few species of mohua in the forest that would economically benefit the collectors of MFP. Development in the tribal regions is, therefore, possible by regenerating the environment with the local endemic flora.

Forest Communities and Forest Policies

The history of relationships between humankind and the forest is complex and ambivalent. While it is sometimes considered as a refuge, a home and a source of raw materials, at some other times, it has been feared and attacked as an obstacle to development and welfare. Over the generations, the forests have been meeting the food, medicine and other material needs of the tribals. But at the same time, intimate social relationships between tribes and forest is exemplary, as revealed in many metaphors they use to express this varied human-forest relationships (Bird-David 1993). These relationships have a direct bearing on the sustainable management of the forests, which balanced human and ecological needs and ensured intra- and inter-generational equity (Minority Rights Group International 1999: 19). But now when the forest coverage in India is declining at an alarming rate, although it is generally recognized as a national crisis, the hardest hit are the tribals, for their very subsistence is crucially linked to the forest. The state of impoverishment and marginalization of the tribal communities in India may be largely attributed to lopsided forest policies from the colonial times till the present.

According to a very moderate estimate, there are still about 5,000 forest villages inhabited by about 48 million forest dwellers in India. These forest dwellers almost entirely depend upon the forest for their requirements of food, fodder, fuel, fibres, timber and a large variety of forest produces, including leaves, seeds, gums, waxes, dyes, resins, bamboo, canes, grasses, honey etc. (Arora 1994: 691). But from the later part of the British administration in India till the recent times, state intervention in the forestry sector has confounded the forest dwellers, as their customary rights over the forest and forest produce have been withdrawn. Attempts have been and are being made to keep the forests free from these communities in order to preserve it for posterity. This kind of approach depriving the tribals of their rights in their own habitats is totally misconstrued. In this volume, Misra's paper (Chapter 6) precisely deals with the history of forest legislation in India and its impact on the tribes that inhabit the forest regions.

It is observed by Misra that till the end of the 18th century, the British administration did not pay much attention to the tropical forests and the tribals living in these regions in India. Only when the British government realized that the Indian forest resources are essential for ship building, iron smelting and tanning in Britain, the Malabar forest was declared as reserve in 1806. Subsequently, Indian Forest Acts of 1865, 1878 and 1927 were promulgated to ensure firm grip of the state over the forests. These Acts, in fact, sought to establish that the customary use of forests by these communities was based not on 'right' but on 'privilege' granted to them by the local rulers (Guha 1983: 1884). Even after the Independence, the National Forest Policies of 1952 and 1988 further consolidated the state monopoly over the forest, reducing the status of the tribals from owners of the forest to mere collectors of MFPs (*cf.* Prasad in this volume). Further, The Wild Life (Protection) Act of 1972, The Forest (Conservation) Act of 1988 and The Wild Life (Protection) Amendment Act of 1991 etc. portrayed the image of the forest communities more as forest criminals than as ordinary, peace-loving natives of this country.

When there was a clash of values between the tribals and the government, with regard to the withdrawal of customary rights over the forests, the state of tribal agony against the atrocious Forest Department was expressed in no uncertain terms. Misra draws attention to many local rebellions that invariably turned violent in the tribal dominated areas against the increasing state interventions in forest management. He cites some selected examples from among the Saora of the Ganjam Agency, the Rampa uprisings, among the Gond and Kolam of Adilabad, and the Bastar rebellion at Jagdalpur etc.

Having realized the growing frustration of the forest communities, the revised forest policy of 1988 made a provision for joint participation in the protection and development of forests (JFM), from which the people derive some benefits in the form of fuel wood, fodder and small timber. Accordingly, the forest protection committees have been formed in many states. But Misra observes that even JFM ensures unlimited opportunities to the state to intervene more aggressively in the management of forests. But if the Panchyats or the *Gram Sabha* (village committees) in the country become more assertive, particularly in the light of the powers given to them by the 73rd Amendment of the Constitution, there could be some advantages to the people by their participation in Joint Forest Management.

In two other papers in this volume, Sastry and Venkata Rao have taken the example of Andhra Pradesh to examine the relationship between the forest and the tribals. Andhra Pradesh has been the abode of 33 Scheduled Tribes with a population of 41.99 lakh, as per the census of 1991. Out of these 33 communities, 30 have been living in forested and hilly areas. Sastry in his paper (Chapter 12) delineates how the tribes establish mythical relationships with trees, animals, hillocks, streams etc. that reinforces the tribal worldview. In an excellent analysis of the origin myths of many north-east Indian tribes, Saraswati endorses this proposition (Saraswati 1991), which has been further strengthened by the observations of Adhikary among the Oraons of central India (Adhikary 1991). Sastry observes that the tribal customary laws facilitated ownership rights over areas under their jurisdiction individually and collectively. For example, hill slopes for swidden agriculture are treated as common property of the community, including trees, fruits, small game etc., which are available within the jurisdiction of the village. But individual cultivators in the village enjoy usufruct rights over the hill slopes as long as they cultivated them.

Sastry observes that the customary rights of the tribals over the forests and forest produces were gradually withdrawn with the introduction of forest regulations by the British government in India. When the tribes of Andhra Pradesh protested against the government policy in 1873 in the Godavari Agency and again in 1940 in Adilabad, there was some concern shown by the state government in 1967 by granting free collection of wood to the tribals for domestic use. This included construction of houses and manufacture of agricultural implements. Further, utilizing the provisions of the Vth Schedule of the Constitution of India, government of Andhra Pradesh has regulated the trading of MFP and *beedi* (country cigar) leaves. By two separate regulations, the GCC and FDC of Andhra Pradesh have been given monopoly rights of trading with MFP and *beedi* leaves respectively, in order to prevent the exploitation of the tribals from the local traders and moneylenders. While the tribes in the state were heaving a sigh of relief by the success of these regulations, the promulgation of The Wild Life (Protection) Act of 1972 and Forest (Conservation) Act of 1980 has again mounted their problems to a new peak.

Sastry observes that with the declaration of the tribal inhabited regions as sanctuaries, the tribals have lost their traditional food reserves. When most of the tribes hunt small game and catch birds, the Wild Life (Protection) Act regarded the use of traps, snares, bows and arrows illegal. Restrictions were imposed on the movement of the tribals and their livestock in the sanctuary areas. Implementation of development programmes came to a grinding halt, as the Act did not permit infrastructure development, including even the construction of school buildings, permanent houses, access roads etc. in the sanctuary areas. The Forest (Conservation) Act put a blanket ban on the conversion of any forestland for non-forest use. This has created confusion among the tribals, who were cultivating land in forest areas for generations. As a result, there were law and order problems in the districts of

Adilabad, Warangal and Mahaboobnagar. But the situation is gradually improving in the tribal areas after the implementation of JFM programmes in Andhra Pradesh since 1993, as a follow up of the National Forest Policy of 1988. *Vana Samrakshna Samithis* (*VSS* or forest protection committees) have been set up in the tribal areas to give them an opportunity to participate in the management and development of the local forests. The 73rd Amendment of the Constitution and its extension to the Scheduled Areas might bring some hope to the tribals, but the elections to Gram Panchayats in these areas are yet to be held in Andhra Pradesh. With all these problems notwithstanding, Sastry ends up with an optimism that education and training to the tribals might improve the situation, and the future would only tell whether the tribes of Andhra Pradesh would regain their paradise that was already lost.

Venkata Rao in his paper (Chapter 11) in this volume discusses how commercial aspects of forestry during the Nizam's administration dominated the Hyderabad Forest Act of 1355 *fasili*. Massive conversion of forest land into agricultural land between 1938 and 1940; laying of railway lines between Hyderabad and Palwoncha in 1874, Kazipet and Balarsha in 1929 and Visakhapatnam and Raipur in 1960; construction of massive irrigation projects; mining and industrial complexes etc. opened up tribal areas to the non-tribal migrants. The tribals had to lose their land without proportional compensatory benefits. Displacement and related displeasure were rampant in the tribal areas of Andhra Pradesh. When the tribes in the state were an impoverished lot without gainful employment, there was mass rehabilitation of Sri Lankan repatriates in the Visakhapatnam Agency during 1972-78, closing whatever little opportunities the former had in seeking temporary jobs in the government sponsored coffee plantations in the region. Over and above, stringent forest laws snatched away the tribal rights over the forests and MFP. and considered their presence within and in the vicinity of forested regions dangerous to the conservation of forests and wild life. The tribals failed to adopt to small scale and cottage industry sectors despite the government assurance of loans and subsidies.

Given the state of multiple alienation of the tribals in Andhra Pradesh, Venkata Rao finally contends that the state intervention has left the tribals homeless and exposed them to the ruthless exploitation by the economic processes of the dominant non-tribal society. Tribal development programmes drifted away from forest development activities, despite the suggestion of various expert committees to develop tribes and forests together, as one is incomplete without the other. This has led to a perversion in the tribal mind that since forests no more belong to them and there is no viable alternative of living, there need not be any hesitation in cutting the forests, as subsistence is paramount. Therefore, Venkata Rao advocates that before it is too late, the tribes should be taken into confidence, their traditional rights over the forests be restored, and they be made a part of the development process.

Environment, Health and Nutrition

The humans are constrained by certain nutritional requirements as part of the evolutionary history. Like other tropical, tree dwelling primates, they need carbohydrates present in vegetable material and share with other primates the incapacity to synthesize their own vitamin C. Therefore, humans are required the intake of certain dietary constituents in quantities not always easy to obtain in nature (Stini 1975: 64); and lack of these leads to nutritional deficiencies. The tribes in India almost entirely depend upon the environment around them for their dietary requirements, and the quality of environment is an indicator of their nutritional status. Besides their food requirements, their settlement pattern, system of land ownership, production and distribution of crops, demography and socio-cultural life etc. are also influenced by the environmental condition. The combined effect of all these factors on the health and nutritional status of the tribes is evidently clear. But since all the tribal communities do not share similar ecology, differential pattern of nutritional status is easily recognisable.

Hanumantha Rao's paper in this volume (Chapter 13) presents the comparative results of the nutritional surveys among some selected tribal groups in India. The survey included clinical examination of nutritional deficiency signs and anthropometric measurements. It was based on dietary intake studies of the whole family and individual members carried out by 24 Hours Recall Method. The information on the quality of the environment and other related factors were collected by extensively interviewing the people and direct observation by the researcher.

For a comparative study of nutritional status among the tribes inhabiting different ecological conditions, Hanumantha Rao had undertaken the survey among 4 different tribal groups and compared them with the general rural populations in India. His selected groups included the Onge of Little Andaman (hunter-gatherers), the Chenchu of the Nallamalai forest of Andhra Pradesh (forest dependent and subsistence agriculturists), the Savara of Srikakulam district of Andhra Pradesh (swidden cultivators), and the Nicobarese of the Nicobar Islands (settled agriculturists and commercial horticulturists).

Hanumantha Rao observes that severe forms of protein-calorie malnutrition, vitamin-A and B-complex deficiencies are highest among the Chenchu children than that of the Nicobarese. The latter are taller and heavier than not only the Chenchu children but also other tribal and non-tribal groups. Other indicators like body weight deficiency, type and duration of malnutrition, calorie intake etc. indicate that the Nicobarese children enjoy a better nutritional status compared to their Chenchu or Savara counterparts. Hanumantha Rao believes that this could be attributed to the ecological conditions in the Nicobar islands. As a cohesive group, he observes that the Nicobarese inhabit a relatively isolated and not much exploited ecological condition. Along with the exploitation of marine and forest resources, they also harvest coconut and arecanut as commercial crops. Consumption of fish, honey, roots, tubers, pork etc. balance their nutritional requirements and hence, they are the least malnourished. Since they are educationally better than the other groups, they appropriately make use of government health facilities to maintain their health status. The study concludes by stating that the overall role of ecology largely influences the socio-economic condition of a population, on which the subsistence and nutritional statuses depend.

Ethnoecology and Management of Tribal Ecosystem

Although anthropological literature now is replete with many serious studies on ethnobotany (Conklin 1957; Berlin *etal.* 1974 etc.) and ethnozoology (Ellen 1978), which constitute ethnoecology, there has not been much research on ethnoecology *per se.* Ethnoecology here refers to the holistic study of specific ethnic communities in their environment. Awasthi in his paper in this volume (Chapter 10) comprehends that an ethnoecological system has primarily two components. The first one is the ethnic community itself, and the second one is the environmental system with which the ethnic community interacts. This interacting environmental system has a biotic resource component *viz.* systems of agriculture, nature of the forest, livestock etc., and an abiotic resource component consisting of the physical and urban resource systems. When the ethnic population interacts with its resource systems, the ethnoecosystem is maintained by a state of homeostasis, effected by the flow of energy and material relations, and thereby presents a structure which is exclusively its own with characteristic functions.

Awasthi has studied the ethnoecosystem among the Gond of Madhya Pradesh by selecting two agricultural villages, two forest villages, and two urban-dependent villages. A questionnaire based survey was undertaken in these six villages to collect first-hand data on population, livestock, socio-economic status, sex ratio, educational status, utilization of forest and animal resources etc., and to carry out the human component analysis and resource dependence analysis for forest-dependent and urban-dependent villages.

The conclusions drawn from this study highlight the socio-ecological dynamics of an ethnic community and suggest steps for the protection of the ethnic groups and managing the sustainability of natural environments. Awasthi suggests that the Gonds living within and in the vicinity of the forests should be given agricultural land and adequate farming facilities to make them economically stable. If this does not happen, there could be more and more encroachment of forestlands for agricultural purposes, thus leading to large-scale deforestation. Further, since the ethnic system indicates a drift towards more and more urban-oriented consumerist culture, there is a danger of exerting tremendous pressure on the forest resources, as the sale of forest produce could only provide them the required buying power of urban goods. These might lead to the breaking down of forest ethnic systems due to growing economic instability of the forest communities and increased utilization pressure on the forest, unless a proper planning is done at the right time.

Local Culture and Indigenous Environmental Knowledge

In many modernization theories of development, tradition is often projected as opposed to modernity, and even an obstacle to the process of development. But after the failure of decades of development from above, development anthropological thinking is drifting towards the potentiality of indigenous environmental knowledge and grass-root participation in environmental management (Apffel-Marglin and Marglin 1990; Brokensha *etal.* 1980). Although there is an inevitable skepticism in complete acceptance of the local environmental knowledge as alternative adaptive strategies (Ellen 1998; Milton 1996), there is not even an iota of doubt that this knowledge has a sustainable value that has passed the test of time (Misra 1998; Ramakrishnan 1992). Two probing and well-documented papers in this volume highlight the importance of indigenous knowledge in sustainability in two diverse ecological zones of India.

Anthropological researches on diversified human settlement pattern have hypothesized that shifting of human habitat begins with the impending pressure from the growing human and livestock populations. When the land for cultivation and grazing falls short of the requirement of a community, there is a tendency to move in search of greener pastures. In the new habitat, the culture of a community gets adapted so as to utilize the locally available resources to meet the demands of survival. That is how even the higher altitudes of the Himalayas extending upto 2700m. are populated by the humans and their livestock. In the cold deserts of Lahaul, Spiti, Kinnaur and Pooh etc., people continue to live successfully by utilizing the available natural resources with the help of their indigenous knowledge, which is revised, refined and consolidated with the passage of time.

In his paper in this volume, Singh (Chapter 9) corroborates

an ethnographic account of the social, cultural and economic dimensions of the hill societies inhabiting the Himachal Himalaya and their continued interaction with the environment for many generations. Singh observes that despite a great deal of ethnic and cultural diversity, these hill people or the *pahari*, as they are popularly known, depend upon hill farming, supplemented by the income from the livestock and forest resources. Because of constraints like inaccessibility, marginality, ecological fragility, environmental heterogeneity, and economic backwardness, the hill people have evolved a complex farming system with the parsimony of utilizing the available resources for their subsistence. Their way of deriving organic manure, indigenous knowledge of leaving stubble and weeds for the purpose of recycling of the biomass, cooperative farm labour and use of locally designed tools and agricultural implements ensure long term sustainability of this fragile ecosystem. These *pahari* populations also largely depend upon cows, bullocks, buffaloes, sheep, goats, mules, ponies and yak for their livelihood. What is worth noticing is their indigenous practice of yak breeding, as yak, a native breed of Tibet, is well known for its ability to withstand low temperature, snowy conditions, and survivability on coarse fodder. Further, the indigenous knowledge of the population in the utilization of the locally available wild plants as fodder, fuel, manure, food and medicine is remarkable. Particularly, the role of the women in recognizing and collecting these species is very important in this harsh environment. In order to adapt to this environment, Singh notes that the *pahari* practice of fraternal polyandry is a well-calculated adaptive measure, for it prevents overpopulation, division of the meagre family land holdings, and maintains family unity, as the children belong to the common parents. On the whole, Singh maintains that the *pahari* indigenous knowledge is so well adapted to the environment that the latter still sustains the population and livestock there despite natural growth and large-scale migration.

In another paper, Sudhakar Rao (Chapter 14) analyses environmental changes and the resultant adaptive strategies by the local population in the mica mining belt of coastal Andhra Pradesh. His focus of discussion is the district of Nellore, which has been experiencing inconsistent rainfall for the last several decades. Consequently, the local people, who are primarily agriculturists, are the victims of either flood or drought. The agriculturists in the southern part of the district face an additional problem because of mica mining. Mica mining began in Nellore district way back in 1887. Since mica mining goes well over 200 feet below the ground, underground water flows into these mines. As a result, the people find it very difficult to dig wells for irrigation, which must have to be deeper than 200 feet. This has created a situation of environmental hazard for the local people.

To cope up with this environmental change, Sudhakar Rao notes some adaptive strategies by the local people. First, there is a shift from the cultivation of paddy to tobacco, tamarind and soap nut, which apparently require less water. Another viable strategy adopted by the people is to reduce the area of cultivation, but practice intensive cultivation in small areas. Probably, the most remarkable strategy adopted by the farmers here is to allow a wild thorny bush, locally known as *thumma chettu* (*Acacia* sp.), which could sustain the drought conditions and at the same time does not die either during flood or by torrential rain. These wild bushes have multiple uses. These are used for fencing, as firewood, and in making charcoal. In this area, charcoal is an essential fuel in small towns as an alternate source of energy to firewood, kerosene and cooking gas. So the farmers earn a part of their livelihood from these wild bushes without investing any amount, except leaving the land fallow, which is otherwise unproductive without water. Sudhakar Rao maintains that the local people perceive the environmental change and devise suitable alternate strategies to cope up with it, so that the ecosystem still remains sustainable.

CONCLUSION

The history of organic evolution reminds us quite unambiguously that the environment, which once nurtured the birth and development of many organisms, had turned hostile to wipe them out from the face of the earth. But the extant human species, *Homo sapiens sapiens,* have managed to survive the vicissitudes of the environment by devising appropriate adaptive strategies. Since humans are a part of the natural world, their survival and development depends on maintaining harmonious relationships with the nature, rather than destroying it. All the papers in this volume aim at exploring the critical balance between the humans and their environment from prehistoric times to the present. Despite population and other pressures, tribal and forest communities have been striving to keep this balance through their cultural practices. But the worth of indigenous environmental knowledge has faded before the greedy clutches of industrialization and technologization of our culture. All the chapters in this volume debate different facets of environmental degradation, irrespective of the various governmental policies for sustainable management!

REFERENCES

Adhikary, Ashim Kumar (1991). The Tribal World View: Changing Perspective. In B.Saraswati (ed) *Tribal Thought and Culture*, New Delhi: Concept Publishing Co.

Altman, I. and M. Chemers (1984), *Culture and Environment*, Monterey: Brooks Publishing Co.

Apffel-Marglin, F. and S. Marglin (eds) (1990), *Dominating Knowledge: Development, Culture and Resistance*, Oxford: Clarendon Press.

Arora, Dolly (1994), From State Regulation to People's Participation: Case of Forest Management in India, *Economic and Political Weekly*, March 19, 691-697.

Berlin, Brent, D. Breedlove and P.Raven (1974), *Principles of Tzeltal Plant Classification: An Introduction to Botanical Ethnography of Mayan-speaking People of the Highland Chiapas*, New York: Academic Press.

Binford, Lewis R. (ed) (1977), *For Theory Building in Archaeology*, New York: Academic Press.

Bird-David (1993), Tribal Metaphorization of Human-Nature Relatedness: A Comparative Analysis, In Kay Milton (ed) *Environmentalism: The View from Anthropology*, London: Routledge.

Brokensha, D., D.Warrwn, O. Werner (eds) (1980), *Indigenous Knowledge Systems and Development*, Lanham, MD: University Press of America.

Conklin, H. (1957), *Hanunoo Agriculture: A Report on an Integral System of Shifting Cultivation in the Philippines* (Forestry Development Report 12), Rome: FAO.

Ellen, R. (1978), Restricted Faunas and Ethnozoological Inventories in Wallacea,

In P.H.Sttot (ed) *Nature and Man in Southeast Asia,* London: School of Oriental and African Studies.

Ellen, R. (1998), Indigenous Knowledge of the Rainforest: Perception, Extraction and Conservation. In B.K.Maloney (ed) *Human Activities and the Tropical Rainforest,* 87-99, Kluwer: Academic Publishers.

Gadgil, M. and R.Guha (1992), State Forestry and Social Conflict in British India. In David Hardiman (ed) *Peasant Resistance in India, 1858-1914,* Delhi: Oxford University Press.

Guha, R. (1983), Forestry in British and Post-British India: A Historical Analysis, *Economic and Political Weekly,* 18 (44, 45 & 46), 1882-1896 and 1940-1947.

Kothari, A. (1994), *Conserving Life: Implications of Biodiversity Conservation in India,* New Delhi: IIPA.

Leaky, R.E. and R.Lewin (1982), *Origins: The Emergence and Evolution of Our Species and its Possible Future,* London: Futura Publications.

Leone, Mark P. (ed) (1972), *Contemporary Archaeology,* Carbondale and Edwardsville: Southern Illinois Press.

Minority Rights International (1999), *Adivasis in India,* London.

Misra, K.K. (1995), Tribalism and National Integration. In A.K.Singh and M.K.Jabbi (eds) *Tribes in India,* 159-173, New Delhi: Har-Anand Publications.

Misra, K.K. (1998), Local Knowledge, Western Science and Development Imperatives, *Proceedings of 5th Biennial Conference of European Association of Social Anthropologists,* Frankfurt.

Murty, M.L.K. (1993), Environment, Royal Policy and Social Formation in the Eastern Ghats, South India, AD 1000-1500 (Presidential Address), *Proceedings of the Indian Historical Congress,* 53rd Session, Warangal, 615-631.

Murty, M.L.K. (1994), Forest People and Historical Traditions in the Eastern Ghats, South India, in Bridget Allchin (Ed) *Living Traditions in the Ethnoarchaeology of South Asia,* 205-218, New Delhi: Oxford and IBH Publishing Co. Pvt. Ltd.

Ramakrishnan, P.S. (1992), *Shifting Agriculture and Sustainable Development,* Paris: UNESCO and The Parthenon Publishing Group.

Rangarajan, M. (1996), The Politics of Ecology: The Debate on Wildlife and People in India, 1970-95, *Economic and Political Weekly,* XXXI (35, 36, 37), 2391-2401.

Roy, N.R. (1972), Introduction. In K.S.Singh (ed) *Tribal Situation in India,* Shimla: Indian Institute of Advanced Study.

Saraswati, B. (ed) (1991). *Tribal Thought and Culture*, New Delhi: Concept Publishing Co.

Sinha, Surajit (ed). *Tribal Politics and State Systems in Pre-colonial Eastern and North Eastern India*, Calcutta: K.P. Bagchi and Co.

Spate, O.H.K., A.T.A. Learmonth and B.H. Farmer (1972). *India, Pakistan and Ceylon: The Regions*, Bombay: B.I. Publications.

Stini, W.A. (1975). *Ecology and Human Adaptation*, Dubuque, Iowa: W.M.C. Brown Co. Publishers.

2

The Environment in Prehistoric Research: A Case Study of the Kortallayar Basin, Tamil Nadu

Shanti Pappu

INTRODUCTION

Ever since the birth of Indian prehistory in 1863, the environment has featured as an important subject in the study of past cultures. Conceptual approaches in the archaeological study of the environment vary greatly (Alland 1975; Bennett 1978; Bettinger 1991; Butzer 1982; Ellen 1982; Hardesty 1980; Harpending and Davis 1978; Kirch 1980), although they all aim at understanding interrelationships between prehistoric societies and changing environments. In Indian prehistory, two principal approaches can be identified. The first approach documents Quaternary climatic, geomorphic and biotic processes at archaeologically rich sites and regions (Deo 1991; see Pappu 1995; Rajaguru 1993; see Statira *et al* 1995). The second approach utilizes this data along with archaeological evidence and models adapted from human ecology and geography to study past hominid land-use patterns and adaptive strategies (Allchin *et al* 1978; Cooper 1992; Misra 1989; Misra and Rajaguru 1989; Murty 1978-79; Paddayya 1979; Raju 1988; Sharma and Clark 1983). This approach may also involve a consideration of environmental impacts on the formation and preservation of Palaeolithic sites.

This article falls within the second category of research. It examines the way in which environment can be used in Palaeolithic archaeology drawing on a case study conducted in the Kortallayar basin, Tamil Nadu. For this purpose, environment is conceived of as encompassing both natural elements (physical geography, climate, biota) and cultural elements (archaeological sites and present cultural geography), which influence the formation of sites, hominid settlements and subsistence strategies. The paucity of fossil fauna and flora necessitated the use of uniformitarian assumptions drawn from the studies in geomorphology, ecology, ethnography and experimental research to put forward some general observations on past man-land relationships.

The Landscape Approach: Regional Scales of Analysis

Hominid adaptation to changing environment results in the differential use of places across a landscape, which in turn, conditions the structure of archaeological sites. This necessitates the adoption of a regional or landscape approach by the archaeologist, whereby the distribution of artifacts across a region can be studied. The study region consists of an area of 200 sq. km. (79°40′ : 79°56′ E and 13°17′ : 13°10′ N) in the Kortallayar basin, which forms a part of the Palar basin, Chengai-Anna District of Tamil Nadu (see Fig. 2:1). This comprises the Satyavedu plantation surface consisting of the north-northeast and south-southwest trending Allikulli hill ranges (200-380 m AMSL), surrounded by undulating lowlands (Muralidharan *et al* 1993). The area is drained by the Kortallayar river (a fourth order stream) and a network of first, second and third order streams. The region falls in an area of wet tropical moderate climate and uneven rainfall regime with an annual range of 105-125 cm., characterized by cyclonic rains from September to November and a mean temperature of 36°C. Vegetation consists of the *Albizzia amara* and *Acacia* series of semi-evergreen scrub, woodland, closed and discontinuous thorny thickets and scattered shrubs (Gaussen *et al* 1964).

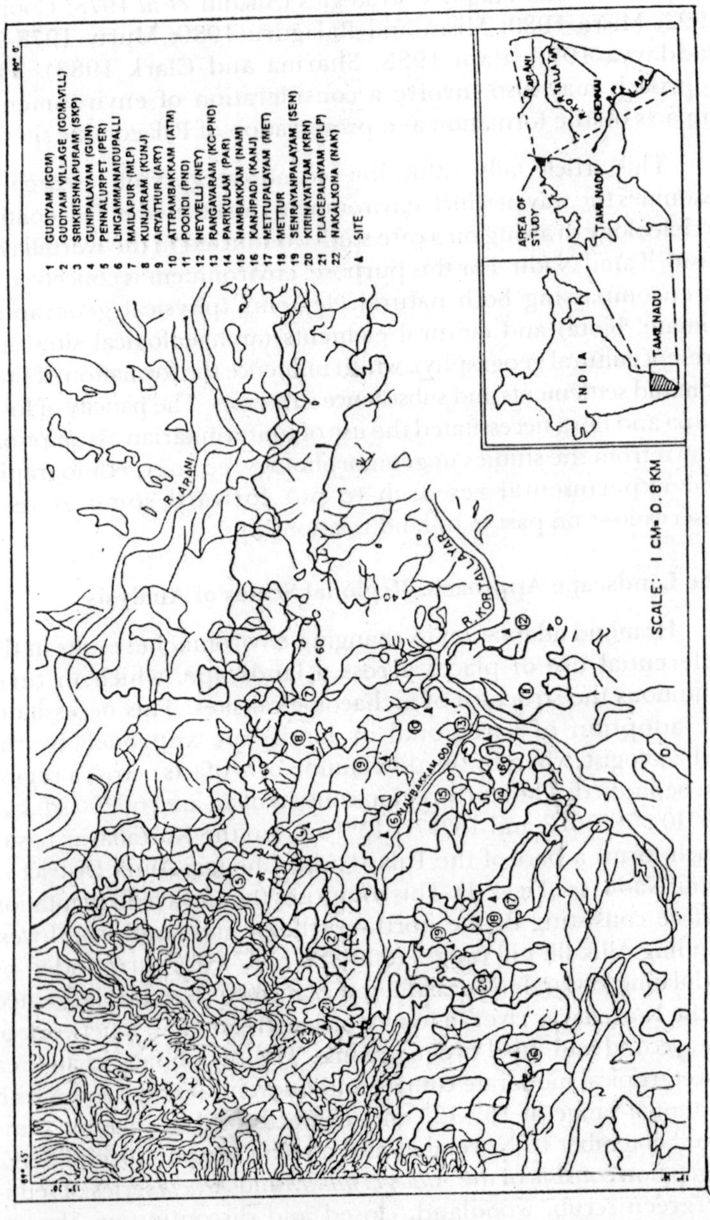

Map 2.1 : Kortallayar Basin

The focus in this paper is on palaeoenvironments vis-a-vis early hominid adaptations in the Kortallayar Basin basing on the archaeologically visible residues (the artefact scatters). In cultural terms this represents the Palaeolithic and Mesolithic cultures. This study proceeds by an analysis of the distribution of artefacts across the landscape in differing zones (defined by elevation and sedimentary context) and by plotting them, taking into consideration both high density artefact clusters or 'sites' and 'off-sites' or isolated scatters of artefacts (Dunnel and Dancey 1983; Ebert 1986; Foley 1981).

Reconstructing Quaternary Environment

As human kind evolved during the Pleistocene (the first epoch of the Quaternary, the second being the Holocene — the most recent), a meticulous scientific study of these deposits is crucial for an interpretation of the palaeoenvironments. Quaternary deposits in the Palar basin consist of the Erumaivettipalayam surface (fluvial-erosional comprising lateritic gravel), and the Palar-Kortallayar formation (comprising channel-bar, channel-fill, channel lag, flood basin, levee, pointbar and terrace deposits), ranging in age from the Middle Pleistocene to the Holocene (Muralidharan *et al* 1993: 9). Within the study area, weathering of the bedrock clasts, winnowing of their siliceous and ferruginous matrix as well as erosion of Tertiary ferricretes were the principal processes contributing to the source material in the form of gravels, silts, sands and clays, which constitute the Pleistocene deposits in the region. Subsequent transport and deposition by colluvial processes, sheet and stream floods and stream channel processes, followed by weathering of the profiles and ferricritization, has resulted in the formation of the Pleistocene landscape (Pappu 1996a; 1996b).

Quaternary ferricretes or ferricritized gravels containing, in general, Late Acheulian to Middle Palaeolithic artefacts, disconformably overlie the bedrock. Ferruginous gravels (30cm to 4.10m thick) vary greatly in age and in the factors responsible for their deposition and subsequent reworking. Two phases of Quaternary ferricretes are noted. Older ferricretes contain Acheulian to Middle Palaeolithic tools. These are 1.5m to 2.5m thick and comprise mainly coarse sands to silts with a few outsize clasts and pebble lenses. Chemical analyses of ferricretes reveal that in general the Fe_2O_3 values are low (13.40 per cent to 26.39 per cent) reflective of immature ferricretes with weak mobilization of iron, lithodependency on parent material and pointing to a predominant role of groundwater in a zone with a fluctuating water table (Subramaniam and Mani 1981; Tardy 1993). Iron is derived from the ferruginous matrix of the Sriperumbudur and Satyavedu formations, and from Tertiary ferricretes. The principal zones represented include the cuirasse and the superficial dismantling horizon. Subsequent dismantling and transport of the duricrust is attributed to block gliding and thermal breakdown.

A 50cm thick deposit of clayey silts is noted overlying ferricretes and covering an area of 4 sq.km. These are capped by ferricrete lag and sheet gravel containing Late Middle Palaeolithic to Microlithic tools. Holocene deposits comprise a 1.2m thick deposit of alluvium of the Kortallayar and Arani rivers, and are archaeologically sterile. Gullies dissecting these deposits can be dated to the Early Holocene humid phase (Rajaguru *et al* 1993: 463). A sub-fossil bone of *Boselephas tragocamelus* (Pappu *et al* 1994) was found and dated to the Middle Holocene. Climatological and geomorphological studies point to the existence of drier climate through most of the Pleistocene, although ferricrete formation points to greater humidity and pronounced seasonality during the Middle Pleistocene (Pappu 1996b; Rajaguru *et al* 1991). In the absence of any organic material, further generalization are to be avoided at this stage.

The Archaeological Record

A total of 22 sites belonging to the Lower (i.e. Acheulian) and Middle Palaeolithic and the Mesolithic were studied. Prior to reconstructing past life, the impact of environmental processes on the formation of the Palaeolithic sites needs to be considered.

Site Taphonymy

Post-depositional processes influencing artefact distribution and morphology include a combination of geomorphic processes (fluvial, gravitational, soil formation, neotectonic), biogenic processes, as well as current and historical land use patterns. These condition the nature of the sample available for the archaeologist and thus influence interpretations of the hominid behaviour (Binford 1982; Goldberg *et al* 1993; Issac 1989; Nash and Petraglia 1987; Schick 1974; Schiffer 1987; Stein 1987; Stern 1993). Variables considered for this study included site sedimentary contexts, horizontal and spatial distribution of artefacts, and artefact morphology (size, shape, abrasion, weathering, rounding, patination). Based on these parameters sites were classified into different types on the basis of their sedimentary context and potential for informing about hominid behaviour. These fall into a continuum between sites possessing a high degree of integrity, indicating areas of hominid activity in varying degrees; moderately reworked sites, where natural processes have operated with a greater intensity; and sites which are completely reworked or in unclear contexts. It was seen that the process of ferricrete formation, duricrust dismantling, atrefact raw material types and the process of iron encrusting, all play an important role in influencing the integrity of sites. Thus caution should be exercised when commenting on the factors thought to arise from hominid behaviour.

Stone Tool Technology

An analysis of 2012 Middle Palaeolithic stone tools in terms of studying their manufacture, use, transport, reuse and discard was attempted. Raw materials comprised of quartzites, quartzitic sandstones, sandstones, and quartz cobbles, pebbles, nodules and thermal fracture flakes derived from weathered bedrock. Choices were exercised as regards the nature of raw material and type of clast preferred. Although no site is more than a distance of 4 km from raw material sources, geomorphic processes and hominid exploitation through time, affected the distribution and ease of accessibility of these sources. Thus while bedrock could be easily exploited by the earlier Acheulian groups, during the Middle Palaeolithic this was buried by ferricretes in some regions. Through time, gravels deposited by seasonal sheet floods or stream floods built up new sources of raw material. Variation in the type of blanks used for the manufacture of tools (cobbles, pebbles, thermal fracture flakes, cortical, non-cortical flakes, prepared core flakes, flake-blades, blades, debitage, older tools) are noted in different regions with a predominance of the first four types in regions close to raw material sources. This may be associated with strategies with raw material conservation (Andrefsky 1994; Montet-White and Holen 1988). Artefact sizes correspond largely to the size of locally available raw materials; thus where there are larger natural clasts larger tools are noted. Sites having smaller clasts also display a lower frequency of the Levallois element and more naturally backed flakes. Lithological studies point to transport of clasts, cores and flake across the landscape (see Pappu 1996b).

Modified cobbles and trimmed nodules representing early stages in the reduction sequence are found at almost all sites, but no site bears evidence of preliminary raw material trimming and core reduction. Cores are few in number at all sites and are of many types (Levallois, discoidal, flake, flake-blade and blade). In some cases, broken cores have been rechipped and converted into other tools. Differences in the type of debitage, i.e. whether a result of early or late stage trimming is noted. A wide range of tool types is also seen. Standardization of forms is generally low, and in some cases debitage and thermal fracture flakes have been rechipped and used. Retouch is mild, causes for tool discard are unclear, as excluding blades very few tools are broken. Reuse of older tools is seen.

The Environment and Modern Hunter-Gatherers

Analogies drawn from modern hunter-gatherer settlement and subsistence strategies, and general principles of human ecology are utilized to discuss alternate adaptive strategies and their possible archaeological correlates. For this purpose a study of the Irulas (inhabiting the study region) and other South Indian and Sri Lankan foragers was considered. Despite shortcomings associated with the use of analogies drawn from such 'acculturated' foragers, it is felt that a general flexibility has enabled this mode of life to survive and thus, principles linking hunting, sharing, politics and social life are relevant here. Particular emphasis was laid on understanding Irula and other hunter-gatherer settlement and mobility strategies, subsistence strategies, technology and their

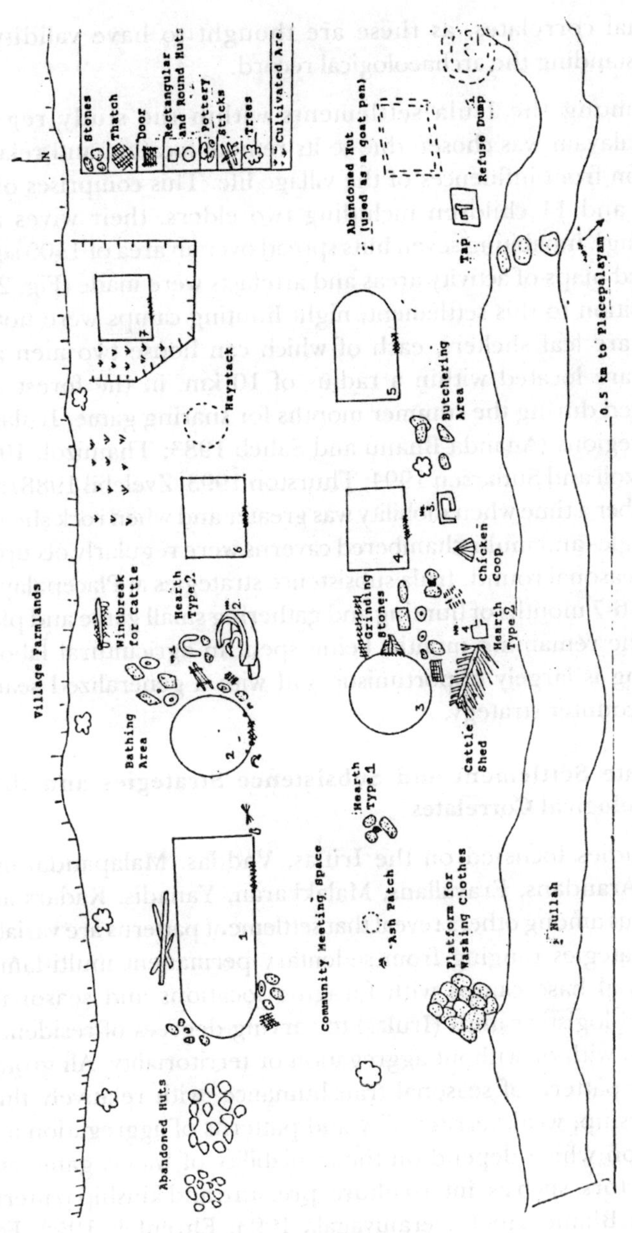

Map 2.2 : Activity Areas

material correlates, as these are thought to have validity in understanding the archaeological record.

Among the Irula settlements within the study region, Placepalayam was chosen due to its remote location and relative freedom from influences of the village life. This comprises of 17 adults and 11 children including two elders, their wives and offsprings, inhabiting seven huts spread over an area of 1500 sq.m. Detailed maps of activity areas and artefacts were made (Fig. 2.2). In addition to this settlement, night hunting camps were noted. These are leaf shelters, each of which can house two men and which are located within a radius of 10 km. in the forest and inhabited during the summer months for snaring game. Irulas in other regions (Ananda Bhanu and Saheb 1983; Thamizoli 1994; Thamizoli and Sudarsen 1994; Thurston 1993; Zvelebil 1988) also remember a time when mobility was greater and when rock shelters and single- and multi-chambered caverns were regularly occupied in the seasonal round. Irula subsistence strategies at Placepalayam involve 6-7 months of hunting and gathering small game and plant food; the remaining months being spent in agricultural labour. Foraging is largely opportunistic and with a generalized search and encounter strategy.

Alternate Settlement and Subsistence Strategies and their Archaeological Correlates

Studies focussed on the Irulas, Vaddas, Malapandarams, Allars, Arandans, Eravallans, Malakkaran, Yanadis, Kadars and Chenchus among others reveal that settlement patterns are variable with strategies ranging from sedentary permanent multi-family residential base camps with foraging locations and seasonally occupied logistic camps (Irulas) to varying degrees of residential mobility, with or without aggregation or territoriality. All groups follow a pattern of seasonal transhumance, with relatively fluid membership, weak territoriality and patterns of aggregation and dispersion which depend on the availability of water, game and other factors, such as, inter-cultural pressure and kinship patterns (Ananda Bhanu 1989; Deraniyagala 1993; Ehrenfels 1952; Fox 1969; Fuchs 1973; Furer-Haimendorf 1943; Jebadhas and Noble 1989; Luiz 1963; Morris 1982; Raghaviah 1962).

Types of sites, their sizes and spatial organization were next considered in terms of the effect they may have on assemblage composition. At the first level, differences in the assemblage composition arising from whether a site is a residential camp, a special purpose site, or a foraging loci were considered (following Binford 1982; Chatters 1987; Kelly 1992; Kent 1991; Winterhalder and Smith 1981). At the second level, systems of mobility-residential versus logistic, were considered and possible assemblage composition arising from such systems were discussed. Depending on the type of mobility, technological organization as reflected in whether tool-kits are transportable, versatile, flexible or economical of raw material was examined. Tools were looked at from the point of view of whether they reflect expedient or curated strategies of manufacture. Variables considered included recycling, reuse, resharpening and causes for discard (Bamforth 1986). Causes of reoccupation or multiple occupation of a site and the effect on site size and artefact density were examined. With respect to subsistence strategies, most of the groups studied follow a generalized immediate return strategy with a search and encounter mode (Woodburn 1982). Expectations on possible technological organization were then put forward.

Reconstructing Palaeolithic Man-Land Relationships

Taking into consideration these expectations, the following general observations are made about the past man-land relationships.

Site Types

Site types are difficult to determine owing to the fact that localities may have been used differently through time as necessitated by change in resource structure, social composition and mobility strategies. Based on expectations considered earlier, two broad categories of residential sites and varying categories of special purpose sites were identified within systems of logistic or residential mobility. These included (a) short-term foraging sites, including find spots representing possibly short-term foraging/collecting episodes (Placepalayam jungles, Nakalkona, Kirinayattam); (b) short-term special purpose camps (Placepalayam,

Senrayanpalayam). Other sites possibly represent residential base camps. The latter display evidence of early and later stages of core reduction and artefact trimming. The sites of Aryathur and Attrambakkam display evidence of preliminary trimming of the cores, high artefact diversity, and a higher percentage of debitage to tools. Debitage is never commensurate with the number of finished tools suggesting considerable movement of tools across the landscape. Sites like Attrambakkam and Aryathur with high artefact densities within small areas could possibly represent periodic aggregation of several groups. At most sites, no spatial resolution or specific tool clusters are noted. Reuse of particular localities as indicated by resharpening or reuse of tools is limited.

Mobility Strategies

The large number of sites located close together within a small area with evidence of reoccupation and high occupational intensity and high artefact density could point to a moderate degree of mobility with territoriality. Causes for abandoning are unclear. However, at Attrambakkam and Aryathur, a sterile layer of clayey-silt indicates a break in occupation and possibly represents a palaeo-pond situation formed during the Late Pleistocene period (Rajaguru, personal communication).

Subsistence Strategies

Artefact types tend to indicate both generalized and specialized strategies. The presence of specialized tools like blades, points and Levallois flakes may be considered to represent a strategy aimed at risk reduction and energy conservation with prey being either unreliable or to be exploited within a short span of time. If this is the case then, sites like Gunipalayam, Attrambakkam, Aryathur and Placepalayam may reflect such strategies. Tool types at sites lying close to raw material sources tend to reflect relatively generalized strategies while those in the lowlands reflect relatively specialized strategies. This could once again be related to the distribution of large and small games.

One possible pattern emerging is seasonal aggregation and dispersal towards and away from the river and local ponds at Attrambakkam and Aryathur. Wet season dispersion from these sites and other low-lying areas close to river towards the hills is indicated. Reoccupation of sites over vast time periods as seen at all sites within the region could imply stability in resource structure.

CONCLUSION

This study focused on the ways in which past man-land relationships could be looked at for understanding the Palaeolithic archaeological record. A regional approach was adopted, sites were plotted and a study of Quaternary environments was conducted. Studies of site taphonomy and post-depositional processes helped to isolate assemblage variability created by natural processes. Following a study of lithic technology, some general principles related to subsistence and settlement strategies of modern foragers were considered; their archaeological correlates were examined, and some general ideas on past man-land relationships were proposed. In general, no comparison with patterns emerging from a study of modern foragers was noted. While this may be the result of the structure of archaeological record and sampling bias, it may also reflect alternate behavioural strategies of the Late Pleistocene hominids.

REFERENCES

Alland, A. (1975), Adaptation, *Annual Review of Anthropology*, 4, 59-73.

Allchin, B. *et al* (1978), *The Prehistory and Palaeogeography of the Great Indian Desert*, London: Academic Press.

Ananda Bhanu, B. (1989), *The Cholanaiken of Kerala*, Calcutta: Anthropological Survey of India.

Ananda Bhanu, B. and S. Yaseen Saheb (1983), *Tribes in Contemporary India: The Irular of Tamil Nadu*, Mysore: Anthropological Survey of India.

Andrefsky Jr., W. (1994), Raw Material Availability and the Organisation of Technology, *American Antiquity*, 59(1), 21-34.

Bamforth, D. (1986), Technological Efficiency and Tool Curation, *American Antiquity*, 5(1), 38-50.

Bennett, J.W. (1978), *The Ecological Transition: Cultural Anthropology and Human Adaptation*, New York: Pergamon.

Bettinger, R.L.B. (1991), *Hunter-Gatherers: Archaeological and Evolutionary Theory*, New York: Plenum Press.

Binford, L.R. (1982), The Archaeology of Place, *Journal of Anthropological Archaeology*, 1, 5-31.

Butzer, K.W. (1982), *Archaeology as Human Ecology*, Cambridge: University Press.

Chatters, J.C. (1987), Hunter-Gatherer Adaptations and Assemblage Structure, *Journal of Anthropological Archaeology*, 6, 262-296.

Cooper, Z.M. (1992), The Relevance of the Forager/Collector Model to Island Communities in the Bay of Bengal, *Man and Environment*, 17(2), 111-122.

Deo, S.G. (1991), *Geomorphic Study of Palaeolithic Settlements in the Ghataprabha Basin, Karnataka (A Study in Environmental Archaeology)*, Unpublished Ph.D. thesis, Pune: University of Poona.

Deraniyagala, S.U. (1993), *The Prehistory of Sri Lanka. An Ecological Perspective. Memoir*, Volume 8. Part I, II, III, Commissioner of Archaeology, Government of Sri Lanka.

Dunnell, R.C. and W.S.Dancey (1983), The Siteless Survey: A Regional Scale Data Collection Strategy, in M.B.Schiffer (Ed.), *Advances in Archaeological Method and Theory*, Volume 6, New York: Academic Press, 267-287.

Ebert, J.I. (1986), *Distributional Archaeology*, Ph.D. Dissertation, Albuquerque: University of New Mexico.

Ehrenfels, U.R. (1952), *Kadar of Cochin*, Madras: Madras University Anthropological Series, No. 1.

Ellen, Roy (1982), *Environment, Subsistence and System: The Ecology of Small Scale Social Formation*, Cambridge: University Press.

Foley, Robert (1981), *Off-site Archaeology and Human adaptation in Eastern Africa: Analysis of Regional Artifact Density in the Amboseli, Southern Kenya*, Cambridge Monographs in Africa Archaeology 3, Oxford: Bar International Series.

Fox, R.G. (1969), Professional Primitives: Hunters and Gatherers of Nuclear South Asia, *Man in India*, 49(2), 139-160.

Fuchs, S. (1973), *The Aboriginal Tribes of India*, Delhi: Macmillan and Co.

Furer-Haimendorf, C. (1943), *The Chenchus: Jungle Folk of the Deccan*, London: Macmillan and Co.

Gaussen, H. *et al* (1964), *International Map of the Vegetation and Environmental Conditions at 1/1,000,000. Notes on the Sheet Madras*, New Delhi: International Council of Agricultural Research.

Goldberg, P. *et al* (1993), *Formation Processes in Archaeological Context*, Madison: Prehistory Press.

Harpending, H. and H. Davis (1978), Some Implications for Hunter-Gatherer Ecology derived from the Spatial Structure for Resources, *World Archaeology*, 8(3), 197-213.

Issac, B. ed. (1989), *The Archaeology of Human Origins. Papers by Glynn Issac,* Cambridge: University Press.

Jebadhas, W.A. and W.A. Noble (1989), The Irulas, in P.Hockings (Ed.) *Blue Mountains. The Ethnography and Biogeography of a South Indian Region,* Delhi: Oxford University Press, 281-303.

Kelly, R.L. (1992), Mobility/Sedentism. Concepts, Archaeological Measures and Effects, *Annual Review of Anthropology,* 21, 43-125.

Kent, Susan (1991), The Relationship between Mobility Strategies and Site Structure, in E.M.Kroll and T.D.Price (Eds.) *The Interpretation of Archaeological Spatial Patterning,* New York: Plenum Press, 33-57.

Kirch, P.V. (1980), The Archaeological Study of Adaptation: Theoretical and Methodological Issues, in M.B. Schiffer (Ed.) *Advances in Archaeological Method and Theory,* Volume 3, New York: Academic Press, 101-156.

Misra, V.N. (1989), Stone Age India: An Ecological Perspective, *Man and Environment,* 14(1), 17-64.

Misra, V.N. and S.N.Rajaguru (1989), Palaeoenvironments and Prehistory of the Thar Desert, Rajasthan, India, in K.Frifelt and R.Sorensen (Eds.) *South Asian Archaeology 1985,* Copenhagen: Scandinavian Institute of Asian Studies, Occasional Paper No. 4, 296-320.

Morris, B. (1982), *Forest Traders. A Socio-Economic Study of the Hill Pandarew* Jersey: The Athlone Press.

Muralidharan, P.K. *et al* (1993), *Geomorphology and Evolution of the Palar Basin,* Abstract of Papers, Workshop on Evolution of East Coast of India, Tanjore, Tamil University.

Murty, M.L.K. (1978/79), Symbiosis and Traditional Behaviour among the Kunchapuri Yerukulas of South India: A Predictive Model, *Purattatva,* 10, 50-61.

Murty, M.L.K. (1981), Hunter-Gatherer Ecosystems and Archaeological Patterns of Subsistence Behaviour on the Southeast Coast of India: An Ethnographic Model, *World Archaeology,* 13(1), 47-58.

Nash, D.T. and M.D.Petraglia (1987), *Natural Formation Processes and the Archaeological Record,* Oxford: Bar International Series 352.

Paddayya, K. (1982), *The Acheulian Culture of the Hunsgi Valley (Peninsular India): A Settlement System Perspective,* Poona: Deccan College.

Pappu, R.S. (1995), The Contribution of Earth Sciences to the Development of Indian Archaeology, in Statira Wadia *et al* (Eds.) *Quaternary Environments and Geoarchaeology of India,* Bangalore: Geological Society of India, 414-434.

Pappu, S. (1996a), Reinvestigation of the Prehistoric Archaeology Record in the Kortallayar Basin, Tamil Nadu, *Man and Environment*, 21(1), 1-23.

Pappu, S. (1996b), *Pleistocene Environments and Stone Age Adaptations in the Kortallayar Basin, Tamil Nadu*, Unpublished Ph.D. Dissertation, Pune: University of Poona.

Pappu, S. *et al* (1994), Discovery of a Middle Holocene Sub-Fossil Bone from Tiruvallur Taluk, Chingelput District, Tamil Nadu, *Current Science*, 67(6), 431-433.

Raghaviah, V. (1962), *The Yanadis*, Delhi: Bharatiya Adimjati Sevak Sangh.

Rajaguru, S.N. *et al* (1993), *Changes in Physical Environment of Western India during the last 200 Ka: a Geoarchaeological Approach*. Abstract of Papers, *Proceedings of the International Symposium on Global Climatic Change (IGBP)*, Shinjuku, Tokyo: Waseda University.

Schick, K.D. (1974), *Processes of Palaeolithic Site Formation: An Experimental Approach*, Ph.D. Dissertation, Berkeley: University of California.

Schiffer, M.B. (1987), *Formation Processes of the Archaeological Record*, Albuquerque: University of New Mexico Press.

Sharma, G.R. and J.D. Clark eds. (1983), *Prehistory and Palaeoenvironments in Middle Son Valley*, Allahabad: Avinash Publications.

Statira, W. *et al* eds. (1995), *Quaternary Environments and Geoarchaeology of India*, Bangalore: Geological Society of India.

Stern, Nicola (1993), The Structure of the Lower Palaeolithic Archaeological Record: A Case Study from the Koobi Fora Formation, *Current Anthropology*, 34(3), 201-227.

Subramaniam, K.S. and G. Mani (1981), Genetic and Geomorphic Aspects of Laterites on High and Low Landforms in Parts of Tamil Nadu, India, *Proceedings of the International Seminar on Lateritisation Process*, Trivandrum, 237-245.

Thamizoli, P. and V. Sudarsen (1994), *Irulas of Pzhayur*, Unpublished document, Madras: Department of Anthropology, University of Madras.

Tardy, Y. (1993), Diversity and Terminology of Lateritic Profiles, in I.P.Martini and W. Chessworth (Eds.) *Weathering, Soils and Palaeosols*, Amsterdam: Developments in Earth Surface Processes 2, Elsevier, 379-405.

Thurston, E. (1903), *Uralis, Sholagas and Irulas*, Madras: Bulletin of Madras Government Museum.

Winterhalder, B. and E.A. Smith eds (1981), *Hunter-Gatherer Foraging Strategies: Ethnographic and Archaeological Analyses*, Chicago: The University of Chicago Press.

Woodburn, J. (1982), Egalitarian Societies, *Man* (N.S.), 17, 431-451.

Zvelebil, K. (1988), *The Irulas of the Blue Mountains*, Syracuse: Maxwell School of Citizenship and Public Affairs, Syracuse University.

3

Environment and Stone Age Cultures of Kalahandi, Orissa

Pradeep Mohanty and *Baba Mishra*

INTRODUCTION

The present paper primarily reports the nature of prehistoric sites discovered in Kalahandi district of Orissa over the course of three seasons of fieldwork in 1996-97, 1997-98 and 1998-99 and their environmental correlates. A review of the literature revealed Kalahandi to be largely *terra incognita*. Although a few sites were reported earlier (Prusty 1992; Dash 1997), no in depth research into the Stone Age cultures of Kalahandi was ever attempted. The present project, which was initiated in 1996-97, could therefore be in some respects a pioneering one. Despite the fact that this survey has brought to light several sites belonging to Palaeolithic to the Medieval period, the discussion here is restricted only to the Stone Age cultures of Kalahandi.

The Study Region

Kalahandi literally meaning 'black pot' or 'pot of arts' was territorially much larger in the ancient and medieval periods. The region had variegated identity in different historical epochs, culminating in the present official name of Kalahandi after the merger of the erstwhile princely kingdoms with the state of Orissa in 1947 (Mishra 1993: 69). It is situated in the south-west part of Orissa between 19°3′ N and 21° 5′ N latitudes, and 82° 20′ E and 83° 4′ E longitudes. It is surrounded by the districts of Balangir and Sambalpur of Orissa and Raipur of Madhya Pradesh to the north, to the south by the district of Koraput, to the west by the districts of Koraput and Raipur, and to the east by the districts of Koraput and Boudh-Phulbani. Its extreme length from north to south is 220 Km and its extreme breadth from east to west is 140 Km.

The district has two distinct physiographic units—the plain land and the hilly tracts, each accounting for an equal share in the total geographical area. The former constitutes the river valleys of the Tel, the Jonk and their tributaries, while the latter chiefly comprises of the hill ranges which run from the northeast to the southwest of the district. The principal hill ranges belong to the Eastern Ghats, while those falling under the Nuapada region belong partly to the Chotanagpur mountain system and partly to the Eastern Ghats. The hill sides used to be covered with dense forests and many of them are still the home of a large variety of flora and fauna. At higher elevations of the hill tracts, open valleys are found. These valleys are fertile and abundantly watered by a cross-section of perennial streams. The hill slopes are most commonly used for shifting cultivation by a number of indigenous communities inhabiting the region.

The Tel, the Indravati and the Jonk, which form the tributaries of large rivers like the Mahanadi and the Godavari are the major rivers of Kalahandi. The Tel is the longest and the most important river in the district. The important feeders on its right bank include the Moter, the Hat, the Sagada, the Ret, the Utai, and the Rahul. On the left bank, The Tel is joined by the Udanti. Unlike the Tel and its tributaries that flow northwards, the Indravati originating near Thuamul village flows southwards. Besides these rivers, the district's hilly tracts are criss-crossed with a large number of streams, most of which are perennial.

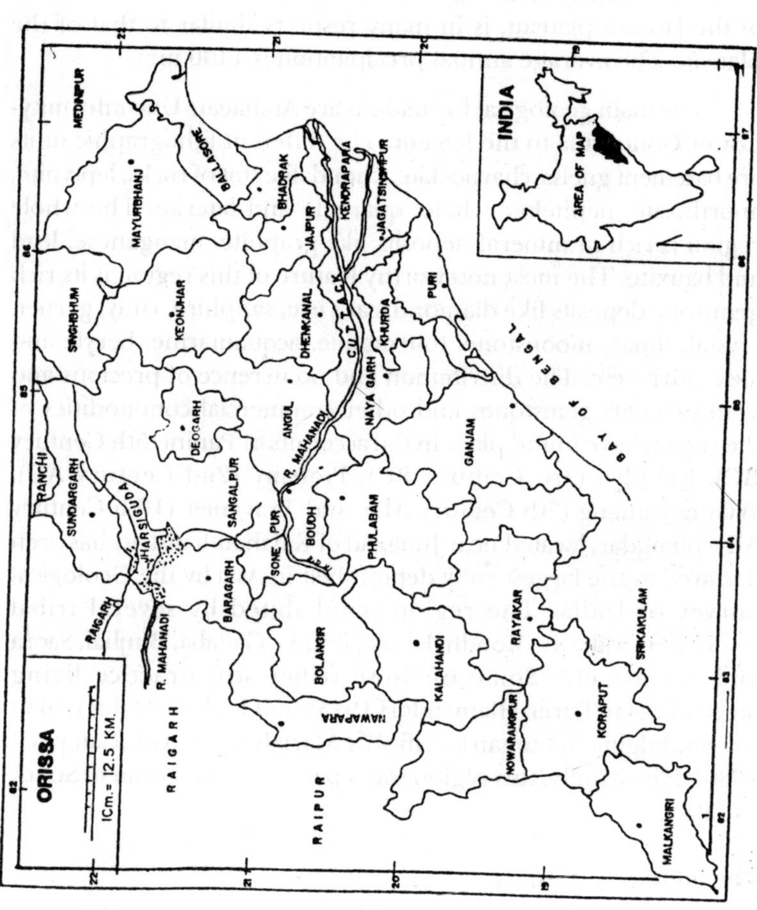

Map 3.1 : Kalahandi District

The vegetation of the region is from tropical to subtropical wet hill type with evergreen species and of dry mixed deciduous forest. The climate of the region, which is in the northeastern corner of the Deccan plateau, is in many respects similar to that of the plateau. The average annual precipitation is 1400 mm.

The main geological formations are Archaean-Unconformity-Lower Gondwana to the Recent. The different lithographic units are basement gneiss, charnockite, khondalite suit of rocks, leptynite, anorthosite, nepheline, shale, quartzite and laterite. The whole region is rich in mineral deposits like graphite, manganese, lead and bauxite. The most noteworthy feature of this region is its rich gemstone deposits like diamond, cat's eye, sapphire, ruby, garnet, crystal, topaz, moonstone, tourmoline, acquamarine, beryle and alexandrite etc. The distribution and occurrence of precious and semi-precious gemstones and other commercial commodities of the region have found place in the accounts of Panini (5th Century BC), Kautilya (3rd Century BC), Ptolemy (2nd Century AD), Wuang Chuang (7th Century AD), and Travenier (19th Century AD). Jillingdar, located near Junagad of Kalahandi district has been declared as the largest ruby deposit belt in Asia by the Geological Survey of India. The region is inhabited by several tribal communities like the Kondh, Paraja, Bonda, Gadaba, Binjhal, Saora and Munda etc. Some of these tribes still practice living megalithicism (Furer-Haimendorf 1943), and Kondhs of this region were indulging in human sacrifice or Mariah in the past (Campbell 1986). Historically, this region was a part of the kingdom of South Kosala.

The Sites

Intensive explorations in Dharamgarh, Rampur-Madanpur, Kesinga and Bhawanipatna sub-divisions, spanning three seasons, resulted in the discovery of several Mesolithic and post-Mesolithic sites in different geomorphic contexts. The sites are: Bhimkhela, Medinpur, Jamapadar, Kuturkhamar, Mahimapadia, Churiagarh, Tersinga, Pipalnala, Tikirapada, Upara Jaregi, Bija Dongar, Kora Dongar, Shilpa, Bichakhamam, and four localities, such as, Jamugadapadar, Dongargad, Bijapur and Jamugadapadar near Ichapur village. Sites like Bhimkhela, Medinpur, Bichakhamam and Jamapadar are extensive in nature and run into several hectares. These sites have preserved evidences from Mesolithic to Chalcolithic, and sometimes upto the Early Historic period. An interesting observation about these Mesolithic sites is that some of them have yielded only heavy-duty tools like choppers and core scrapers; some others have both microlithic artefacts and heavy-duty tools together; there are sites which have revealed microlithic artefacts and heavy implements in different clusters; and there are sites yielding only microlithic artefacts. Another important feature pertaining to these sites is the occurrence of celts and ringstones. These two objects have their appearance in the Mesolithic phase and have continued throughout into the Early Historic period.

Most of these sites are associated with low hillocks, foothill regions, or river banks. The artefactual spreads at individual sites vary widely; some are very large and some others being very small. At large sites, big and small boulders and quartz blocks characterize the locality. The majority of the sites discovered are primary in nature and still preserve habitational deposits. Various site features noted during the survey (location away from the river bank, discreteness of scatters of stone artefacts, regular association of raw material blocks and waste products, and lack of certain features like surface smoothing of artefacts associated with river action) indicate that most of the sites are well-preserved and are unconnected with any fluvial activity. The occurrence of isolated Mesolithic artefacts in foothill areas was also observed at a few sites. Although these occurrences may not be regarded as 'sites' in the conventional sense, their significance for interpreting the character of the Mesolithic cultural system cannot be entirely ignored. These sites may be interpreted as short duration, single episode spots involving an individual or a small group engaged in food collecting of food processing activities lasting from a few hours to a few days. As such, these sites may have served as satellites of larger sites (Foley 1981: 164-166; Mohanty 1993: 89; Paddayya 1991: 131; Thomas 1975: 62).

Most of these open-air sites seem to have been connected with occupational activities. Many of these sites are located on higher elevation, about 10m above the plains. The possibility of obtaining a commanding view of the surrounding plains, the availability of hard ground for habitation purpose, and the ubiquity of rock boulders for raising shelters must have been among the considerations that influenced the settlers to select these spots as locales for their encampment. Also noteworthy is the nearness of the sites to rivers and streams. The dense forests and the hills around would have provided a variety of game and wild plant foods. The raw materials for stone tool making may have been obtained from the nearby veins and dykes, and also from river beds.

The Lithic Industry

The lithic industry of Kalahandi Mesolithic sites consists of two distinct yet complimentary components: microlithic and heavy-duty tools. The lithic assemblages of these components occur separately at some sites and occur together at many others. These two components distinguish themselves from each other in several ways in terms of raw material and functional attributes. These distinctive features notwithstanding, these two lithic assemblage types constitute complimentary aspects of a unitary process of Mesolithic adaptation in the area. Chronologically, the sites may differ, as there are sites with edge ground tools, ringstones and crude handmade potsherds; and there are sites without these features.

The microlithic assemblages from these sites show differences with one another in terms of both raw material and typotechnological features. At sites like Kuturkhamar, Jamapadar and Bichakhamam blade tools with chert as raw material dominate the assemblages, whereas at other sites flake tools with quartz as the predominant raw material characterize the assemblages. Overall, chert and quartz are the most common raw materials used for manufacturing microlithic artefacts and for producing shaped artefacts. Other materials, in descending order, are chalcedony, dolerite and quartzite. Sites whose microlithic assemblage is dominated by quartz have a low proportion of shaped artefats and a high proportion of chips.

Developed blade and flake technologies are the most outstanding features of the microlithic assemblages. The industry is evident in blades, flakes, and nodules of various sizes. The flakes and blades of different shapes and sizes have been struck off from a variety of cores. A few cores, especially the fluted ones, indicate that the blades have been removed in one of several ways: in one direction, in two directions either from one end and side or from both ends, in three directions, or sometimes in multiple directions. The flake cores generally show both regular and irregular scars. A few small cores are roughly round in shape and have centrally directed scars—an indication that they were probably prepared before removing the flakes. The blade and flakes have been removed by a soft hammer of bone or wood, by punch, or by pressure technique.

Several blades and flakes have further been worked by various kinds of retouch and converted into tools. The microlithic industry of this area consists of mostly retouched blades, backed blades, notched blades, denticulate blades and points. All these tools are prepared by both unifacial and bifacial working. Unlike in other districts of Orissa, Kalahandi microlithic assemblages contain very few tools like triangles, trapezes, lunates and burins. The flake tools and the tools made on nodules, such as various types of scrapers, small core scrapers, borers, points generally have a fine unifacial and bifacial retouch.

However, the most outstanding feature of these assemblages is the common occurrence of heavy-duty implements. These differ radically from the microlithic component of the lithic technology in terms of both raw material and typotechnological features. At many sites, these artefacts occur together with microlithic artefacts. There is no stratigraphic data to separate the two components or to suggest that they were deposited at different times. Although the co-occurrence of heavy implements and microliths appears definitely to be a phenomenon strongly conditioned by environmental factors, evidence from different parts of India and around the world demonstrates that it is a common phenomenon (Mohanty 1988; 1988-89; 1989; 1992; 1993; 1997-98; 1998; 1999).

The lithic types comprise choppers (both uni- and bifacial) and core scrapers. These artefacts are made of quartzite. Technologically, the heavy tools show sophisticated workmanship. Suitable raw materials were exploited to achieve an effective working edge relative to the shape and size of the tool fabricated. Choppers are mostly made on river worn pebbles of quartzite. They are broad, rounded and massive. Many of them have flat base with most of the cortex intact. The working edge is sharp. The flake scars are deep and tapering from butt end to the working edge. Core scraper is the other tool type of heavy-duty implements. In general, these tools have sharp edges obtained by means of steep flaking. Most of these specimens were prepared by minimum flaking along their margins, leaving much cortex intact. In all cases, the flat bottom of the raw material has been retained. Flake scars are generally shallow and do not show any prior preparation of the core. The nature of flaking suggests the use of a controlled hammer technique and the secondary working along the margin is quite common.

It is generally agreed that these core scrappers served as wood-working tools (Kamminga 1978: 309). It has been hypothesized through edge-angle analysis (Ferguson 1980: 56-72; Hayden 1979: 124-125; Wilmsen 1968: 156-161) of various classes of tools that specimens with high edge-angle (above 55-60°) were meant for such wood-working operations as scrapping or planning or smoothing of a wood surface, while the specimens with low edge-angles were used for cutting or chopping. The edge-angle analysis of core scrappers and choppers from the Kalahandi sites shows that most of the core scrappers are in the range of 55-80°, and choppers in the range of 40-50°, lending support to the hypothesis of wood-working, and chopping and cutting by the core scrapers and choppers respectively.

Celts

Celts constitute an extremely important economic and symbolic resource from the Mesolithic period onwards. Celts were used both for functional tasks and ceremonial activities (Tilley 1996: 250). Celts, fashioned by means of flaking, pecking, grinding and polishing, are another interesting category of heavy implements in Kalahandi Stone Age sites. As mentioned earlier, celts make their appearance in the Mesolithic phase and have continued throughout upto the Early Historic phase. Celts mostly comprise of axes, adzes and chisels.

The raw materials used for fabricating celts are fashioned on locally available rocks, of which the most important is dolerite. This rock occurs abundantly in the form of dykes all over the district and the prehistoric artificer exercised a clever sense by selecting this raw material for making celts. The other raw material used was sandstone. In plan form, majority of the artefacts are rectangular with a few elongated-triangular to triangular. The cutting edge of most of the celts is straight to convex with bevelled edges. The cross-section of most of the celts is rectangular, whereas a few are planoconvex. A majority of the celts are chipped and pecked and partially ground at the distal end. One specimen shows unifacial chipping at the distal end. A few broken specimens with the proximal and distal ends have also been found at these sites. The most noteworthy feature about these celts is its wide variety in its length. They range from as small as 3cm to as large as 47 cm. The biggest axe measuring 47cm and weighing 2.5kg comes from the site of Medinpur, which is a Neolithic-Chalcolithic site. This particular axe shows very sophisticated workmanship. It is double-ended, chipped, pecked and partially ground. Its production must have required considerably long time and effort. Its enormous length makes it completely unsuitable for functional uses. The pristine state of many of these finds indicates that they were never used for everyday tasks. The lack of damage to these small axes and the big ones indicate that they were possibly prestigious symbolic items having aesthetic importance (Tilley 1996: 253). It is also possible that these celts were made by specialized craftsmen (Cross 1993). Already the Chalcolithic site of Sankarganj in Dhenkal district of Central Orissa has revealed a large number of ground and polished axes which measure between 33 and 39 cm in length with rectangular cross-sections. However, difference of opinion exists regarding the use of these celts. Yule *et al* (1990) argued that these were the earliest musical instruments preserved in South Asia and were similar to those found in Vietnam. Dash (1986; 1994) is of the opinion that these tools bear thrashing mark of grains and hence, might have been used in pounding or comcrunching, or as mallets, or even as nut-crunchers. We are more inclined to believe that these enormously long axes were made as votive offerings. In many tribal shrines of the northern and central Orissa one gets to see iron swords as votive offerings.

Ringstones

Ringstone is another category of implement which makes its appearance in the Mesolithic, and like celts, has continued throughout till the Early Historic period. It has been variously interpreted as net-sinkers, as an aid to digging sticks etc. Ringstones of Kalahandi are mostly made of sandstone and dolerite. These are about 8 to 12cm in diameter, and are either round or oblong in shape. However, the ethnographic use of ringstone is very interesting. Local people of the area collect them from archaeological sites and keep them hanging in their cow sheds. These are locally called 'Panaka Pathara'. Their main use in the cow shed is to drive away a bird locally called 'Panaka Chadhei'. Sometimes ringstones are put around the neck of the sheep or goats to cure them from a particular kind of disease.

CONCLUSION

Kalahandi district forms part of a distinct ecological zone. As described above, it receives high rainfall and has tropical deciduous vegetation. All the known Stone Age sites are surrounded by stretches of thick forest. Given the locational features of the sites, it is reasonable to assume that the Stone Age cultures flourished in a comparable forested ecological setting. The present population of the area, mainly the Kondh and the Bondo, practice extensive forest clearing and wood working as a part of their daily sustenance. In carrying out forest clearance and other domestic and outdoor wood-working activites, the Stone Age people might have employed a large number of heavy-duty tools of the types that are recovered from the Stone Age sites delineated above.

Heavy implements have been documented in regular association with microlithic artefacts at the Stone Age sites in Kalahandi district. Although these have been found in many Mesolithic sites in India, the functional-ecological role the implements might have played has not yet been deliberated. Coexistence of heavy implements and microliths is consistent with similar occurrences in other areas within and outside India. This heavy-duty tool component pertained to forest clearing, wood-working, house construction and food procurement and preparation in the Stone Age period.

ACKNOWLEDGEMENT

The Authors are grateful to Mr. Dana Mishra, who assisted them in the fieldwork.

REFERENCES

Campbell, J. (1986), *Human Sacrifices in India*, Delhi: Mittal Publications (reprinted).

Dash, R.N. (1993), Sankerganj: A Chalcolithic Site in Orissa, *Orissa Historical Research Journal*, 32, 95-125.

Dash, R.N. (1994), Unique Stone Objects from Sankerganj, in H.C.Das *et al* (Eds.) *Krishna Pratibha*, New Delhi: Sandeep Prakashan, 23-28.

Dash, R.N. (1997), Pre and Protohistory of Kalahandi, *Souvenir*, District Council of Culture, Kalahandi, 46-51.

Ferguson, W.C. (1980), Edge-Angle Classification of the Quininup Brook Implements: Testing the Ethnographic Analogy, *Oceania*, 15, 56-72.

Foley, R. (1981), Off-site Archaeology: An Alternative Approach for the Short-sighted, in I. Hodder *et al* (Eds.) *In Pattern of the Past: Studies in Honour of David Clarke*, Cambridge: University Press, 157-183.

Furer-Haimendorf, C. V. (1943), Megalithic Ritual among the Gadabas and Bondos of Orissa, *Journal of Royal Asiatic Society of Bengal*, 9, 149-178.

Hayden, B. (1979), *Palaeolithic Reflections: Lithic Technology and Ethnographic Excavations among the Australian Aborigines*, Atlantic Highlands: N.J.Humanities Press.

Kamminga, J. (1978), *Journey into Microcosms: A Functional Analysis of Certain Classes of Prehistoric Australian Stone Tools*, Unpublished Ph.D. Dissertation, University of Sydney.

Mishra, Baba (1993), Kalahandi: A Toponomical Study, *Proceedings of the Orissa Historical Congress*.

Mohanty, P. (1988), Five Seasons of Exploration in Keonjhar District, Orissa, *Indo-Pacific Prehistory Association*, 8, 47-53.

Mohanty, P. (1988-89), The Mesolithic Culture of Keonjhar District, Orissa, with Special Reference to the Heavy-Duty Tool Components: A Functional Interpretation, *Deccan College Bulletin*, 47-48, 227-237.

Mohanty, P. (1989), *Mesolithic Settlement System of Keonjhar District, Orissa*, Unpublished Ph.D. Dissertation, Poona University.

Mohanty, P. (1992), Stone Age Research in Orissa: An Overview, *Man in India*, 72, 207-232.

Mohanty, P. (1993), Mesolithic Hunter-Gatherers of Keonjhar District, Orissa. *Asian Perspectives*, 32, 85-104.

Mohanty, P. (1997-98), The Prehistory, Protohistory and the Early Historic Cultures of Orissa, *Pragdhara*, 8, 69-103.

Mohanty, P. (1998), The Mesolithic Culture of Keonjhar District, Orissa: A New Prespective, in A. Dutta (Ed.) *History and Archaeology of Eastern India*, New Delhi: Books & Books, 59-95.

Mohanty, P. (1999), The Mesolithic Culture and Ethnography of Keonjhar District, Orissa, in K.K.Basa and P.Mohanty (Eds.) *Archaeology of Orissa*, New Delhi: Pratibha Prakashan.

Nassaney, M.S. (1996), The Role of Chipped Stone in Political Economy of the Social Ranking, in G.H.Odell (Ed.) *Stone Tools; Theoretical Insights into Human Prehistory*, New York: Plenum Press, 181-224.

Paddayya, K. (1991), The Acheulian Culture of the Hunsgi-Baichabal Valleys, Peninsular India: A Processual Study, *Quarter*, 41-42, 111-138.

Prusty, R. (1992), Palaeolithic Vestiges from Kalahandi, *Orissa Historical Research Journal*, 37 (1-4), 55-61.

Tilley, C. (1996), *An Ethnography of the Neolithic: Early Prehistoric Societies in Northern Scandinavia*, Cambridge: University Press.

Tacon, P.S.C. (1991), The Power of Stone: Symbolic Aspects of Stone Use and Tool Development in Western Arnhem Land, Australia, *Antiquity*, 65, 192-207.

Thomas, D.H. (1975), Non-Site Sampling in Archaeology: Up the Creek without a Site ? in J.W.Muller (Ed.) *Sampling in Archaeology*, Tuscon: University of Arizona Press, 61-81.

Wilmsen, D.N. (1968), Functional Analysis of Flaked Stone Artefacts, *American Antiquity*, 33, 156-161.

4

Cultural Ecology of the Eastern Ghats (South India) from Prehistoric Times to the Ethnographic Present

M.L.K. Murty

INTRODUCTION

Eastern Ghats (11° 30' and 22° N: 76° 56' and 86° 30'E) is a term (like the Western Ghats) popularly used for a group of disjointed hill ranges, running more-or-less parallel to each other in a crescentic fashion, in the interior of the southeast coast of the Bay of Bengal. The major part of these hill ranges is in the State of Andhra Pradesh, with their southern and northern extremities in the States of Tamil Nadu and Orissa, respectively. The area covered by the Eastern Ghats is about 70,000 km; it is a landscape of marine; hinterland; hilly and forested lowland and upland plateaus, and forms a part of the Deccan. This region.is characterized by varied ecosystems, and the archaeological evidence unfolds valuable record of prehistoric human adaptive strategies right from the Stone Age times to the induction of agro-pastoral village system.

Geographically (Spate *etal* 1972: 700-707, 715-727), the region of the Eastern Ghats forms a part of the peninsular interior. The northwestern part of the Eastern Ghats region, called Telangana (contiguous with the southern Maharashtra and eastern Karnataka plateaus), is a zone of senile peneplains developed on the Archean gneisses (which form the basement), intersected by broad, open, almost completely graded valleys and littered with monadnocks. The elevation of the Telangana region ranges from 530m to 660m above the mean sea level (AMSL). The bioclimate in the northwest and east along the Godavari valley is a rainy variant of the tropical accentuated type: the average temperature in winter remains around 20° C, the annual rainfall is high being 1000 mm to 1500 mm, and the dry season lasts for seven to eight months (Gaussen *etal* 1965). The Telangana is drained by the Godavari and the Krishna, and the catchment areas of these river systems have dry deciduous woodlands of the *Tectona- Terminalia* series.

The southwestern part of the Eastern Ghats is the Rayalaseema, and in this region the gneisses and granites form only a broad outer rim on the west, south and east, and the remaining central part consists of rocks of the Purana group. These are the Cuddapahs (*Algonkian-Torridonian*) and the Kurnools (Lower Vindhyans). The Cuddapahs and Kurnools comprise a series of mountain ranges, which are separated from each other. These are collectively known as the Eastern Ghats. According to Spate (Spate *etal* 1972 : 721-22) 'the term "Eastern Ghats" is honoured by time but nothing else; its use gives a misleading impression of comparability with the Western Ghats, and suggests an entirely non-existent homogeneity. The hills which border the Peninsular interior have in fact no continuity, structural or topographic . . . it seems best to use the non-committal term "Eastern Hills" for these hill ranges.' Beyond the Krishna lie the most interior of the Eastern Hills, which from their rocks and position may be collectively styled the Cuddapah Ranges and Basins (*ibid*). These hills are the Velikonda and Nagari in the east, the Palkonda and Seshachalam in the southwest, the Erramalai in the northwest and Nallamalai in the centre. The altitude of these hills rarely exceeds 900 m, and the summits and high plateaus of the Nallamalai hills rise to above 500 m to 600 m AMSL. Between these hill ranges are situated basins at an altitude of over 200 m, and the Nandyal Basin (215 m to 245 m) is a typical limestone country with drastic landforms. It is drained by the river Kunderu.

The other major river systems of the Rayalaseema are the Krishna, Tunghbhadra, Penner, Cheyyeru, Papagni, Swarnamukhi and several hill streams. The summits and high plateaus of the Nallamalai hills receive an average rainfall of 1000 mm, a dry season of six months and temperature cooler than on plains. The Nallamalai hills have a thick forest cover of woodlands of *Anogeissus-Terminalia -Tectona* series which extend from the Nandyal in the south to the Amarabad plateau in the north (Gaussen *etal* 1964). These woodlands degrade into savannah woodlands and scrub savannahs on the slopes. To the west of Nallamalais are the Erramalai hills which have low plateaus, and it is a typical semi-arid zone with a low rainfall ranging between 800 mm and 500 mm, and vegetation of *Albizzia-Acacia* series presenting scrub woodland, shrub savannah and thorny thicket facies. Further to the south, between the Palkonda ranges and the higher Mysore levels, are a series of basins around the middle courses of the Penner and its tributaries. The region slopes down to the southeast, joining the Nellore/Coromandel plains through the intermontane basins of the Nagari hills and the Swarnamukhi valley, which occupies a fault trough under the Palkondas. These are low to medium rainfall zones, with the rainfall ranging between 1000 mm and 800 mm. The vegetation from the hills down to the plains presents woodland, woodland savannah, scrub savannah, continuous/discontinous thorny thicket and shrub facies of the *Albizzia-Acacia* series and *Hardwickia-Pterocarpus-Anogeissus* series. Further east, the eastern littoral is marked by the great deltas of the Godavari and the Krishna; sand dunes stretching several kilometres inside; and expanses of alluvium between the low level plains and dunes. Finally the southeast coast of the Bay of Bengal comprises vegetation of halophytic, mangrove and semi-evergreen species of *Manilkara-Chloroxylon* series, and the rainfall varies between 1500 mm and 1000 mm.

The varied physiographic zones of the Eastern Ghats are rich in prehistoric occupations right from the Palaeolithic to the Neolithic- Chalcolithic periods. Interestingly enough, the location of a majority of prehistoric occupations is within the habitation zones of the ethnographic present in the lowlands, uplands, river valleys and forested zones. This indicates that the prehistoric ecosystems, despite the fact they suffered varied degrees of degradation form the historic times to the present, continue to provide optimal resources to the numerous indigenous social groups (the tribal populations). That being the case, the adaptive patterns of these communities provide analogies to explicate the possible modes of living strategies in the prehistoric environments of the Eastern Ghats. Suffice it would, in this context, to give a brief review of the Palaeolithic (Lower, Middle, and Upper), Mesolithic, and Neolithic-Chalcolithic cultures.

SETTLEMENT SYSTEMS

Palaeolithic and Mesolithic

They represent hunting-gathering cultures and date from the Late Middle Pliestocene to early Holocene periods. The nature of their occupations can be distinguished, and related to the environment, by the occupation scatters (i.e. the dispersal of artifacts in various modes) within the confines of a site. The topographical location of the Paleolithic and Mesolithic occurrences indicate the following types of settlement patterns:

1. On fluviatile deposits, especially eroded flood plains and shingle beds, with sporadic but localized clustering of artifacts. These are essentially dry season temporary camps connected with the exploitation of aquatic niches, and occupations of this nature are very common in the riverine zones of the Eastern Ghats. Examples are furnished by various Lower Palaeolithic (Acheulian), Middle Palaeolithic, Upper Palaeolithic and Mesolithic occurrences around Renigunta at different localities along the stretch of the Rallakalava in the Swarnamukhi valley, Paleru, Penner and Kunderu valleys; and by Acheulian and Middle Palaeolithic occurrences along the Gundkakamma river etc.
2. On sandy or red sandy loamy patches along the courses of braided seasonal runnels in alluvial flats, within the catchment limits of a river, ephemeral stream, or even a feeder. Typical occupations of this type range from Acheulian to the Mesolithic around Renigunta, at Narayana Nellore and Upper Palaeolithic at

Peddarajupalli (also Peddarachapalli), both in the Gunjana valley; Middle Palaeolithic at Nadenamarella, in the Paleru basin; and extensive Middle Palaeolithic scatters at Julapalli, in the Godavari basin.

3. Extensive river terrace occupations overlooking the water course of a river or stream at those niches where there are perennial water pools. Striking examples of this category are the Upper Palaeolitic scatters at Konamadugu on the Rallakalava near Renigunta and at Peddarajupalli on the Gunjana.

4. Horizontal diffuse scatters on flat rock surfaces, or boulder-strewn rock surfaces, at times covered by alluvio-colluvial sediments, in close proximity to a stream, a waterhole, or a lake. Among the best examples are a lakeside Middle Palaeolithic occupation near Guravarajupalli at Renigunta on granite surfaces (which are now weathered); Acheulian occurrences at Thummachetlapalli and Narayana Nellore, both in the Gunjana valley; a Middle Palaeolithic occurrence at Venkataraopalli, in the Godavari basin; an Upper Palaeolithic occupation at Pochera on the Peddavagu river; and Mesolithic scatters at Buchaiahpalli in the Godavari basin and at Kanvamadagala Bugga (a perennial spring) in the Kurnool cave area.

5. Artifact spreads in a limited area amidst exposed rock outcrops in different physiographical settings, ranging from a defunct channel to the outliers of a deciduous forest. Interesting examples are the Acheulian within a circle of boulders in the channel of Rallakalava (close to the airport) at Renigunta; and the Upper Palaeolithic, also within a circle of boulders at Wankdi right in the deciduous forest of the Godavari basin.

6. In gallery forest or gallery bush ecotones along the foothills and hillslopes, at times forming a component of the colluvial breccias, in close proximity to a hillside stream, spring or waterhole. Typical occurrences are vertically diffuse Acheulian occupation scatters on the Tirupati foothills; a horizontally diffuse Acheulian

occupation scatter at Amarabad; and a vertically diffuse Mesolithic occupation at Gourigundam falls (Godavari valley).

7. Occupations in the riverine catchment zones but away from the main channel and within the outliers of dry deciduous open forests. Examples are the Acheulian occupation at Cherla and Mesolithic at Alabaka both in the Godavari valley.
8. Occupations on upland mountain plateaus in a thickly wooded country where water resources are meagre, being available only in seasonal streams, or springs, and ponds. An Upper Palaeolithic occurrence at Gundla Brahmeswaram, on the Nallamalais, is a striking site, and Chenchu settlements are scattered here and there in these niches.
9. Open-air and cave occupations in the limestone country of Nandyal Basin in the Kurnool reigon. Examples are surficial sporadic Upper Palaeolithic and Mesolithic find spots and a cave occupation at Muchchatla Chintamanu Gavi, all in the region of Betamcherla.

Occupations of the first to fifth category, being located in the active floodplain zones, are essentially dry season camps; however, sites like Wankdi, situated away from the river and at a higher elevation, could be all-season camps. Scatters of the sixth to ninth categories can be broadly termed all-season camps reflecting exploitation of various microenvironmental niches in different seasons (but mostly during the wet seasons) within a site catchment area, taking a radius of 20km. hypothetically as the potential range for exploitation.

PALAEOLITHIC (ARTIFACT CATEGORIES)

Lower Palaeolithic

The Lower Palaeolithic culture is distinguished by a lithic tool technocomplex, the Acheulian (other synonyms being hand axe-cleaver technocomplex or biface technocomplex). The diagnostic artifact categories are predominantly hand axes and cleavers; and the other types are choppers, scrapers on core and flake; utilized flakes; simple (unmodified) flakes; core dressing flakes; cores; and debitage.

The Lower Palaeolithic in the Eastern Ghats, as in other parts of the peninsula, represents an Early Acheulian and a Late Acheulian (Issac 1960; Krishna Sastry 1983; Madhusudhana Rao 1979; Murali Mohan 1994; Murty 1981; Nagabhushana Rao 1966; Raju 1988; Sankalia 1974; Singh 1979; Sudarsen 1976; Thimma Reddy 1968; Vijaya Prakash 1981). The artifact categories though are generally common to both the Early and the Late Acheulian, the former represents a crude technology, and the latter is marked by refinement in artifact manufacture, standardized shapes and symmetrical forms. The Early and Late Acheulian of this region share several typo-technological traditions with the industries in other parts of the Indian subcontinent. Some of the industries at sites such as Nevasa, Singhi Talav, Yedurwadi and Hunsgi have been dated by Thorium/Uranium method and these dates are in the range of > 0.4 myr (Mishra 1992). Likewise there are TL dates for the Son valley (Williams and Clarke 1995) and Saurashtra (Pappu 1995), associated with the Lower Palaeolithic. The TL date for (a) the Sihawal formation near Baghor II (northern Madhya Pradesh) in the Son valley is 103,800 + 19,800 (uncalibrated) and (b) the Thorium/ Uranium dates for the Acheulian associated with miliolites at Junagad and Umrethi (Saushtra) indicate a time range of 69 kyr and 190 kyr B.P. Thus by cross-cultural comparison, the Lower Palaeolithic (Early and Late Acheulian) in the Eastern Ghats may be ascribed a relative dating within the range of > 0.4 myr and 69 kyr.

Middle Palaeolithic

The Middle Palaeolithic is wide spread in all the ecological zones of the Eastern Ghats (Issac 1960; Krishna Sastry 1983; Madhusudhana Rao 1979; Murali Mohan 1994; Murty 1981; Nagabhushana Rao 1966; Raju 1988; Sankalia 1974; Singh 1979; Sudarsen 1976; Thimma Reddy 1968; Vijaya Prakash 1981). A noteworthy feature is its distribution in ecotones in which traces of Acheulian occupation are not noticeable, especially in the western peneplains and in the interiors of upland plateaus. It is a flake tool technocomplex with the general characteriztic features of the peninsular sites. The typical tools are predominantly scrappers (side, concave, convex, notched, end, discoid and ovate) on flakes, cores and nodules; points (asymmetrical in most cases) on flakes (including Levallois flakes), flake-blades and cores; irregularly retouched flakes; borers and awls on flakes; small sized unifacial/ bifacial choppers on pebbles and nodules; utilized flakes; discoid cores and Levallois cores; and debitage. In the western peneplains (in woodland savannah and thorny thicket zones) the flake tool technocomplex is more of an amorphous nature (artifacts excepting scrappers being mostly atypical) though made on rocks of the cryptocrystalline family such as chert, jasper, chalcedony, agate etc. This kind of amorphous lithic tool kit is suggestive that it is more an accessory for the manufacture of a variety of non-lithic (wood, bone etc.) hunting, trapping and snaring contrivances. On the other hand the lithic component of the low foot-hill ranges and riverine ecosystems of the Eastern Ghats (in the Cuddapah Basin) display a distinctively different pattern. The artifactual occurrences in these zones show a continuity of refined Late Acheulian tradition (miniature bifaces and cleavers) in association with the conventional flake tool forms. The raw material is predominantly green fine grained quartzite, though chert and jasper were also used. Based on radio carbon dates (halflife 5730 BC) from other parts of the country (Possehl and Rissman 1992 : 460), the Middle Palaeolithic in the Eastern Ghats may possibly fall in the time-frame of ca. 32000 BC to 23000 BC.

Upper Palaeolithic

The Upper Palaeolithic in the Eastern Ghats is one of the striking entities in the Indian sub-continent (Issac 1960; Kasturi Bai 1982; Krishna Sastry 1983; Madhusudhana Rao 1979; Murali Mohan 1994; Murty 1969, 1981, 1985; Nagabhushana Rao 1966; Raju 1986-87, 1988; Sankalia 1974; Singh 1979; Sudarsen 1976; Thimma Reddy 1968; Vijaya Prakash 1981). This technocomplex is characterized by a blade tool tradition and a blade and burin tradition. The blade tool tradition consists of long parallel sided blades; irregular blades; flake-blades; scrapers (side, convex, concave, a few end); retouched blades, flake blades and flakes; a few points, burins and bores; and blade cores, flake cores and debitage. What is conspicuous in the blade tool tradition is again the predominance of unmodified blades, flake blades and flakes, and the amorphous element. And the backed blade element is markedly low, perhaps <5% of the assemblages at the respective sites. The blade tool tradition is characteriztic of occupation scatters in the woodland savannahs, savannah grasslands of the Erramalai low plateaus and the Kunderu valley (in which Kurnool cave sites are situated), and also the woodland zones of higher Nallamalai plateaus. The southwestern outliers and lowlands of the Eastern Ghats, and the deciduous woodlands of the higher Nallamalai ranges is the domain of the blade tool tradition. The distribution pattern of the blade tool scatters indicates low density and short term occupations, and these are separated by a distance of several kilometres. The Kurnool caves have yielded a variety of Late Pleistocene fauna (food refuse) along with blade tools, bone tools, and grinding slabs (Murty 1975, 1985). The most striking and distinctive feature of the Upper Palaeolithic of the southeastern outliers of the Eastern Ghats is the blade-and-burin lithic tradition. The typical artifact categories are parallel sided blades; irregular blades and pointed blades; end, side and notched scrapers on blades; ovate and discoid scrapers on flake, flake blade and core; denticulates; horse hoof scrapers made on blade cores; prismatic core scrapers; backed blade variants such as straight back and curved back points; backed knives; macro lunates as big as an orange segment which are comparable to the Australian elouera; macro triangles; a variety of burins made on blades and split cores; borers; utilized flakes; cores; bored stones; grinding slabs and debitage. The burins, backed blade variants and end scrapers of these assemblages are of finest quality. And some of these assemblages reveal a tendency towards microlithization. The occupations consisting of blade and burin assemblages are extensive in the riverine ecosystems of the southeastern fringes of the Eastern Ghats, especially between the Penner and Swarnamukhi valley systems. Some of these scatters extend over 20,000 m^2, and the occupational loci are on ancient aggradational terraces and close to ephemeral streams. The association of bored stones (some of them are on flat nodules) suggests their use, more than anything else as net sinkers; and the large quantities of grinding slabs (some with pit marks) certainly provide indirect evidence for the possible processing of plant foods. The raw material used for the artifacts are green fine grained quartzite and lydianite. The blade tool and blade-and-burin lithic co-traditions of the Eastern Ghats strikingly point out, by their very nature of geographical location, that the former indicates upland/open woodland/grass land cultures and the latter are distinctively confined to the riverine/scrub woodland/ thorny thicket zones. Considering the radiocarbon dates (half-life 5730 BC) from other parts of the country and the TL date from the Kurnool caves, the Upper palaeolithic of the Eastern Ghats falls in the range of 23460 BC to 8090 BC (Possehl and Rissman 1992: 460).

A striking feature of the Upper Palaeolithic adaptive pattern in the southeastern fringes of the Eastern Ghats (blade-and-burin lithic cotradition) is demographic concentration in the riverine zones marked by a degree of sedentism; long-term occupations (with the artifactual counts going into several thousands); and a tendency towards microlithization. Such a kind of archaeological record indicates the cultural links of the succeeding Mesolithic with the Upper Palaeolithic. This kind of evidence, viewed in the light of evidences from the thickly forested zones of the Son/Belan/Ganga valleys in Uttar Pradesh (Sharma *et al* 1980; Sharma and Clark 1983), indicates sub-regional patterns of Mesolithic emergence, with certain broad similarities, in the Indian situation.

Mesolithic

The Mesolithic in the Eastern Ghats, as elsewhere is characterized by a microlithic technocomplex (Issac 1960; Kasturi Bai 1982; Krishna Sastry 1983; Madhushana Rao 1979; Murali Mohan 1994; Murty 1981, 1985, 1988; Nagabhushana Rao 1960; Raju 1988; Sankalia 1974; Singh 1979; Sudarsen 1976; Thimma Reddy 1968; Vijaya Prakash 1981). The tools are made on blades and bladelets and the predominant types are backed points, obliquely blunted blades, lunates, triangles and trapezes; flake scrapers; worked flakes and nodules; and fluted cores of finest quality. The Mesolithic occupation in the Kurnool caves has also yielded a well finished shouldered arrowhead on limestone; a perforator with needle sharp end on limestone, finished by grinding; sling balls; quartzite hammerstones and grinding slabs.

The raw materials in the western peneplains and the Kurnool cave areas are chert, jasper and chalcedony, whereas in the southeastern Eastern Ghats the raw material is quartz and crystal. The latter industries are comparable to the coastal *teri* sites of Tamil Nadu. In the thickly forested zones of the lower Godavari valley inhabited by the shifting cultivators (Murty 1988), microlithic occurrences occur in three contexts. One type is the association of bifacial heavy-duty tools on quartzite and dolorite along with microliths made of chert, jasper, agate, chalcedony and quartz. The second types of context is heavy-duty implements, microliths and polished celts of the Eastern Neolithic complex. Several surficial findspots were reported in the forested ecotones of the Eastern Ghats, north of the river Godavari which have yielded faceted tools and shouldered celts typical of the Eastern Indian Neolithic complex (Subrahmanyam and Raju 1983) in association with microliths, perforated stones and potsherds of gritty fabric with red-slipped surfaces. Occupational debris of distinctive entities consisting of heavy-duty tools, microliths and polished celts of the Eastern Indian Neolithic complex is a widespread Mesolithic tradition in the Indravati Basin (Nanda 1983) and the Mahanandi river systems (Ota 1986) of Orissa which lie in the easternmost outliers of the Eastern Ghats. The nature of this technocomplex with microliths, amorphous tools, and heavy-duty implements, indicates a Mesolithic adaptation to closed woodlands, and the artifacts, especially the heavy-duty tools, in functional terms suggest their use for clearance of patches of forests and tree felling, to begin with, at least to make settlements.

Ecologically this zone right from the lower reaches of the Godavari valley upto Santal Paraganas and extending into the northeast (and linking up with Southeast Asia for that matter) is the belt of swidden agriculture (or shifting cultivation, called *podu*). Considering the contiguity of (Upper Palaeolithic and) Mesolithic sites with the shifting cultivator habitats, and drawing analogies from the land use pattern and subsistence strategies of the latter, we can predict that fire was as much an important tool in the prehistoric past as it is today, for forest clearance, to raise settlements and food procurement through fire-aided hunting. Bits of charcoal do occur in some of these Mesolithic sites but their provenance and clear-cut association with the Mesolithic is yet to be confirmed. Use of fire as a tool (for landscape manipulation and hunting) has its greatest impact on the local ecotones. It has been suggested in the context of Stone Age occupations in the shifting cultivation zone of the Eastern Ghats (Murty 1988) that fire aided forest clearance created fire-climax ecosystems and favourable habitats for colonizing plant species of graminae and promoted symbiotic association between human groups and certain pyrophilous species. These fire-climax ecosystems result in environmental changes with no relationship to any climatic changes, and moreover increase in plant and animal productivity. The shifting cultivators (e.g. Konda Reddi, Konda Dora, Koya, Khond etc.) of the Eastern Ghats provide valuable insights to make propositions of the man-land associations, taking cues from the present and going back into the past. These shifting cultivators practice bush fallow and short fallow agriculture and the general pattern is that of both monocrop and polycrop agriculture in two cycles annually: (1) *punasa panta* (June to August) and (2) *Pedda panta* (January to June). For *punasa panta* the major crop is rice, a variety called *budama dhanyamu,* the seeds of which are usually stored but they are also obtained, if the need arises, from the Odiya who migrated from Orissa. Incidentally *budama dhanyamu* also grows without cultivation along hillslopes and stream banks, where it is also harvested. For the *punasa panta* two other crops are also grown, namely, *samalu (Panicum miliare)* and *sollu (Eleusine coracana)*, but the yields are small.

For *pedda panta* which is also known as *konda panta* (hill crop) mixed cropping in *podu* fields is the pattern. That is, a variety of crops in different combinations are raised by broadcasting and covering with the ashes of burnt trees, shrubs and undergrowth. These crops are millets such as *samalu, sollu, korralu (Setaria italica), gentelu (Pennisetum typhoideum), varigelu (Panicum miliaceum) and arikelu (Paspalum scrobiculatum), chamalu (Echinichola frumentacea);* two varieties (red and white) of *jonnalu (Sorghum bicolor); mokka jonna (Zea mays);* grams like *alasandalu/ bobbarlu (Vigna catjang), kandulu (Cajanus cajan), minumulu (Phaseolus mungo), pesalu (Vigna radiatus), sanagalu (Cicer arietinum),* and *ulavalu (Mycrotyloma uniflorum);* oil seeds like *anusulu, nuvvulu (Sesamum indicum); arise (Linum usitatissimum); avalu (Brassica juncea)* and *amudalu (Ricinus communis);* several kinds of beans (*Chikkudlu),* the common varieties being *Dolichos lab-lab and Vicia fabra;* squashes like *gummadi (Cucurbita maxima)* and *an-pa (Lagenaria vulgaris);* leafy vegetable the most common being a few varieties of *Amaranthus* sp. and *Hibiscus* sp.; *konda mirapa* (a hill variety of chili); yarns and tuber crops (not less than thirty varieties including a few of *Dioscorea* sp.); and several kinds (landraces) of rice. It is no wonder that the Konda Reddis not only believe there is comfort in the *podu* cultivation, but also compare the *podu* field to a grocer's shop.

The most important crop in this zone is rice. At a rough estimate there are about three thousand local rice varieties (landraces) in this region. What is important there are still extant two species of wild rice in the Eastern Ghats which are *Oryza nivara* and *Oryza* var. *spontanea.* The local name for *Oryza nivara* over a wide tract is *passer* (or *phasser/passei/phassei).* Some of the other names for local rice varieties are *balunga, jhar, uridhan, janglidhan, deobhat, akasatadi* and *vanji* (used by the Gonds and Kolams of Adilabad); and *balludan* (black rice); *batadan, sapoordan, ninnudan, bogadu sapoor* and *oldu sapoor* (scented variety) are the names of local rice varieties in the Araku valley. Though most of the local varieties are certainty landraces, there could be wild strains, if the names can be taken as suggestive. For instance *uridhan* refers to rice that grows near the settlements; *janglidhan* means rice that grows wild; *deobhat* suggests the rice given by god; and *akasatadi* is the rice that springs up with the onset of monsoon. Thus there are a few varieties of rice which are not cultivated, and all these are harvested by the shifting cultivators.

The presence of wild rice in the Eastern Ghats, occurrence of wild and domesticated rice respectively, in the contexts of Mesolithic and Neolithic (the Vindhyan Neolithic) in the Son, Belan and Ganga valleys (Sharma *et al* 1980; Sussman *et al* 1983; Possehal and Rissman 1992); and the calibrated radiocarbon date of 3385-3135 BC at Chopani Mando III (Belan valley), all point out the plausibility of harvesting and cultivation of rice going back to the prehistoric times. In the context of archaeological evidences and ethnoecological practices, the whole belt extending from the northeast down to the Eastern Ghats at least forms a part of secondary centre of rice domestication.

An interesting feature of the Mesolithic in the Eastern Ghats is preserved in the Kurnool Caves (Murty 1995). Here the Late Mesolithic occupational deposits yielded Neolithic Chalcolithic pottery, copper objects such as bangles, spiral ear ring, copper rod, and a steatite disc bead along with microliths and food refuse of wild game. A red ware potsherd from one of the caves gave a TL date of 1800 BC. Archaeological evidence in the Kunderu valley, in which the Kurnool caves are situated, have brought to light numerous Neolithic-Chalcolithic sites (see below) and radiocarbon dates from excavated sites in the southern Deccan point out that the induction of Neolithic-Chalcolithic cultures began around Ca. 3000 BC. What is important in the context of Late Mesolithic vis-à-vis Neolithic-Chalcolithic in this region is the culture contacts between the former and latter and the occurrence of Neolithic-Chalcolithic in the Late Mesolithic can be attributed to some kind of exchange system between the former and latter.

Subsistence Economy (Palaeolithic and Mesolithic)

The artifact categories of the Palaeolithic (Lower, Middle and Upper) and Mesolithic, in functional terms, indicates a strategy of hunting wild game. As attention has already been drawn, some of the lithic tools of the Palaeolithic and Mesolithic could only have been used to work on wood/bone/antler to make hunting contrivances such as wooden spears, projectile points (flake points hafted in wooden shafts); bow and arrow and harpoons (especially from Upper Palaeolithic times); and a variety of traps and snares. Since these sites (excepting the Kurnool caves) are open-air sites no organic remains survived. But the food refuse in the Upper Palaeolithic and Mesolithic of the Kurnool Caves (Murty 1975) belongs to both small and big game. Some of these are langur (*Presbytis entellus*), jungle cat (Felis *chaus*), rusty spotted cat (*Felis rubiginosa*), Indian grey mongoose (*Herpestes edwardsi*), sloth bear (*Melursus ursinus*), large bandicoot rat (*Bandicota indica*), Indian bush rat (*Golunda ellioti*), black naped hare (*Lepus*), ox (*Bos* sp.), buffalo (*Bubalus* sp.), nilgai (*Boselaphus tragocamelus*), chinkara (*Gazella gazella bennetti*), blackbuck (*Antilope cervicapra*), four-horned antelope (*Tetracerus quadricornis*), sambar (*Cervus unicolor*), chital (*Axis axis*), barking deer (*Muntiacus muntijak*), mouse deer (*Tragulus meminna*), wild boar (*Sus scrofa cristatus*), pangolin (*Smutsia gigantea*), monitor lizard (*Varanus dracaena*), and bones of birds and aquatic fauna which are too fragmentary for identification. It would not have been possible to hunt this big and small game represented in the Kurnool caves without specialized hunting technologies. All the indigenous communities inhabiting varied ecotones of the Eastern Ghats (e.g. the Chenchu, Yanadi, Yerukula, Boya, Konda Reddi, Konda Dora, Koya etc.) have exploited the above cited game in earlier times, before prohibition of hunting (Annexure I). During the present times they mostly depend upon small game birds and fish, and prey upon big game in change encounters. Drawing analogies from the ethnographic present the hunting strategies during the Palaeolithic and Mesolithic times plausibly were (a) group hunting; (b) chasing and stalking the game; (c) use of a variety of net traps, noose traps, and gravity traps; (d) use of different kinds of bows and arrows, and slings, (e) fire-aided hunting; and (f) opportunistic scavenging. Insofar as the exploitation of wild plant foods during the prehistoric period there are no archaeological traces, but from the wild plant foods exploited by the ethnographic present (Annexure II) it is possible to expect considerable reliance on such flora in the subsistence behaviour the prehistoric past.

The Neolithic-Chalcolithic

While the Palaeolithic and Mesolithic are hunting-gathering cultures, the Neolithic-Chalcolithic are that of the forest farmers. The emergence of Neolithic-Chalcolithic cultures in the Eastern Ghats is not a gradual tradition from the preceding Mesolithic but due to minicolonization by the farming societies which moved in form. These cultures elsewhere are widespread in the river valley systems of the lower Godavari, Krishna, Tunghabhadra, Penner, and Kunderu. These sites, in most cases, are not in deltaic zones, but in semi-arid, low rainfall (800mm to 1000mm) and red and black sandy loams regions which are suitable for dry farming and best for pastoralism. The radiocarbon dates (5730 BC half life) from the excavated sites indicate a time range of 2465 BC to 955 BC (Ehrich 1992 : 466) for the southern Neolithic.

The salient features of these farming cultures are (a) sedentary village settlements with semi-permanent to permanent structures (mostly wattle and daub); (b) stone tools finished by grinding and polishing (polishes stone axe industry) and made on hard rocks like dolorite and basalt, (c) long and thin blade artifacts made on cryptocrystalline rocks like chart, jasper, chalcedony and agate; (d) pottery which is handmade in the earlier stages and wheel thrown in the later stages; and (e) an economy based on millet farming, and cattle and sheep/goat pastoralism. The presence of remains of wild animals in food refuse also indicate that the dietary requirements are supplemented by wild game. The economy is thus basically agro-pastoral with a sedentary village life.

On the basis of evidences from excavated sites (see Allchins 1982, 1997; Sankalia for details and references), Allchins suggested three phases. Phase I represents the earliest settlements on tops of granatoid hills, on leveled terraces on hill sides, or in the valleys between two or more hills. The material culture consists of a polished stone axe industry, a blade and bladelet tool technocomplex with ash mounds (i.e. mounds formed by burnt cattle among accumulations), and it has been suggested that the ashmounds are cattle pens or places where domesticated cattle (*Bos indicus*) are herded, and that the major economic activity depended on cattle husbandry.

Some of the pottery types of this phase (e.g. those with applied ring feet and hollow pedestals recall those of pre-Harappan Amri or Kalibangan. In the context of the latter, it should be noted that the origins of the Neolithic-Chalcolithic (referred to above as minicolonization) in the southern Deccan are linked to some epicenter in the northwestern part of the Indian subcontinent. Radicarbon dates indicate a date of Caesalpiniaceae 2800-1800 BC for these levy farming settlements.

In the succeeding Phase II the settlement pattern continues without any change but the structures, circular huts of wattle and daub on wooden frames with mud floors, are well made. In the material culture new elements in pottery (e.g. perforated and spouted vessels) appear, recalling the early Harappan types of the Indus valley and Baluchistan. Copper and bronze artifacts appear for the first time in this (hence, the term Chalcolithic) phase and increase in frequency towards the end of this phase. Because of the use of metal (copper/bronze) Phase II occupations are metal using Neolithic cultures. This phase is ascribed to ca. 1800 to 1500 BC on the basis of radiocarbon dates.

In the next (and last) phase (Phase III) there is an increase in the occurrence of copper/bronze tools, while the rest of other items of material culture (e.g. polished stone axes, blade and bladelet tools, pottery) continue. An entirely new pottery type wheel made unburnished ware with people paint appears; and this has affinities with the Chalcolithic Jowar ware of Maharashtra. The appearance of domestic horse (*Equus caballus*), rock paintings showing horses with riders, and caches of swords or disks of copper or bronze (as at Kallur in the Raichur district, Karnataka) are associated with this phase. These copper/bronze objects though are stray occurrences display similarities to those of Iran (database to the middle of second millennium BC), which again suggests movement of people from the Indo-Iranian borderlands. This phase is ascribed to Caesalpiniaceae. 1400-1050 BC on the basis of radiocarbon dates.

Economy

Farming

The epicenters for these early farming village settlements are favourable resource zones for agro-pastoral economies (Murty 1989). From the general pattern of their distribution in respective physiographic zones, the preferred landforms are low hilly ranges away from major watersheds but in proximity to streams; tropical black clays, tropical red and black sandy loams, sandy or sandy-loamy ferruginous tropical soils, and some sites are also in the deltaic alluvium. Considering the settlement pattern in relation to landscape ecology, it is clear that areas which were mainly suited for rainfed gravity-flow irrigation were essentially colonized. Palaeobotanical evidences preserved at some of the excavated sites in the southern Deccan point out that millets and pulses were the main cultivated crops. There are finger millet (*Eleusine coracana),* kodo millet (*Paspalum scrobiculatum*), horse gram (*Dolichos biflorus*), green gram (*Vigna radiata*), black gram (*Phaseolus mungo*), hycianth bean (*Dolichos lablab*), rice (*Oryza sativa*) and barley (*Hordeum vulgare*) is known from one site.

The remains of these millets and grams and the location of these settlements, seen in the context of prevailing agricultural practices in this semi-arid region suggests that the prehistoric crop management pattern could not have been much different from that of today. Proceeding on the premise that crops were cultivated on levelled terraces of hills and foothills and gravity-flow irrigation was the land use pattern, it would be worthwhile to consider the dispersal polished stone axes in the hilly areas with no occupational debris. These polished stone axes in functional terms can be associated with tree felling and land clearance; and these surfacial findspots point out landscape manipulation of hilly and forested areas to make farmlands for dry farming, not very different from the present day practices in these areas.

Animal husbandry

The faunal remains recovered from the excavated Neolithic-Chalcolithic sites belong to domesticated species and also some wild game. The domesticated species which may vary from site to site consist of cattle (*Bos indicus*), buffalo (*Bubalus bubalis*), sheep (*Ovis aries),* goat (*Capra hircus aegagrus*), pig (*Sus scrofa cristatus*) and fowl (*Gallus* sp.). Cattle predominate among the domesticated species at all the sites indicating maximum reliance on cattle management in the economy of these early farming communities. While the cattle remains (which also include food refuse showing cut/crop marks and roasting) are not less than 50.00 per cent (more at some sites), the remains of sheep/goat are a meager 05.00 per cent was because of primarily cattle pastoral (sheep/goat to a much less extent)-cum-dry farming. Even today cattle pastoralism linked to sedentary farming villages is the chief economic activity in the upland semi-arid and low rainfall zones of Telangana and Rayalaseema.

Sheep/goat Pastoralism

As mentioned above the sheep/goat remains in these early farming settlements is very low and poorly represented, thus making it obvious that sheep/goat herding received less attention in the agro-pastoral sedentary villages. In such a situation, as a methodological approach, we can take recourse to ethnoecological and oral traditions of the present day sheep/goat pastoralists of this region, i.e. the Kurubas, Kuruvas, Kurumas and Gollas. The western peneplains of this region (the Telangana and Rayalaseema plateau) with extensive grasslands, scrub woodlands and thorny thicket zones is vastly inhabited by the abovementioned sheep/goat pastoral communities. This oral narrative centered on their god betrays metaphorical representations recapitulating the social memory of their past (Murty 1993).

The sheep/goat pastoral communities claim their origin from an ancestral agricultural stock. To give a brief summary, their god, before his deification, happened to be the youngest of the seven sons of an agricultural Kapu family (Adireddi the husband and Ademma the wife). Their last son Elanagireddi was born due to a boon given by the god Siva. Elanagireddi therefore had supernatural powers, and he was also the headman of seven villages. The power and prestige enjoyed by Elanagireddi causes envy among his six brothers and sisters-in-law and they hatch a plan to drive him out. They make several allegations against him, one of which was that he attempted to molest one of his sisters-in-law. They ask him to move out of the family, procure his own bullocks and cultivate a land in a distant forest. In the piece of land where Elanagireddi was asked to cultivate, there was a termite mound (*putta*). At this juncture let us turn to an episode in the narrative regarding the origin of sheep. In the primeval past, in the heavenly abode of Kailasa, god Siva's consort, Parvati, asks Siva that she wants sheep. To her delight he creates a ram and an awe. In course of time, these two multiply into a big herd, and become a nuisance. They filth the gardens in Kailasa, keep pulling the hair of Parvati and trouble her. Vexed with the sheep, Parvati asks Siva to send the sheep away. Then Siva brings all the sheep, keeps them in the termite mound (*nagaloka*), and this is the place where Elanagireddi, starts felling the trees, clearing and burning the shrub to prepare the field for cultivation. While Elanagireddi was ploughing, his plough gets stuck in the termite mound. Perplexed he prays to god Siva. Siva and Parvati manifest to him at the termite mound and tell him that he is not suited for agriculture. They tell him to let the sheep out of the termite mound and herd them. Elanagireddi lets the sheep out of the termite mound and as ordained by Siva and Parvati he starts rearing the sheep, and then becomes a shepherd. He moves for twelve years in the forests for pasture with his flock of sheep. The narrative thus explains, the origin of sheep/goat pastoralism as a distinctive economic organization. And the present day Kurubas/Kuruvas are his progeny and Elanagireddi becomes a god. He is equated with Siva, and is a warrior-god. The narratives of other sheep/goat pastoralists (Golla/Kuruma), of which there are numerous intra-regional versions, depict the origin of sheep/goat pastoralism from an ancestral agricultural stock.

CONCLUSION

The cultural ecology of the Eastern Ghats embodies an array of adaptive strategies encompassing social groups adapted to hunting-gathering, fishing-hunting-gathering, shifting cultivation, agro-pastoralism (leaving aside wet rice agriculture in the deltaic zones) and sheep/goat pastoralism. The archaeological evidence unfolds various patterns of man-land associations and adaptive strategies. The traditions of the ethnographic present and the medieval historical sources (the latter not discussed here) reveal the rich diversity, symbiotic association between different social orders, a past-present continuum in the interaction of native (indigenous/tribal) social groups and the 'State' level societies.

REFERENCES

Allchin, Bridget and Raymond (1982), *The Rise of Civilization in India and Pakistan*. London: Cambridge University Press.

Allchin, F.R. and Bridget Allchin (1997), *Origin of a Civilization: the Prehistory of Early Archaeology of South Asia*. New Delhi : Viking (Penguin Books).

Ehrich, W.R. (1992), *Chronologies in Old World Archaeology (Third Edition)*, II: 447-474.

Gaussen, H., P. Legris, and M. Virat (1964), *International Map of the Vegetation and Environmental Conditions at Scale 1/1,000,000: Madras with Notes on the Sheet*, New Delhi : Indian Council of Agricultural Research.

Gaussen, H., P. Legris and M. Virat (1965), *International Map of the Vegetation and Environmental Conditions Scale 1/1,000,000 Godavari, With Notes on the Sheet*. New Delhi : Indian Council of Agricultural Research.

Isaac, N. (1960), Stone Age Cultures of Kurnool District. Ph.D. Thesis, Poona University.

Kasturi Bai, M. (1982), The Stone Age Cultures of the Eleru River Valley in East Godavari District, Andhra Pradesh. Ph.D. Thesis, Nagarjuna University.

Krishna Sastry, V.V. (1983) *The Proto and Early Historic Cultures of Andhra Pradesh (Archaeological Series 58).* Hyderabad: The Government of Andhra Pradesh.

Madhusudhana Rao, V.V. (1979), Stone Age Cultures of Prakasam District. Ph.D. Thesis, Nagarjuna University.

Mishra, S. (1992), The Age of Acheulian in India, *Current Anthropology,* 33: 325-328.

Murali Mohan, S. (1994), Patterns of Pre-Neolithic Settlements in Coastal Andhra. Ph.D. Thesis, Nagarjuna University.

Murty, M.L.K. (1969), Blade and Burin Industries near Renigunta on the South-East Coast of India. *Proceedings of the Prehistoric Society.* 34 : 83-101.

Murty, M.L.K. (1975), Late Pleistocene Fauna of Kurnool Caves, South India. In A.T. Clason (ed.), *Archaeozoological Studies.* 132-38. Amsterdam: North Holland Publishing Company.

Murty, M.L.K. (1981), Hunter-Gatherer Ecosystems and Archaeological Patterns of Subsistence behaviour on the Southeast Coast of India : An Ethnographic Model, *World Archaeology.* 13(1): 47-58.

Murty, M.L.K. (1985), Ethnoarchaeology of the Kurnool Cave Areas, *World Archaeology.* 17(2): 192-205.

Murty, M.L.K. (1988), Rice and Tuber Crops in the Eastern Ghats (India): An Ethnoecological Perspective, *Bulletin of the Indo-Pacific Prehistory Association.* 26-36.

Murty, M.L.K. (1989), Pre-Iron Age Agricultural Settlements in South India: An Ecological Perspective, *Man and Environment.* XIV (1): 65-81.

Murty, M.L.K. (1993), Ethnohistory of Pastoralism: A Study of Kuruvas and Gollas, *Studies in History.* 9(1), n.s.: 33-41.

Nagabhusana Rao, S. (1966), Stone Age Cultures of Prakasam District, Andhra Pradesh. Ph.D. Thesis, Andhra University.

Nanda, S.C. (1983), Stone Age Cultures of Indravati, Koraput District, Orissa. Ph.D. Thesis, Poona University.

Ota, S.B. (1986), Mesolithic Culture of Phulbani District (Orissa) With Special Reference to the Heavy Duty Component, *Bulletin of the Deccan College Research Institute.* 45 : 79-88.

Pappu, R.S. (1995), The Contribution of the Earth Sciences to the Development of Indian Archaeology. In S.Wadia, R. Korisettar and V.S. Kale (eds). *Quaternary Environments and Geoarchaeology of India Essays in Honour of Professor S.N.Rajaguru. Geological Society of India Memoir 32.* Pp.414-434. Bangalore; Geological Society of India.

Possehl, G.L. and P.C. Rismann (1992), The Chronology of Prehistoric India : From Earliest Times to the Iron Age. In R.W. Ehrich (ed.), *Chronologies in Old World Archaeology (Third Edition)*, Vol. 1 & 2: 465-474.

Raju, D.R. (1986-87), Fresh Light on the Upper Palaeolithic from the Eastern Ghats, Andhra Pradesh, *Bulletin of the Indo-Pacific Prehistory Association*. 7: 17-22.

Raju, D.R. (1988), *Stone Age Hunter-Gatherers: An Ethnoarchaeology of the Cuddapah Region, Southeast India.* Pune: Ravish Publishers.

Sankalia H.D. (1974), *Prehistory and Protohistory of India and Pakistan*, Pune: Deccan College.

Sharma, G.R., V.D. Misra, D. Mandal, B.B. Misra and J.N. Pal (1980), *Beginnings of Agriculture*, Allahabad: Abinash Prakashan.

Sharma, G.R. and J.D. Clark (eds.) (1983), *Palaeoenvironment and Prehistory in the Middle Son Valley*, Allahabad: Abinash Prakashan.

Singh, Thakur Raja Ram (1979), Prehistoric and Early Historic Sites in Karimnagar Region, Andhra Pradesh, *Journal of Andhra Pradesh Archaeology*, 1(1): 1-12.

Spate, O.H.K., A.T.A. Learmonth and B.H. Farmer (1972), *India, Pakistan and Ceylon The Regions*, Bombay: B.I. Publications.

Subrahmanyam B.R. and David Raju (1983), The Neolithic Phase in Coastal Andhra —Distribution Pattern, *Journal of the Andhra Historical Research Society*. XXXVIII(1): 37-45.

Sudarsen, V. (1976), Environment and Archaeology of Nellore District. Ph.D. Thesis, Andhra University.

Sussman, C., R. Blumenschine, J.D. Clark and B.B. Misra (1983), Preliminary Report on Excavations at the Mesolithic Occupation Site at Baghor II Locality. In G.R. Sharma and J.D. Clark (eds.), *Palaeoenvironmental and Prehistory in the Middle Son Valley*. 161-96. Allahabad: Abinash Prakashan.

Thimma Reddy, K. (1968), Prehistory of Cuddapah District. Ph.D. Thesis, Poona University

Vijaya Prakash, P. (1981), *Lithic Cultures and Palaeoenvironment in Gambhearam River Valley, Visakhapatnam Coast*. Ph.D. Thesis., Andhra University.

Williams M.A.J. and M.F. Clarke (1995), Quaternary Geology and Prehistoric Environments in the Son and Belan Valleys, North Central India. In S.Wadia, R.Korisettar and V.S.Kale (eds). *Quaternary Environments and Geoarchaeology of India Essays in Honour of Professor Rajaguru*. 282-308. Bangalore: Geological Survey of India, Memoir 32.

Annexure I

Important Big and Small Game Hunted by the Indigenous Communities in the Eastern Ghats

Common Name	*Latin Name*
Hanuman langur	*Presbytis entellus*
Rhesus macaque	*Macaca mulatta*
Sloth bear	*Melursus ursinus*
Small Indian civet	*Vivericula indica*
Palm civet	*Paradoxurus hermaphroditus*
Jungle cat	*Felis chaus*
Mouse deer	*Tragulus meminna*
Wild boar	*Sus scrofa cristatus*
Spotted deer	*Axis axis*
Barking deer	*Muntiacus muntjak*
Sambar	*Cervus unicolor*
Nilgai	*Boselaphus tragocamelus*
Four-horned antelope	*Tetracerus quadricornis*
Indian blackbuck	*Antilope cervicapra*
Indian gazelle	*Gazella gazella bennetti*
Indian pangolin	*Manis crassicaudala*
Indian giant squirrel	*Ratufa indica*
Indian porcupine	*Hystix indica*
Indian hare	*Lepus nigricollis*
Monitor lizard	*Varanus dracaena*

Annexure II

Wild Plant Foods Commonly Exploited By The Indigenous Communities in the Eastern Ghats

Botanical name	*Family*	*Food Value*
1	2	3
Anona squamosa L.	Anonaceae	Fruits are eaten.
Poinciana elata L.	Caesalpiniaceae	Pods are eaten raw and leaves made into a curry.
Tamarindus indica L.	Caesalpiniaceae	Pulp of the pods is thoroughly mixed with wood ash to reduce acrid taste and consumed. Tender leaves of the new foliage are made into dal, chutney etc.
Bauhinia vahlii Wight & Arn.	Caesalpiniaceae	Seeds are roasted and eaten. Leaves are used for making leaf plates and umbrellas.
Pithecolobium dulce Benth.	Mi moseae	Pods are commonly eaten raw by tribals and other groups.
Prosopis spicegera L.	Mimoseae	Pods are eaten raw.
Alangium lamarckii Thwaites	Cornaceae	Fruits are eaten.
Ficus glomerata Roxb.	Moraceae	Fruits are eaten.
Ficus bengalensis L.	Moraceae	Fruits are eaten.
Ficus religiosa L.	Moraceae	Fruits are eaten.
Artocarpus integrifolia L.	Moraceae	Fruits and seeds are eaten.
Urtica tuberosa R.	Urticaceae	Tubers are boiled and eaten.
Flacourtia ramontchi L'Heritier	Bixaceae	Drupes are eaten.
Trema orientalis Blume.	Ulmaceae	Leaves mixed with any type of gram are made into a curry.

{Cont.}...

1	2	3
Capparis sepiaria L.	Capparaceae	Fruits are eaten.
Melothria heterophylla Cogn.	Cucurbitaceae	Tubers are boiled and eaten.
Opuntia dillenii Haw.	Cacataceae	Fruits are eaten.
Grewia asiatica L.	Tiliaceae	Fruits are eaten.
Grewia salvifolia Heyne.	Tiliaceae	Fruits are eaten.
Grewia tiliaefolia Bedd.	Tiliaceae	Fruits are eaten.
Grewia hirsuta Vahl.	Tiliaceae	Fruits are eaten.
Streculia foetida L.	Streculiaceae	Seeds are eaten.
Malva parviflora L.	Malvaceae	Leaf vegetable made into a curry.
Erythroxylon monogynum Roxb.	Linaceae	Leaves and drupes are eaten.
Bridelia retusa Spreng.	Euphorbiaceae	Drupes are eaten.
Phyllanthus emilica L.	Euphorbiaceae	Fruits are eaten.
Givotia rottlerformis Griff.	Euphorbiaceae	Fruits are eaten.
Careya arborea Roxb.	Myrtaceae	Seeds are roasted and eaten.
Eugenia alternifolia Wight.	Myrtaceae	Fruits are eaten.
Eugenia jambolana Lam.	Myrtaceae	Fruits are eaten.
Terminalia belerica Roxb.	Combretaceae	Fruits are eaten.
Memecylon edule Roxb.	Melastomaceae	Fruits are eaten.
Zizyphus jujuba Mill. Non Lam.	Rhamnaceae	Fruits are eaten.
Zizyphus oenoplia Mill.	Rhamnaceae	Fruits are eaten.
Zizyphus xylopyrus Willd.	Rhamnaceae	Fruits and kernels are eaten.
Sageretia oppositifolia Brong.	Rhamnaceae	Fruits are eaten.

{Cont.}...

1	2	3
Vitis quadrangularis L.	Vitaceae	Tender branches mixed with gram and tender leaves of the tamarind tree are made into dal.
Diospyros melanoxylon Roxb.	Ebenaceae	Fruits are eaten.
Mimusops hexandra Roxb.	Sapotaceae	Berries are eaten.
Bassia Latifolia Roxb.	Sapotaceae	Flowers are a seasonal source of food. Kernels are also eaten. Flowers are distilled into an alcoholic beverage (*ippa sara*).
Glycosmis pentaphylla (Retz.) Correa.	Rutaceae	Berries are eaten.
Aegel marmelos (L.) Corr.	Rutaceae	Pulp of the ripened fruits is roasted and eaten.
Balnites roxburhii Planch.	Zygophyllaceae	Fruits are eaten.
Garuga pinnata Roxb.	Burseraceae	Fruits are eaten and leaves are made into curry.
Balsamodendron berryi Arn.	Burseraceae	Fruits are eaten.
Azadirachta indica A.Juss.	Meliaceae	Drupes are eaten.
Buchanania angustifolia Roxb.	Anacardiaceae	Fruits and seeds from an important item of food and are collected on a large scale during the season.
Buchanania latifolia Roxb.	Anacardiaceae	Flowers, fruits and seeds are eaten.
Strychnos nux-vomica L.	Loganiaceae	Berries are eaten.
Carissa caranadus L.	Apocynaceae	Berries are eaten.
Carissa spinarum A. DC.	Apocynaceae	Berries are eaten.
Gardinia lucida Roxb.	Rubiaceae	Fruits are eaten.

{Cont.}...

1	2	3
Gardinia gummifera L.	Rubiaceae	Fruits are eaten.
Canthium parviflorum Lam.	Rubiaceae	Leaves and fruits are eaten . An important item of food during times of scarcity.
Nymphaea esculenta R.	Nymphaceae	The tuberous roots are eaten .
Nymphaea cyanea R.	Nymphaceae	Berries are eaten.
Nymphaea lotus Willd.	Nymphaceae	Berries are eaten.
Nasturtium officinale R. Br	Cruciferaceae	Leaves are made into curry.
Trianthema obcordata R.	Aizoaceae	Leaves are made into curry.
Amaranthus tristis Willd.	Amaranthaceae	An important leaf vegetable for curry.
Amaranthus spinosus Willd.	Amaranthaceae	A very common leaf vegetable for curry.
Amaranthus polygamus Willd.	Amaranthaceae	An important leaf vegetable for curry.
Amaranthus giganteus Konig.	Amaranthaceae	Leaves and the tender succulent parts of the stem and branches are made into curry.
Amaranthus polygonoides Willd.	Amaranthaceae	An important leaf vegetable for curry.
Cordia fulvosa Wight	Boraginaceae	Fruits are eaten.
Cordia myxa L.	Boraginacae	Fruits are eaten.
Colocasia esculenta Schott.	Araceae	Tubers are eaten.
Dioscorea bulbifera L.	Dioscoreaceae	Tubers are boiled and regularly consumed.
Dioscorea oppositifolia Willd.	Dioscoreaceae	Tubers are boiled and regularly consumed.

{Cont.}...

1	2	3
Dioscorea pentaphylla L.	Dioscoreaceae	Tubers are eaten. Some of the noxious forms are made edible by repeated washing and boiling.
Borassus flabellifer L.	Palmaceae	Pulp of the fruits, jelly-like pyrenes inside the fruits and tender shoots (after roasting) are eaten.
Phoenix slyverstris Roxb.	Palmaceae	Apical meristem and berries are eaten.
Tacca pinnatifida Forst.	Taccaceae	Tubers which taste like arrow-root are eaten.
Bambusa arundinacea (Retz.) *Willd.*	Graminaceae	The young buds are eaten. Bamboo grain is an important item of food especially during times of scarcity; and the tabashir has various uses in medicine.
Dendrocalamus strictus Nees.	Graminaceae	B,amboo shoots are eaten. Bamboo grain is an important item of food.

5

Biodiversity and Society: The North-South Tangle

Rajiv K. Sinha and *Shweta Sinha*

INTRODUCTION

Every human civilization on earth has been rooted in the biodiversity of nature. The domestication of wild crops made the first farming possible. Genetic resources taken from the wild still sustain modern societies, providing food, fodder, medicines and industrial raw material. Biodiversity—the vast array of species of plants, animals and microorganisms created by nature is the 'foundation of human life' on earth. They have provided the basic necessities of our social, cultural, economic and biological life. Human life on earth would have been simply 'impossible' if there were no microorganisms, no wild plants, animals and insect species. How much do we realize about those thousands of wild worms, insects, birds and bats that work day and night in the soil, in the farm-land, and in the forest to provide food and fodder to us. Human life depends upon their survival, as they are all linked up in a complex chain of food web. If the chain becomes 'weak' (by extinction of species) at any point, it will be translated all along the chain. If the chain continues to be weaker at several points, as it is becoming today due to large-scale extinction of species, the chain of life on earth would finally break and disintegrate.

Ironically, human life on earth depends only upon the narrow spectrum of those species of plant life, which provides our entire food, fodder, fuel, fertiliser, furniture (timber), and medicinal needs. We have not yet explored those millions of species which nature has created. A number of them are getting extinct even before we come to know about them. Modern human society has retained only a few varieties of high yielding (HYV) crops, which they grow in modern agriculture. What if they are devastated by some new pests and disease?

With major change in earth's climate already on the way due to 'green-house effect' and 'global warming', accompanied by depletion of stratospheric ozone layer, preserving earth's biodiversity of plants, particularly crop plants, holds the key to human survival. The justification lies in the need for maintaining genetic variability for plant breeding. The maximum genetic diversity is going to provide the raw material with which the human society would adapt to change.

The loss of tropical forest causes the extinction of increasing number of species and reduction in the 'genetic diversity' of others. Preserving the 'gene pools' found in tropical forest is vitally important. The future of our agriculture vitally depends upon the gene pool of the wild relatives of modern crop plants, which are found in the tropical forests. With only 8 crops supplying 85 per cent of the world's food, new types of crops would be essential for human survival on earth.

Biodiversity, in wild and domesticated forms, is the source of most of human needs: food, fuel, fodder, fertiliser, fibre, timber and medicine for our living, clothing and housing. Many species have been fundamental to stabilization of climate, protection of watersheds, protection of soil, and to the protection of nurseries and breeding grounds. Undoubtedly it is the very basis of human existence on earth. One cannot imagine the situation in which the fungus *Pencillium* or the *Cinchona* tree were to become extinct before mankind discovered 'pencillin' and 'quinine' respectively from them. Both these drugs saved millions of lives during the World War II and after (Myers 1986). Besides, there are many socio-economic benefits of biodiversity, some of which are mentioned below :

1. In Asia, by the mid-1970s genetic improvements had increased wheat production worth $2 billion and rice production worth $1.5 billion a year by incorporating 'dwarf genes' into both the crops from their wild relatives. This formed the basis for green revolution.
2. Genes from a 'wild wheat' in Turkey saved an epidemic of the wheat disease in the USA in the 1960s. It provided resistance to that and other diseases and is saving worth $50 million annually to the US alone.
3. A particular gene from a single Ethiopean barley plant now protects $160 million worth of annual barley crop from the 'yellow dwarf virus'.
4. An ancient wild relative of corn (*Zea diploperennis*) from Mexico can be crossed with modern corn (*Zea mays*) varieties to produce a perennial, high yielding, disease resistant variety of maize called *Zea perennis* with potential world-wide savings to the farmers estimated at $4.4 billion annually in terms of agro-chemicals. This miracle maize has increased the value of corn in the US by $150 to 200 million per year.
5. Worldwide, medicines from wild products are worth some $40 billion a year.
6. In 1960, a child suffering from leukemia had only one chance in five of survival. Now the child has four chances in five due to the treatment with drugs containing active substances discovered in the rosy periwinkle (*Catharanthus roseus*), a tropical forest plant originating from Madagascar.
7. In 1970 when an epidemic called, grassy stunt virus, destroyed more than 160,000 hectares of rice in Indonesia, it could be controlled from a 'single gene' of wild rice, *Oryza nivara* from the forest of South India.

8. A wild coffee gene from Ethiopia's fast dwindling forest saved the Brazilian coffee species in 1970.
9. Among other medical products of biodiversity, the 'birth pill' that is swallowed by some 80 million women each day contains sex hormone combinations derived from a Mexican forest yam (*Dioscorea spp.*). Sales of this herbal birth pill are now worth $1 million per year.

Germplasm in Crop Improvement

Crops need to be given new protection every 5 to 10 years because pests and diseases-causing organisms change their races and physiological specializations for food requirements. The only effective way to counter this is to inter-breed them with new strains, often wild ones with resistant germplasm. There are several instances where the wild relatives have contributed in the improvement of their cultivated varieties. Rice, maize, potato and sugarcane are the prime examples.

Interbreeding with wild varieties increase yields and extend the area under crops. Nearly 10 million sq.km. of land around the world is too saline for agriculture. Vast areas in Thar desert have saline soils. If they are made productive or any such crop plant are produced which thrived in saline soil of Thar desert in Rajasthan, their germplasm could be used to create new crops for reclaiming the saline land of the world.

The wild plant and animal species became the foundation for agriculture and animal husbandry which began 5,000 to 10,000 years ago. Humanity has since recognized and utilized wildlife through conscious and unconscious selection pressure to develop and spread domesticated plants and animals for its use. Wild relatives of our crop plants and cattle are still needed and are indispensable to maintain their productivity (Pal 1940).

New and Alternative Food from the Wild

The future of human food security is highly dependent on biodiversity and genetic resources. Ancient civilizations depended upon a variety of food products with great nutritive value; but with the loss of biological diversity the range of food available for mankind on earth has narrowed down. Just three crop species, wheat, rice and maize provide half of the world's food; anoter four, potato, barley, sweet potato and cassava, bring the total to three quarters. Such overwhelming dependence on a few crops could prove dangerous for the civilization. Disease can wipe out these handful of crops, as it happened in the case of Irish potato famine in the 1940s, causing a fifth of the country's people to die.

Some 5,000 plant species have been used as food by the civilization across the world, and another 75,000 are expected to be edible which are not yet known. These need to be domesticated. A grass called job's tears from tropical forest is an extremely nutritious cereal so far not known to man. Tribes of North-East India grow *Amaranthus polygamous, Fagopyrum esculentum* and buckwheats, which are 'pseudo-cereals' rich in protein, particularly the amino acid, lysine. Amaranth is all set to make a re-entry into the food chain of human ecosystem as a major food crop of the world after 1519. Although not a grass, it produces huge quantities of seeds with high lysine content. Other new and promising sources of food for the humanity which can be domesticated from the wild are buffalo gourd (*Cucurbita foetidissima*), winged beans (*Psophocarpus tetragonolobus*), tree tomato, yeheb nut, pumello, and cope gooseberry from plant diversity, and green iguana, kouprey, pigmy hog, and tilapia fish from animal diversity. The seeds of *Cicer songaricum*, a wild plant from the Ladakh Himalayas has high protein and phospholipid contents. It also has about 1 per cent lecithin. Paraguayan plant produces calorie-free substance which is 300 times sweeter than sugar. A coffee entirely free from caffeine has been discovered on the Comoros Islands near Madagascar. These can enter into our modern food system.

Industrial Raw Materials from Biodiversity

We utilize materials from wild species every time we apply a shampoo or sun screen lotion, every time we paint a wall or varnish a table, every time we use a golf ball or jet engine or oil drilling equipment, every time we employ goods containing tin plate or glycerine, or every time we get to the doctor to take vaccine or to the dentist to make a mould of our teeth. Wild plant derived industrial materials include fats, oils, waxes, latex, pectins, resins, gums, and other exudates, vegetable dyes and tannins, lignin, cellulose, starch, hydrocarbons, and hosts of biochemical compounds. Palm oil is used in a hundred products from lipstick to tinplate, icecream to jet engines.

Raw Materials for Explosive Industries

Candelilla wax, which has great potential in explosive industry has been isolated from *Euphorbia antisyphilitica*, a wild desert plant of Mexican origin.

Raw Materials for Drugs and Pharmaceutical Industries

Diosgenin, an important raw material for production of steroid hormones and oral contraceptives, has been isolated from *Dioscorea deltoidea* and the roots of the desert plant, *Balanites aegyptiaea*. Nearly 95 per cent of all steroids are now being obtained from Mexican yam, *Dioscorea*, which is the main source of sex hormones (androgens, estrogens and progesterone), oral contraceptives, cortisones and other anti-inflammatory drugs. Scoparone, now under clinical trial as a hypotensive and tranquilizing agent, has been isolated from the inflorescence of *Artemisia scoparia*.

Isohexenylnaphthazarins are considered to be a new class of drugs and some of them possess anti-cancer activity. Five isohexenylnaphthazarins have been isolated from the roots of *Arnebia hispidissima*.

Withanolide-D and Withaferin-A are the chemical compounds extracted from the leaves of *Withania somnifera* have been found to have significant anti-tumour activity *in-vivo* against Sarcoma-180 cells in mice. They also inhibit RNA synthesis in them. The root powder of *Withania somnifera* has been found to be anabolic. It accelerates growth in children and retard the process of ageing in older people.

Raw Materials for Perfumery

The essential oil extracted from the leaves and inflorescence of *Cymbopogon* has been found to have great perfumery properties. Jojoba (*Simmondsia chinensis*) oil is in high demand in perfumery industries. Its oil is comparable with sperm whale oil.

Raw Materials for Petroleum Industries

Some species of xerophytic plants like, *Euphorbia caducifolia, Jatropha curcus* and *Calotropis procera* are very promising sources of rich hydrocarbons (C-15 compounds), and are classed as petro-crops. The oil obtained from the latex of *Jatropha curcus* is very close to diesel oil in its chemistry.

Life Savings Drugs from Biodiversity

Worldwide, medicines from the wild products worth some $40 billion a year is being utilized by the mankind. WHO has listed over 21,000 plant species around the world which have medicinal use. Wild species have provided most of our medicines in the traditional medical practices like Ayurveda, Siddha and Unani. In modern medicine too around 119 pure chemical substances extracted from about 90 species of plants are used. More than 40 out of the 90 species listed as plants useful in modern medicine are available in the wild. Each time we take a medicine, there is one chance in two that our purchase owes its origin, in some way or the other, to start point materials from the wild species (Myers 1986). The product may be an analgesic, an antibiotic, a diuretic, a laxative, a tranquilizer, or a cough postile. A host of microbial, anti-viral, cardioactive and neurophysiologic substances have been derived from the poisonous marine wildlife.

Foxgloves (*Digitalis purpurea*) have saved the lives of millions of heart patients by giving digoxin to modern medicine. Pacific yew (*Taxus wallichiana*) was found in 1991 to contain the most important drug, taxol, for the treatment of lungs, uterine, prostrate and breast cancer. The Madagascar rosy periwinkle (*Catharanthus roseus*) has provided the anti-leukemic drug, vincristine, and raised the hope of survival of leukemic children upto 80 per cent. Alkaloid from the Australian Moreton Bay Chestnut, the twiner *Ancistrocladus korupensis* from Korup in Cameroon yielding the chemical Michellamine-B, and the plant *Homolanthus nutans* from the Samoa islands in South Pacific yielding the chemical prostatin show great promise in combating the HIV, AIDS virus, the biggest human killer. *Rauvolfia serpentina* which gave antihypertensive drug reserpine; *Gymnema sylvestere* which gave hypoglycaemic drug gymnemic acid; *Bacopa monniera* and *Evolvulus alsinoides* which gave mental tonic to increase memory power and relief from mental anguish, stress and strain; *Phyllanthes nururi* for treatment of viral hepatitis; and *Commiphora wightii*, the gum resins of which have the property to lower serum cholesterol and triglycerides are proving to be a boon for the modern man.

The importance of alkaloids, codeine and morphine, obtained from *Papavar bracteatum* and *P. somniferum* respectively; ephedrene from *Ephedra gerardiana* and quinine from *Cinchona officinalis* in human life is already known to us. Quinghasu is a most promising anti-malarial herbal drug discovered in China in 1971. Ginseng (*Panax ginseng*) is emerging as another wonder drug. It is now being actively investigated all over the world for its effects on tumours, corneal opacity and for increasing resistance to infection.

Biodiversity: Key to Sustainable Agriculture

The stability of sustainable agriculture depends upon biodiversity. Throughout the world the traditional agro-forestry system, which is based on biodiversity, contains well over hundred annual and perennial plant species per field that yield diverse plant products, from food, fodder to fuel, fertiliser, timber and herbal drugs. Biodiversity renews the soil fertility without the use of chemical fertilisers and controls agricultural pests without the use of pesticides. The intercropping of diverse plant species in a polyculture farming system helps provide habitats for the natural enemies—the benevolent insects and predators for biological control as well as an alternative diversionary host plants for the pests.

The new environmentally benign agricultural inputs for sustainable agriculture i.e. the herbal biopesticides and biofertilisers are also the products of biodiversity.

Indirect Benefits of Biodiversity to Man

The indirect benefits of biodiversity include:

1. Absorption of green-house gas carbon dioxide through photosynthesis and regulation of climate.
2. Decomposition of wastes and pollutants by diverse microorganisms—bacteria and fungi, and cleaning of the environment.
3. Pollination of flowers of the fruit and vegetable bearing plants by insects, bats, birds and butterflies in the absence of which there will be no fruiting. A million dollar 'durian' fruit industry in Malaysia collapsed in the 1970s when the single species of bat pollinating the durian fruit trees migrated from the area due to their habitat destruction.
4. Operation of bio-geochemical cycles in the biosphere.
5. Soil production, protection and prevention of erosion.

Biodiversity and Environmental Quality

Biodiversity is not only the bio-indicator of a healthy and sustainable human environment, but also helps in the maintenance of a conducive environment essential for human survival.

National Botanical Research Institute (NBRI) of India has identified several plants which act as natural pollutant sink, intercepting and absorbing various air pollutants and dusts from the atmosphere. There are several aquatic weeds like *Eichhornia, Lemna, Salvinia* and *Azolla* which accumulate and remove heavy metals and other toxic chemicals like nitrates, phosphorous etc. from waste water and help in its purification. The water hyacinths (*Eichhornia crassipes*) have also been reported to absorb radioactive wastes from waste water. The seeds of *Moringa oleifera* and *M. stenopetala* work as natural coagulants to clean the muddy water.

Diverse species of microorganisms (both bacteria and fungi) in the soil and air work as the decomposer and scavenger in the natural ecosystem, biodegrading all the wastes including personal excreta from humans and animals, and also decomposing their bodies after death and decay to recycle back the minerals for the continued operation of the ecosystem. In their absence, the surface of the earth would have been stacked with human and animal carcasses and vegetable debris, unfit for life to exist. There are a number of microorganisms coming to light, which have the capacity to biodegrade even the toxic chemicals and hazardous wastes in the environment. In Germany, genetically tailored bacteria have been used to clean up polluted soils and oil spills in water. Bacteria eat pollutants, gobble them up, and chemically alter them in their bodies. When pollutants are finished the bacteria die leaving clean soil and a biomass of dead bacteria containing harmless minerals. There are bacteria which can also ingest cyanide from water. It is hoped that in future, scientists would be able to genetically tailor such microorganisms, which would also biodegrade the otherwise non-biodegradable plastics.

The earthworm species are emerging as one of the best environmental managers by biodegrading wastes and detoxyfying polluted soils. Earthworms have also been found to ingest several pesticides from the soil. Several species of reptiles and predator birds maintain the environmental quality and a balance in the ecosystem by eating the harmful pests and insects. The role of scavenger birds and animals like vultures and jackals are particularly benevolent as they help clean the human environment by scavenging on dead animal carcasses.

Biodiversity Conservation and Indigenous People of India

Animism and naturalism are parts of the cultural life, beliefs and practices of the tribal population in India. Plants and animals are considered sacred by them. Nature worship is a form of belief that reinforces the view that all nature's creation has to be protected. This faith of the indigenous people in nature's creation has greatly helped in the preservation and protection of many natural ecosystems in India. Such tribal beliefs have survived several patches of virgin forests in India in their pristine glory, which are termed as the 'sacred groves'. It is believed that such virgin forest patches date back to several thousand years when human society in India was at the state of hunting and foraging. Within such groves, even birds and animals are not disturbed. The Garo and Khasi tribes in Northeast India completely prohibit any human interference in their sacred groves. The Gonds of Central India prohibit cutting of trees from the sacred groves, but fallen branches are only allowed to be removed out. Sacred groves are not peculiar to a handful of tribal communities, but are found all over India. In the states of Maharashtra and Goa, Andhra Pradesh, Madhya Pradesh, Meghalaya, Karnataka, Kerala, Orissa etc., there are several sacred groves found. Nearly 30,000 tribes inhabit the Attapady valley of the Western Ghats in Kerala which is a part of the Nilgiri biosphere. The biodiversity of this region is inextricably linked to the indigenous knowledge of these tribes. The Kerala tribes use about 245 wild species of plants as food, fodder, fuel and fertiliser. In Maharashtra these groves cover 5,000 to 10,000 hectares (Gadgil 1993). They are perhaps the last refuge of the endangered and vulnerable species of plants and animals. Sacred groves have also been reported from China, Ghana, Syria and Turkey. In China, the Dai ethnic group of Yunnan province maintains roughly 400 sacred hills (*Nong*) covering about 50,000 hectares.

These virgin forests of the tribals also preserve several wild varieties of biologically diverse flora and fauna in their undisturbed state. Since many of them are on the extinction list of nature, their survival in these sacred groves is of great ecological significance for the biosphere. One of such species is *Rauvolfia serpentina* yielding reserpine drug for the treatment of high blood pressure, which has disappeared from its natural habitat except these sacred forests emotionally preserved by the tribal communities in India. Therefore, the sacred groves of the ancient times have become part of the biosphere reserves of India today.

In the sacred groves of Cherapunji in Meghalaya, four dominant tree species, viz., *Englehardtia spicata, Echinocarpus dasycarpus, Sysygium cuminii* and *Drimycarpus racemosus* contain high level of Nitrogen, Potassium and Phosphorous in the leaf tissues, in spite of the fact that these trees grow on highly infertile soils. These are 'keystone species' performing valuable role of nutrient conservation in these protected ecosystems. These species contribute to supporting and conserving biodiversity in these relict forests preserved by the indigenous people of India.

Many aboriginal societies in India have deep reverence for particular trees also. The Munda and Santhal of Bihar worship mahua (*Bassia latifolia*) and Kadamba (*Anthocephalous cadambe*) trees. Similarly, the Bhuyian and Gond of Madhya Pradesh consider palash (*Butea monosperma*) tree as sacred. Bishnois in Rajasthan have reverence for khejri (*Prosopis cinenaria*) trees, for which they sacrificed 363 people in 1887 to save these trees from felling by the axemen of the king.

Conservation of Crop Diversity by Tribes of India

Many rare and primitive cultivars of cereals, preudo-cereals, pulses and vegetables, which have probably disappeared from the modern agricultural society, are found being grown by the tribal communities in the Himalayas and in the Western Ghats of India. The tribes of Kerala grow 26 different varieties of rice crops. Therefore, the Indian tribes are said to have preserved—1) landraces of important crop plants; 2) useful domesticated plants and animals; 3) useful wild plants and animals as a source of food and medicine; and 4) wild relatives of economically important cultivated crop plants. They hold the 'genetic key' of many valuable characters such as disease and drought resistance, which the modern plant breeders need for crop improvement.

Shifting cultivation is practiced by many tribal communities all over the country. A patch of the forest is cleared for cultivation; the plant biomass is burnt and the ashes containing essential nutrients are dumped in the field. After 2-3 years of cultivation, the land is left fallow for a few years to regain and renew its fertility through natural regeneration, while the farmers shift to a new patch of land. What is noteworthy is that while practicing shifting cultivation, the tribes do not level the whole forest like modern cultivators do, but selectively retain the species like jack fruit (*Artocarpus heterophyllus*), mango (*Mangifera indica*), mohua (*Bassia latifolia*), myrobalans (*Emblica myrobalan*) etc., which ensure additional seasonal food to them. The North-Eastern Himalayan region has several pockets inhabited by the tribes with enormous biodiversity, e.g., citrus, musa, mango, rice, maize, etc. There is particularly enormous genetic diversity of citrus in this region. They are the products of many years of natural and human selection and contain genetic treasures for resistance to pests and diseases and adaptability to stress conditions.

The manner in which the indigenous people preserve biodiversity for the functional integrity of the ecosystem is very interesting. Under a 60-year shifting agriculture cycle, the number of crop species are over 40. Here the emphasis is towards cereals which are mostly placed towards the base of the slope as these are less nutrient use efficient, while the more nutrition use efficient tuber crops are placed towards the top of the slope, where the level of soil fertility is usually low. Under shorter shifting agriculture cycle for 10 to 5 years, the cropping pattern shifts with emphasis on tuber crops. In the settled agricultural system, a high level of biodiversity is maintained by rotation of crops in space and time, and co-existence of mixed and monocropping systems. In the rainy season, paddy is grown with maize, millets and pseudo-millets, such as, amaranths (*Amaranthus paniculatus*), buckwheats (*Fagopyrum debotrys, F. esculentum, F. tataricum*), fingermillet (*Eleusine coracana*) etc. The pulses grown together are black bean (*Phaseolus mungo*), french bean (*Vigna sinensis*), horse bean (*Dolichos uniflourus*), green gram (*Vigna mungo*), pea (*Pisum sativum*) and soyabean (*Glycine max*). All crops are local cultivars. In the winter season, both the traditional and HYV wheats (*Triticum aestivum*) are grown with barley (*Hordeum vulgare*).

About 250 samples of rare cultivars collected from the tribal belt of India are deposited in the National Bureau of Plant Genetic Resources, New Delhi. It may be remembered that in 1963, a gene from a wild variety of rice cultivated by the tribes of Uttar Pradesh saved about 30 million hectares of paddy (*Oryza sativa*) from pest attack (Gadgil 1993).

Rich Nations' Fortune from Poor Nations' Forest

Utilization of biodiversity through biotechnology holds out big promise for the human kind in future. Better seeds, unconventional methods of propagation and higher yields from plants resistant to pests, droughts etc. spell new hope for a hungry, crowded world. Faster diagnostic techniques, more vaccines for a variety of diseases, better medicines tapped from plants and microbial genetic resources assure comfort to the sick and suffering humanity.

Advances in biotechnology have raised the economic value of biodiversity, because any species can now become raw material for genetic engineering. Vast profits are being made by the Multi-National Corporations (MNCs) of the North with advanced biotechnology from the products based on genetic material collected from the poor developing nations of the South. Pharmaceutical companies see great fortune in bioprocessing of natural products.

Biotechnology has increased biodiversity's value in agriculture too. Genes for pesticide resistance are now being transferred from bacteria to plants. The distant wild relatives of modern crops, once considered useless for breeding purpose, contain unique traits that can now be bred into commercially elite varieties within a matter of one year. Biotechnology offers developing countries a means of tapping their enormous genetic diversity for sustainable economic development. Kenya, Senegal, Egypt and Brazil are exploring biological fertilisers based on nitrogen-fixing organisms, which it is estimated, could cut the world's chemical fertiliser bill by $15 billion a year.

Ownership of Biodiversity: The North-South Tangle

Now that the enormous value of genetic resources is being recognized, developed and developing countries and their companies are fighting over the issue as to who really owns them. Developing countries are rich in biodiversity but poor in biotechnology, while the developed countries are rich in biotechnology but poor in biodiversity. Developing countries regard their genetic resources as their property and stop them from being exported to technologically advanced countries. Some developed nations, particularly the US, claim proprietorial rights over all the genetic materials it imports from anywhere in the world. The National Cancer Institute of the US, which extracted the alkaloid, Michellamine-B, inhibiting replication of AIDS virus from the Cameroon plant, *Ancistrocladus korupensis*, patented the drug before a negotiation could be made with the Cameroon government. This was both morally and ethically wrong. Private companies in the US are buying seed firms in developing countries. Ten of them control a third of all the cereal crop species listed by the OECD.

The developing countries of the South incur enormous annual losses due to 'genetic piracy' by the MNC. According to UNDP report, developed countries of the North owe at least $5.3 billion a year as royalty from the global seed industries for products derived from crop diversity and indigenous knowledge to the farmers in the South. The report lists over 100 cases where the developed countries benefited from the knowledge of the farmers in the South. One glaring example is the profits made from the single Ethiopean barley gene, which protects $160 million annual barley crop from yellow dwarf virus.

It is now established that the vast majority of the world's biological wealth is contained in the tropical forests of the South. Yet in recent history, access to this wealth has been cornered by the industrial nations of the North by the process of colonization and by other weapons of economic and military dominance. The benefits accruing in the North out of the use of biological resources, including from biotechnology, have not been shared by the South. Unfortunately, the decision-making elite in the South follow the footsteps of their counterparts in the North (Kothari 1994).

Traditional knowledge and wisdom about biodiversity conservation and use has been flowing from the South to the North, while information on the products of biotechnology and genetic engineering in the reverse direction. But while Northern technology is protected as intellectual property right, Southern knowledge is not. It is merely respected, preserved and maintained—and given free. The nations in the South, lured by the glamour of genetic engineering, did not think much of the rich knowledge they possess, and have been giving it away. It has been like a one-way traffic. In exchange for its biological diversity, the South expects to share the benefits of its commercialization by the North (Swaminathan 1994).

Throughout the human history, biological varieties, technologies and knowledge related to them, have been openly exchanged between societies and individuals, resulting in all-round enrichment of cultural capitals. This was also the spirit with which the Biodiversity Convention was formulated.

But in an unequal world a common heritage of mankind has

every chance of getting misused. In reality, a common heritage has been turned into a colony for the North. There are many examples to substantiate this statement. From Peru, the US scientists obtained the germplasm of the wild tomato plant, *Lycopersicon chemielewskii*, to produce a new strain of tomato, which was larger and 2.5 per cent sweeter, and yielded $20 million every year to the tomato ketchup industry. Another selection No. 832 of tomato from Latin America helped in changing the solid content of commercial tomato varieties, *Lycopersicon esculentum*, from 4.5 to 6 per cent. The profit of ketchup industry increased further by $8 million per year, and during the last 10 years the industry has earned $80 million (Anderson 1992). What share out of this accrued to Latin American farmers who conserved this variety of tomato? Similarly, the US Scientists produced a miracle disease resistant perennial variety of maize, *Zea perennis*, by crossbreeding with a wild maize species, *Zea diploperennis*, conserved by the Mexican farmers. This crop yielded $50 to 200 million per year in the US. What the Mexican farmers got from such scientific marvel? A multimillion drug industry for fighting Leukemia was established in the US, based on rosy periwinkle species from Madagascar, but the country of the origin of the drug got what? Common heritage, therefore, should include not just genetic resources, but also genetic diversity related knowledge, both traditional and modern biotechnological. Considerable part of the South's genetic variability is present in the gene banks of the North, including species and varieties, which are impossible or very difficult to find at their original locations in the South any more (Querol 1988). Moreover, utilizing the biological resources and knowledge of other countries and producing new biological materials, and patenting them, go against the letter and spirit of the Biodoversity Convention agreed upon at the Rio Earth Summit in 1992.

Indian Biodiversity and American Patenting

In the US, anything which has not been previously patented or described in a printed publication, is considered to be novel, and therefore, is possible to be patented. At least 32 US patents have been granted so far on various properties of neem, *Azadirachta indica.* Out of 12 patents issued in 1994 on neem, 3 (Nos. 5298241, 5298247 and 5281218) were for fungicide, pesticide and storage stable high azadirachtin solution. Among them, one was for reversible fertility control in women and others were pesticide formulations. While the issue of neem biopesticide patented by the American Company, W.R.Grace, is still fresh, other life forms collected from India are being patented in the US.

Turmeric (*Cucurma longa*), which for centuries has been used in India as a traditional medicine to treat various sprains and inflammatory conditions and heal up wounds, is now been patented in the US. The patent (No. 5401504) was granted on 28 March 1995 to two Americans born in India, besides a German, an Indonesian and an American. But the right to exploit it has been granted to the University of Mississippi Medical Centre. The patent application claimed: 'The present invention is directed to the use of turmeric to promote wound healing. The present inventors have found that the use of turmeric at the site of an injury by topical application or oral intake will promote healing of wounds.' But, in reality, the healing properties of turmeric was discovered in India centuries ago, which is supported by its mention in Ayurveda and *Charak Samhita.* The broad nature of patents on turmeric will affect the plans of India to commercially utilize its products, which is widely grown and used in India. However, recently, India succeeded in getting the patent claim withdrawn from others through judicial intervention.

Shocking evidence has recently been surfaced about the patenting of microorganisms collected from India by American firms. Bags of soils were taken away from the Western Ghats region of India, along with millions of microbes of diverse species in the garb of soil, and stored at American Type Culture Collection (ATCC) at Maryland. These have been used by various companies and agencies like, Bristol-Myers, Pfizer, Merck, Lepetit and Lederle etc. for industrial purposes, primarily for production of pharmaceutical products like antibiotics. According to a Canadian research and action group, Rural Advancement Foundation International, at least 28 microorganisms have already been patented and another 6 are under patent claims. ATCC alone has 381 fungal and 90 bacterial accessions from India (Kothari 1994).

The Ill-effect of Patenting

Since the discovery of neem's anti-feedant properties in 1962 at Indian Agricultural Research Institute (IARI), New Delhi, several scientists have been proving its efficacy on a wide range of farm pests. Patents on neem, if broad enough, can make it illegal for farmers in India to use what they have been using for centuries for such purposes. The additional danger is that neem seeds and their extracts will be exported in enormous quantities, forcing the prices to rise and depleting the domestic supply. Commercialization could wipe out the neem tree (*Azadirachta indica*) in a few years from India and also cause indigenous knowledge about its pesticidal use to fade away.

Farmers' and Fishermen's Rights over Biodiversity

India has nearly a quarter of the world's farming and fishing communities. Seeds with genes that give them tolerance or resistance to a wide spectrum of biotic and abiotic stresses provide their best safety net against crop failure. Both their own livelihood as well as national food security systems depend on the efficient and equitable use of genetic diversity. Divergent gene pools are also the feedstock for the modern genetic engineering industry.

Indian farmers have adapted the genetic materials from crop diversity, which was available to them from nature, and diversified their own skills and practices of cultivation. The diversity of crops and cattle is not there by any chance, nor it is purely natural. It is rather as much the outcome of thousand of years of deliberate man-made selection, planned exposure to a variety of environment, field-level cross-breeding and other agricultural manipulations which the Indian farmers have tried out for centuries.

It is imperative at this juncture that the farmers, fishermen, traditional medicinemen and the rural folk to conserve genetic variability, both among and within the species. There is an economic stake in the utilization of biodiversity, but there is no corresponding stake in its conservation. Ownership is a question not just of nations, but of communities as well. Traditional doctors' intellectual contribution to the development of pharmaceutical industries is immense. So economic benefits must necessarily be provided to rural farming and fishing communities for their painstaking work in genetic conservation. Some of the genetic resources conserved by indigenous societies are of great value in improving the quality of human life. These species have significant food and medicinal value.

Over centuries of agricultural practice, traditional societies have developed an incredible variety of crops and livestock. Some 200-250 flowering plant species have been domesticated, and genetic diversity among each of these species is astonishing. In India alone, for instance, farmers have grown over 50,000 varieties of rice (*Oryza sativa*). In a single village in Northeast India 70 varieties are being grown. Modern practices of intensive, high-yielding agriculture has pushed out this diversity in favour of a monotonous uniformity. Now in India, over 70 per cent of rice-growing land is sown with a handful of modern varieties.

Throughout the developing world, rural communities are well ahead of their governments in recognizing the importance of biodiversity and in taking action to safeguard its survival. For farmers, fishermen and medicinemen biodiversity conservation is not a luxury, but a necessity for the present generation, as well as for those to come in future. Now, not only do poor farmers and fishermen lose their indigenous seeds, not only are they not compensated for their genetic and intellectual contributions, but also have to pay through their nose for the seeds developed from their own genetic contributions. The challenge lies in developing a system which both recognizes and rewards the rural people, who have helped to preserve genetic diversity in plants and animals for posterity, and have stimulated scientific research to convert genetic resources into products which can enhance food and health security and economic prosperity for the mankind.

The Rio Earth Summit and the North-South Divide

Biodiversity of the tropical forest became an important socio-political issue at the Rio Earth Summit in Brazil in 1992 and was included in the global political agenda. On this particular issue the whole world was divided into two political blocks. One was the block of 'biological powers' or the developed nations of the North, which were poor in biodiversity but rich in biotechnology. The other was the block of developing nations of the South with rich biodiversity but poor biotechnology. The North wanted the South to agree to a list of especially valuable areas in the tropical rain forest, rich in biodiversity, as a common property for protection, while foregoing their sovereign rights over them. It was a blatant ecoimperialism, which the North wanted to force upon the South. Developing nations, however, stuck to their demand of sovereign rights on their forest and biodiversity. While Germany, Japan, France and the UK agreed, the US under the former President, George Bush, backed out and was completely isolated.

Biodiversity Convention gives sovereign rights to the developing countries over their tropical forests and the genetic resources within their political boundary. This means that the South, including India, can now legitimately demand fair returns for the use of their biodiversity by the developed nations. It would be particularly rewarding for them in the field of food and medicine, as the future of world economy and trade would particularly depend upon biodiversity. This can be used as an economic weapon and as a lever for political bargain with the rich nations. But to do this will require an unprecedented show of political solidarity among the 'gene rich' nations of the South. But this leads to another problem. For example, India shares a considerable part of its biodiversity with neighbouring countries in South and South-East Asia. Our natural ecosystem extends over and meets the political boundaries of other adjoining countries. For instance, the Sunderban mangroves of West Bengal cross over to Bangladesh. Similarly, the Manas biosphere reserve extends to Bhutan; and other Himalayan ecosystem crosses over to Nepal. Several species of plants and animals in the Western Ghats of India are also found in Myanmar and China. Some biodiversity is also shared by Maldives, Pakistan and Sri Lanka. Any one of these countries could undermine the position of others by offering commonly held genetic resources on less stringent conditions. It is critical, therefore, that the South Asian Association for Regional Cooperation (SAARC) and similar group of nations reach at an agreement on a minimum set of conditions under which genetic resources from the South could be given to the prospectors in the North. To achieve this objective in the South Asian region, an international consultation on biodiversity including the SAARC and ASEAN countries was held in Bangalore in 1994.

In India, serious gaps exist with respect to patenting of life forms, conservation of crop and cattle diversity, restrictions on the introduction of exotics and genetically modified organisms. In a political decision taken recently, India under the pressure of GATT, has categorically denied for patenting of all life forms. In my view, India should emulate Australia's example of patenting the country's entire plant and animal biodiversity. The government could subsequently prepare an accurate inventory like Australia did. The Indian government must also ensure that all the medicinal plants mentioned in the ancient Indian pharmacoepia of traditional medicine, such as, Ayurveda and *Charak Samhita*, should be kept out of the purview of patenting. The intellectual property rights of these medicinal plants should rest with the tribes and indigenous people of India. There is also a strong need for farmers' rights as suggested by the FAO for the traditional farmers of India, who have been inventing new crop varieties and new techniques of farming since centuries.

There is also a need for an internationally binding legal and political instrument in the form of a 'biosafety protocol' under the Convention. This would protect the weaker nations of the South from becoming an experimental ground for the North's genetically engineered monsters and the 'biological time bomb' held in the hands of the Northern Transnational Corporations.

It was hoped that in the post-cold war and post-apartheid era, there would be greater goodwill and cooperation among nations in the conservation and sharing of common genetic resources of mankind and equidistribution of the benefits derived from them. But divergent political pressures, commercial and political interests, indifferent attitude of the developed countries, population pressure, rampant poverty in the developing countries, ethnic-economic-political conflicts across the world etc. are impeding the realization of this hope.

Biodiversity Erosion: A Potential Threat to Civilization

Large scale destruction of wild plants and animals continues interrupting the process of 4 billion years of evolution. The human ecologist warn that it is a threat to the civilization, second only to the thermo-nuclear war, in its severity. The consequences could be literally incalculable. An extremely ironical and worrying aspect of this situation is that even if all human activities were to cease immediately, species extinction due to the impacts that have already taken place would continue for decades.

As said earlier, the future of mankind is dependent upon just three species of crops, such as, wheat, rice and maize. Such overwhelming dependence on a few crops with narrow genetic diversity can be dangerous for the civilization. There is probably no more serious environmental threat to mankind than continued decay of genetic variability of crop plants. Their cultivars and landraces have already dwindled from a few thousands to a few hundreds since the beginning of agriculture. Once the process has passed a certain critical limit, humanity will have permanently lost the co-evolutionary race with crop pests and diseases, and will no longer be able to adapt to the climatic change. What adds to the tragedy is our limited knowledge of the earth's biodiversity, as an ever-increasing number of species are being lost even without being discovered, much less studied. Species once lost from the face of the earth cannot be brought back. Extinction is irreversible and forever. The destruction of biodiversity undermines basic operation of the ecosystem. The loss of ecosystem function provided freely by the natural forests and vegetation entails real economic and social costs. Biodiversity, the myriad of genes, species and ecosystems that collectively make up what we call 'nature' may have taken 4 billion years to evolve, but it seems destined to be largely destroyed in just 4 human generations.

CONCLUSION

While biological resources and information on biodiversity, which are for the benefit of humanity as a whole, should not be allowed to be shackled by private companies and monopolistic declarations like patents, those who work towards gaining these resources and information should be suitably rewarded. Indigenous peoples who have for centuries been conserving biodiversity and finding new uses for them, farmers who for generations have been discovering wild plants worthy of cultivation and engaging in their own cross-breeding and selection methods to continuously refine agriculture, must be appropriately rewarded. Almost all the miracle discoveries of modern technology are based on this traditional wealth of knowledge and resources.

The issue of equitable sharing of benefits is, of course, a thorny one, especially since genetic resources are not easily accounted for. The price of a wild plant, for instance, can reflect anything between simply the collection and preservation costs, to the foreseeable potential commercial benefits in several million dollars that might accrue from its use.

Two of the valuable assets possessed by the poor nations of the South are genetic resources and traditional knowledge. So far, indigenous people have guided scientists to the discovery of valuable plants in tropical jungles. Scientists have confirmed that around half the folk remedies they analyse bear out their effectiveness in laboratory tests and assays. A new trend in chemical prospecting in the tropics is underway. A pharmaceutical company in the North sends its scientists to the tropics to gather herbs or plants used in indigenous medicines and build up a multi-million dollar market back home. But this profit has not benefited the people and the place of its origin.

In India, too, a number of outfits are currently exporting crude extracts of medicinal plants or plant parts to the North which fetch only minimum returns. The North's discovery of the usefulness of the neem tree (*Azadirachta indica*) has triggered off a rapacious harvesting of not just the seeds but the leaves of the tree as well.

REFERENCES

Anderson, Stacey (1992), The Million Dollar Seed: The Genetic Diversity and Quest for Profit, *Our Planet*, 14(1).

Anonymous (1993), Biodiversity: Practicalities for Sustainable Development, *Our Planet*, 5(4).

Gadgil, Madhav (1993), Biodiversity: Tapping Folk Knowledge, *The Hindu*, January 10.

Kothari, Ashish (1994), *Conserving Life: Implications of the Biodiversity Conservation in India*, New Delhi: IIPA.

Myers, N. (1983), *A Wealth of Wild Species*, Boulder: Westview Press.

Querol, D. (1988), *Genetic Resources: Our Forgotten Treasure*, Penang: Third World Network.

Pal, B.P. (1940), *The Search for New Genes*, New Delhi: IARI.

Sinha, Rajiv K. (1996), *Global Biodiversity: The Library of Life and Secret of Human Existence on Earth*, Jaipur: INA Shree Publications.

Sinha, Rajiv K. (1998), *Human Ecology: Man the Destroyer: Humanity the Sufferer: Human Responsibility and Response to the Environmental Challanges*, Jaipur: INA Shree Publications.

Swaminathan, M.S. (1994), Towards a Rich Genetic Estate, *The Hindu*, January 2.

6

Forest Policies and Forest Communities in India: Customary Rights, State Intervention and Participatory Management

K. K. Misra

INTRODUCTION

In recent times newspapers are flooded with the news of eviction of rural and tribal people from their traditional habitats in favour of constructing massive hydro-electric projects, major industries and industrial townships, or for mining and allied activities. Its outcome, as can be easily imagined, is the painful experience of being a refugee in one's own home-land, which has been customarily owned and enjoyed by the people for generations. They are being alienated from their habitat as well as from the sources of subsistence. An increasing number of cases of such alienation has something to do with state intervention in the rights of the forest communities in their access, control and management of natural resources, as forest policies right from the British period to the present have been perpetually detrimental to the interests of the forest communities in India. It is, however, interesting to note that the recent forest policies of the Government of India are not characteristically different from the policies formulated during the British rule in India, apparently to serve strategic imperial interests. This is a matter of serious concern today for the dwindling forest communities in the country. In this paper, I shall attempt to focus on the continuity between the colonial and post-colonial forest policies in India in overplaying the commercial aspect of forestry, and the contradiction between commercial forestry and the existing values of the hitherto marginalized forest communities in a welfare state like India. I shall also throw some light on the much discussed green agenda of participatory management of the forest ecosystem and its *modus operandi* in India in order to explore whose interest it serves.

About 23 per cent of the total geographical area of India has been declared forest, although satellite imagery shows that actual forest coverage is as low as 19 per cent, against an expected requirement of 33 per cent of the total area for an ideal stable environment. The official estimate states that about 5,000 forest villages inhabited by around 48 million forest dwellers are still within these chunk of forests, which provide food, fodder, fuel, fibres, timber and a large variety of minor forest produces, including leaves, seeds, gums, waxes, dyes, resins, bamboo, canes, grasses, honey etc. for the sustenance of the forest dwellers (Arora 1994: 691). The perception of the government, represented by its officials is that the growing number of forest dwellers and their equally multiplying livestock numbers are mainly responsible for denudation of the forest, and hence, eviction of these groups from the vicinity of the forest and curtailing their access into it might save the 'forest for posterity'. The Forest Department (hereafter FD) of the government views the forest dwellers as plunderers of the forest, and hence, recommends action against the violators of the forest laws. On the other hand, Non-Government Organizations (NGOs) and social workers working closely with forest communities accuse the government of implementing 'anti-people' laws and indirectly encouraging a corrupt FD to plunder the forest in connivance with business interests backing forest contractors. NGOs feel that forest communities are, and have been, the victims of the callousness, indifference and neglect of the FD without any respite (Guha 1983: 1943). While the debate goes on, there is a steep rise in the extent of degraded forest land of about 175 million hectares, threatening the subsistence of forest communities, flooding, soil erosion and heavy siltation of irrigation dams (Arora *op cit.*: 691). The fact remains that even though forest policies continue to be at the cost of the forest communities all these years, there is no real progress in the direction of preserving the valuable humid tropical forest, if the above statistics prove to be correct. The vital question then is whether the state is the ultimate beneficiary in this prolonged exercise? In the later section of this paper, I shall consider why it should be that neither the state nor the forest communities gain anything from forest policies. To begin with, however, I shall discuss the legacy of colonial forest policy in the formulation and implementation of present policies, and the way in which they not only undermine the customary rights of forest communities, but also threaten their very survival.

Forest Management in Ancient and Medieval India

Although it is hard to find any definite historical or epigraphical evidence of forest management in ancient India, reference is quite often made to Kautilya's *Arthashastra*, which suggests the preservation of forests to protect wild elephants (Rangarajan 1996: 2391), a basic military resource for the Mauryan rulers. Besides this there is evidence of forest regulation by the Maratha kings in the 18th century to cater to the needs of naval boat construction (Pouchepadass 1995: 2063). During medieval times, under the control of the feudal chiefs, forest communities had almost free access to the forest, except to those patches earmarked by the king for royal hunting. Probably because of the abundance of forest, under pre-British governments, ' ... anyone was accustomed, without let or hindrance, to get what he wanted from the forest, to graze his cattle where he liked, and to clear jungle growth for cultivation wherever he listed' (quoted in Guha *op cit.*: 1883). In many cases since the *adivasis* were inviting kings of *Kshtriya* origin for the protection of their territories from external aggression (cf. Misra 1986: 226-236), or the tribal chiefs themselves were the rulers of the jungle tracts, the forest dwellers had no particular difficulty in living in and utlizing the resources of the forest. Forest dwellers engaged in shifting cultivation were left to themselves and there was no intervention by the state. In many cases, forest communities were exempted from taxes of any kind, except an annual gift made by the leaders of the communities to the king on very special occasions like *Vijaya Dashami*, the custom still being in practice in the erstwhile feudal states of eastern and north-eastern India (cf. Singh 1972). In some exceptional cases, however, with a nominal annual revenue to the king, the forest communities continued to enjoy free access and exploitation of the forest resources within the jurisdiction of their village boundary. Over time, the relationship between the forest and forest communities was institutionalized through various cultural and religious mechanisms that ensured uninterrupted habitation of the tribes within the forest regions. Tribal identity, therefore, became associated with the forest (as they are called *Vanabasis*—people of the forest), and the forest became the vital life force for the tribes. Even today, many of these forest communities relate myths and legends about their association with the forest, and the remnants of many sacred groves are mute reminders of this emotional relationship between people and the forest (Gadgil and Chandran 1992: 183-187). The material and emotional relationship between people and forest, underpinned by the symbolic significance attached to plants and animal species, religious duties and obligations, legitimized tribal access to forest, and also encouraged restraint and caution in using forest as a resource base (cf. Bird-David 1992a: 19-45).

Forest Management in British India

It is fairly clear that till the end of the 18th century, the British administration in India paid no attention to the rich Indian forests and the forest communities relying on them, and rather preferred to remain indifferent to the need of conserving forest. This neglect was not accidental or without selfish interest of the Raj, for large areas of valuable timber growing forest was denuded day by day. It was an outcome of the colonial policy of expanding the area of cultivation to obtain more revenue for the treasury, and to continue the export of *teak*. The devastation of *teak* and *sal* forests was to a large extent caused by contractors and people from outside the forest communities, who operated without any hindrance whatsoever from the British administration.

When the colonial administration realized that British forests no longer provided sufficient timber for shipbuilding, iron smelting and tanning, it turned to India. The first interest in Indian forests for exporting timber was shown in 1806 by the reservation of *teak* forests in Malabar (Guha *op cit.*: 1883). Captain Watson was appointed as the first Conservator of Forests on the 10th of November 1906 to superintend forest work, so that the supply of *teak* to the Royal Navy remained unaffected. Captain Watson and his immediate successors devastated the valuable forests of Malabar and Travancore to such an extent that the post of conservator was to be abolished in 1823 (Stebbing 1982: 65). Another beneficiary of largescale deforestation was the Imperial Railways. Valuable timber forests in the Himalayan foothills were targeted for railway sleepers, and wood was the main fuel for railway locomotives before the coal mines of Ranigunj came into operation (Guha *op cit.*: 1884). The felling of Himalayan conifers and *sal* trees of Central India for the railways was carried out with the help of private contractors, who were instrumental in denuding the forests for profit, exploiting the demand created by the colonial administration. In this context Atkinson comments: ' ... The forests were denuded of good trees in all places. The destruction of trees of all species appears to have continued steadily and reached its climax between 1855 and 1861, when the demands of the Railway authorities induced numerous speculators to enter into contracts for sleepers, and these men were allowed, unchecked, to cut down old trees very far in excess of what they could possibly export, so that for some years after the regular forest operations commenced, the department was chiefly busy cutting up and bringing to the depot the timber left behind by the contractors' (Atkinson 1882: 852). When the British administration finally realized that immense damage had already been caused to Indian forest resources for half a century, the Imperial FD came into existence in 1864, with the assistance of the German foresters, with an expectation of ensuring the sustained availability of timber for railway sleepers.

In order to control the destruction of the forest by the people and to assert monopolistic rights over the forest, the first Inspector General of Forests was appointed in 1864, and the first Indian Forest Act was passed by the Supreme Legislative Council in 1865. This authorized the government to declare forests and wastelands as reserved forests (Shiva 1989: 63). The Act was further strengthened by the Forest Act of 1878, which empowered the state FD to close reserved forests to people and impose penalties for any transgression of the Act. It certainly hit the forest communities very hard, as ' ... it sought to establish that the customary use of forest by the villagers was based not on "right" but on "privilege", and that this "privilege" was exercised only at the mercy of the local rulers. Since the British were now the rulers, the rights of absolute ownership were held to be vested in them' (Guha *op cit.*: 1884). The forest policy statement of the colonial administration in 1894 further consolidated the monopolistic rights of the state over the forest, when it was made clear that the state was empowered to take over all forests including private and community forests, and therefore, favoured regulation of rights and privileges of the forest communities in the name of 'public benefit'. The Forest Act of 1927 further denied any customary right of the forest communities over the forest, ' ... simply because they were domiciled there' (Arora *op cit.*: 691). The absolute state right facilitated uninterrupted supply of timber not only for the Royal Navy and the Imperial Railways, but also for military purposes during both the World Wars (Guha *op cit.*: 1886-87). During the Wars, the demand for hitherto valueless and unimportant forest produces like bamboo, fodder grass etc. from the Indian forests became regular along with the supply of timber, for which ' .... Felling and sawing were pushed into the remotest forests of the Himalayas and into the densest jungles of the Western Ghats'.

Between 1864, when the Imperial Forest Department was created in India, and the Indian Independence in 1947, the colonial forest policy was to serve strategic imperial interests through various means, and at the cost of millions of forest dwellers. The implementation of the Forest Acts culminated in a series of *satyagrahas* throughout India, as a protest against the reservation of forests for the exclusive use of the colonial administration, against commercial exploitation and the denial of minimum subsistence needs of the forest communities. Mention may be made of numerous social movements in 1916 and 1921 in Garhwal Himalayas and by the Gonds of Central India, which ended with the sacrifice of many lives. Although the traditional rights of forest communities to various products was partially reinstated after these protests and eventual loss of human lives, the colonial policy of forest exploitation continued unabated till Independence (Shiva *op cit.*: 66-67).

Forest Policies after Indian Independence

So far as the charter of the relationship between the state and forest communities is concerned, the period after India's Independence is in no way different from the colonial period. Most surprisingly, the National Forest Policy of 1952 largely retained the fundamental orientation of colonial forest policies, despite its use of populist rhetoric. Like the policy of 1864, it defends and reinforces explicitly the assertion of state monopoly right over forests by retaining the category of 'reserved forest' for 'national interest' at the cost of the forest communities (Guha *op cit.*: 1888). However, the policy has conceded the popular demand by earmarking small 'village forests' to cater to the needs of the forest communities without, of course, granting them the right to manage the forest on their own. Like colonial policies, the National Forest Policy of 1952 has uppermost in its agenda '... the need for the realization of maximum annual revenue in perpetuity', which is a clear indication of the continuity of commercial interest in forestry from colonial times to the present. With the emphasis on massive industrialization in independent India during the initial Five Year Plan periods, forest was indiscriminately exploited to supply raw materials to the industries eventually to make them commercially viable. Moreover, for defence, reconstruction schemes like river-valley projects, expansion of urban centres, modernization of communication network etc., which gained high priority in the development agenda, deforestation continued, much to the discomfort of the forest communities. This was encouraged further by the policy of offering subsidies on forest products to the industrial consumers, who not only maximized their bit in exploiting the forest, but also paid little attention to avoiding waste, thus causing a rapid depletion and degradation of forest resources (Arora *op cit.*: 692).

During the last two decades, there has been a spate of legislation geared towards conservation of the forest and wild life in India. This includes, The Wildlife (Protection) Act of 1972, The Forest (Conservation) Act of 1980, The Forest (Conservation) Amendment Act of 1988, and the Wildlife (Protection) Amendment Act of 1991 etc. In the 42nd Amendment of the Indian Forest Act in 1976, forests were shifted to the concurrent list from the state list, which consolidated direct control and decision-making power of the Government of India over the affairs of the forest, and thereby forest communities in India. Sometimes back, a draft Forest Bill was circulated by the Ministry of Environment and Forests for opinions, prior to its placing before the Parliament. The Draft Bill not only retains all the sections of the Indian Forest Act of 1927, but also proposes addition of some new sections with a view to increasing the power of the forest bureaucracy. The Bill makes the task of withdrawing any right over the forest easier by introducing the undefined concept of 'carrying capacity' and empowering the Forest Settlement Officer to recommend its implementation, if (s)he feels that the carrying capacity of a forest has exceeded its limits. The Bill, however, proposes that forests neither reserved nor protected may be given to the village communities for their use. These village forests may be given loans from the Village Forest Development Fund, to be set up by the state governments for afforestation and other activities. These loans are to be recovered from the proceeds of the sale of forest produces from these forests, thus prioritizing the commercial needs of the village forests over the subsistence needs of the forest communities. Ironically, the Bill cedes absolute power to the state to formulate rules for the regulation of these forests, utilization of the resources and the loans, and duties and obligations of the village bodies to manage them, thus reducing village forestry to more of a government enterprise than a people's enterprise (Chhatre 1996: 1085).

In order to make the provisions of the Act effective and keep the intruders away from encroaching the forest land, the Draft

Bill empowers any forest, police or revenue officer to detain and arrest without warrant anybody suspected of forest offences. The Bill states that an assistant conservator of forests or an officer authorized by him may break into any place at any time, by day or by night, and break open any lock of any door or remove any obstacle to his entry into such place, if he has reason to believe that an offence under this Act has been committed or is being committed. On the contrary, no court shall take cognizance of an offence under this against any officer unless a report in writing is made by an officer or authority competent to remove him from office (*ibid.* 1086). However noble the spirit of this provision may be, it certainly would act as a protective shield for an officer who might indulge in unfair practices. The stringency of the Bill goes against those who make a minimum living out of the forest resources, and it is silent about the accountability of the people at the helm, e.g., the officers of the FD. Among other proposals for alienating forest communities from the forest and undermining any right of anybody on the forest resources other than the state, the Bill warns: 'Any person felling or removing any tree [even] from private land without permission from the tree officer [concerned forest officer] is liable to a maximum fine of Rs. 5000' (*ibid.*: 1086).

Forest Policies and the Tribal Communities

Indian forest policies as revealed in the above account, from the middle of the 19th century till the present, have increasingly cut into the traditional rights and freedom of tribal and other forest communities all over the country. It has had at least two major consequences: one is material, and the other is moral. Needless to say, the material dependence of the tribal communities on forest resources is squeezed day by day, eventually making them to starve. Many of them have migrated for work and have become easy victims in urban and industrial centres (Behura and Misra 1987: 70-80). But what is more deplorable is the moral conflict on the question of customary right over forest and successive attempts by the state either to withdraw or limit it. This is precisely the situation that baffles the forest communities today.

Moral conflict between tribal customary rights and commercially oriented forest policies can be best explained with reference to the tribes that subsist on hunting and foraging. The tribal communities, who were probably never 'original affluent societies' as they are termed (see Sahlins 1971; Bird-David 1992b: 25-47), have been depending on the forest for their daily requirement of food, fodder and fuel. But the hunter-gatherer is strictly guided by his moral code of conduct for his subsistence, and not by sheer greed by transgressing his rights over the resources. For example, it is remarked of the Chenchus of Andhra Pradesh that 'Though extremely poor in material goods Chenchus are nevertheless conscious of the rights in property which may be vested either in groups or in individuals. A group's right to the produce of the tract of land in its possession is generally recognized, and a man is not supposed to collect or hunt in a territory to which he has no claim by ties of either descent or marriage. An animal already wounded, however, may be pursued into another group's territory, and if ultimately found, belongs to the hunter whose arrow caused its death. This rule is in accordance with the important principle that any commodity obtained by an individual through his own efforts, be it game, vegetable produce, or implement, becomes his property over which he or she has complete control. This right of individual ownership is accorded to women and children no less than to adult men, and infringements are ...rare' (Furer-Haimendorf 1967: 19). This should not be taken as a stray example, as in many other hunting and foraging societies, ownership is clearly defined and any infringement is considered to be an immoral act, which deserves supernatural sanction. The act of alienation of hunter-foragers from their forest habitat and restricting their entry into the forest by the FD, therefore, clearly contradicts tribal notions of ownership and morality. What, perhaps, annoyed them most was that while their legitimate occupancy rights over forest resources were withdrawn, there were frequent hunting expeditions in their own territory under their very nose by the British, from the Viceroys to the lower echelons of the British Indian Army (Gadgil and Guha 1992: 267). The same activity is repeated now by the urban and elite Indians in tribal habitats.

Even among the shifting cultivators, who communally own land for cultivation, instances of encroachment are very rare. For example, among the Konda Reddis of Andhra Pradesh, who are traditionally *podu* cultivators, 'Ownership of the land is vested in local groups, whose members may hunt, collect and cultivate anywhere within the territory traditionally belonging to the group. A principle prevailing also among food gatherers provides that any part of the communal property turned to use by the labour of an individual becomes his private possession. Just as the hunter has the right to dispose of the game which falls to his arrow, so the Reddi diverts to his private use the land he makes arable. As long as he cultivates a hill-slope the land and its produce are his undisputed property, but when after two or three years the soil loses its fertility and the plot is allowed to revert to jungle it also returns to the ownership of the group. When after some ten or twelve years it is again ready for cultivation any member of the group may clear the forest, and the previous occupier has no prior right to its utilization' (Furer-Haimendorf *op cit.*: 39). The attempt to curb shifting cultivation, which is not only a means of subsistence for the tribes, but is intertwined with the totality of their culture (cf. Misra 1988: 43-49), started seriously during the middle of the 19th century, when Sir Richard Temple ordered the ban on the practice in the then Central Provinces (Gadgil and Guha *op cit.*: 270-271). From the colonial times till now, shifting cultivation by the tribes has been construed as a wasteful, inefficient and ecologically destructive exercise, and the Draft Bill proposes to replace the practice with 'agro-forests' in the areas where shifting cultivation has been endemic.

Forest Policies and Peasants

The settled plough agriculturists, mostly belonging to various cultivating and occupational castes, but living in the vicinity of the forest were no less affected by the forest policies than tribal hunters, foragers and shifting cultivators. Shrinking forest land meant the shrinking of cultivable land for them, as demographic expansion of a family or a village necessitated extension of agricultural land by forest clearing. Further, despite agriculture being their primary occupation they were dependent on the forest for fodder, fuel, leaf amnure and timber. Although the policy of state control over the forest affected all the caste groups living in the vicinity of the forest, the worst affected were those occupying lower positions in the caste hierarchy, who depended for their livelihood exclusively on the forest for collection of fuel wood to sell in the nearby villages or urban centres.

Forest communities in general, be they hunter-gatherers, shifting cultivators or settled agriculturists, supplement their primary means of subsistence by the collection of minor forest produce (MFP). These include leaves for the manufacture of country cigars, gums, resins, honey, seeds etc., which are collected by these people irrespective of their age and sex. This activity traditionally did not require anybody's permission and was considered to be the right of the people. But the increasing state control over forest has eventually prevented them from collecting MFP, thereby depriving them of their livelihood, as well as undermining their customary relationship with the forest.

Forest Movements

Since forest policies in India from the colonial times till the present threatened the very existence of forest communities by limiting their subsistence opportunities and clashing with their values of ownership and control over resources, there has been resistance to the state control of forests from time to time. Many communities, however, have suffered in silence, because of their small numerical strength and lack of effective leadership. Many other communities, like the Chenchu of Kurnool, had expressed their dissatisfaction by becoming highway bandits and looting the pilgrims visiting the holy shrine of Srisailam in the state of Andhra Pradesh (Furer-Haimendorf 1943: 311-312; 321). Other groups, like the Kadar, had to abide by the dictates of the forest officials and cooperate with them in the collection of forest produce on behalf of the state with a marginal return (Gadgil and Guha *op cit.*: 266). But still some other forest communities have responded violently to the enforcement of forest laws causing serious concern among the state officials, both during the colonial and in more recent times.

The defiance shown by the Saora of the Ganjam Agency in

the 1930s against the state policy of banning axe cultivation greatly embarrassed the administration. When the cultivators did not pay any heed to the official ban, the most obvious option for the administration was to arrest them. But while their men were in jail, the Saora women took over cultivation till the men returned. When the tribals did not relent even after repeated arrests, the FD uprooted crops under the pretext that the land did not belong to them but to the state (Elwin 1945: 154-157).

The restriction to *podu* cultivation and creation of forest reserves in the hills of Andhra Pradesh, among other things, had resulted in the historic Gudem-Rampa uprising of 1922-24. This was the conclusion of a series of uprisings or *fituris* that went on for nearly a century. The Koya, Konda Dora and other tribal communities of the Rampa hill region under the supreme leadership of Alluri Sita Rama Raju initiated successful guerrilla warfare against the British police outposts between 22 and 24 August 1922. The bloody rebellion continued till Rama Raju was captured by the police and shot dead on 6 May 1924 (see Arnold 1982: 88-142), which is still vivid in the memory of the people in this region. Yet another revolt by the Gond and Kolam tribes in Nizam's Hyderabad against the government decision to restrict *podu* cultivation in the Dhanora forest of Adilabad region resulted in angry protests, for which their leader, Kumara Bhimu, laid his life in 1940. The Bastar rebellion of 1910 in Jagdalpur by the Maria and Muria tribes against the local king for reserving the forest and evicting the tribes from their traditional habitat had a very sad ending, when the British police hired by the king, encountered about 900 tribesmen fighting with their traditional weapons of bows, arrows and spears (Gadgil and Guha *op cit.*: 273-274). Voices of protest against the forest laws alienating the forest communities from their homeland was also heard from the Chotanagpur plateau of Central India, in which the Kol, Munda, Santal and the Oraon fought relentlessly for many years. The whole of tribal dominated North-East India also protested against state intervention in their traditional rights over forests during colonial times. Sometimes these protests were with millenarian undertones, and some other times were explicitly political, linking to the freedom movement launched by the Indian National Congress. The situation in the

Himalayan foot-hills was highly explosive. The localized movements of 1904, 1906, 1930 and 1944-48 in the Tehri region bear testimony to the genuine grievances of the forest communities against the policy of separating them from their forests. These movements have been the progenitors of the well-known *Chipko* movement of the recent times (see Guha 1989). In most cases, despite forced suppression of movements by the local or Imperial governments, the forest communities have been able to vent their feelings against the forest laws that contravene their basic rights and their value of honouring individual and communal rights over natural resources, which invariably have supernatural sanctions, the violation of which is considered as immoral. Therefore, all these years, forest communities have suffered from an irreparable sense of cultural deprivation that agitated them to hold arms against the administration many a times.

Participatory Forest Management and Development Imperatives

Despite unfavourable responses from the forest communities—sometimes explicit and some other times implicit—Government of India has consistently adopted forest policies that go contrary to their minimum expectations. Because of emphasis on industrialization during the first few years after the independence forest resources acquired a commodity value at the expense of their subsistence value to forest communities. As a result, deforestation continued at an alarming rate. But partly because of the introspection by the policy makers and partly because of international pressure to preserve the forest for posterity, the Government began to initiate Social Forestry project in the late 1970s. But despite an estimated expenditure of Rs. 60 million till 1988 mostly from international aid, the project failed. As a result, in 1988, it was decided that Indian forests would no longer be exploited commercially. The revised forest policy of 1988 advocated people's participation in the protection and development of forests from which they derive the benefits in the form of fuel wood, fodder and small timber. A circular issued by the Government to this effect in June 1990 proposed that a village panchayat, cooperative or protection committee constituted for the purpose, be given the responsibility of forest regeneration and protection, and the right to have part of the proceeds from sales at a later date, if the scheme succeeds. The FD of the concerned state, however, would supervise the project closely, and the benefits could be withdrawn in case of failure. Although the exact nature of the agreement between the state and the village institution is not the same in all the states, it is ensured that the benefit goes to those and only those involved in the process of protection of the forest. From the point of view of the forest communities, it is envisaged that the policy should induce people to participate in forest protection, making it economically rewarding. From the point of view of the state, it would be most cost effective method of forest management (Arora *op cit.*: 692). Since its notification in 1990, 16 states have already accepted the programme, and it is estimated that 10,000 to 15,000 village forest protection and management groups are currently protecting over 1.5 million hectares of state forest land (Sundar 1997).

However participatory it might look, this programme of Joint Forest Management (JFM) ensures unlimited opportunities to the state to intervene in its real operation, which it has been doing in many instances. I shall cite a couple of examples here. In many cases, the FD allots only degraded forest land for this purpose, and the participants have no right to ask about the quality of the forest land and its possible productivity, as the ownership rights are vested with the state. The number of village committees are generally decided by the FD on the basis of their targets, funding and personpower availability at the Department, and not taking into account the needs of the people. The constitution of committees and their registration are facilitated by the FD with the help of local NGOs, as the people are, in most cases, not aware of the legal implications. In Indian villages, members tend to be hand-picked by the facilitating institutions (e.g. castes) only. In the long run, this becomes a source of group antagonism and ethnic conflict, putting in jeopardy the best intentions of JFM. Moreover, these communities are '... expected to "assist" the forest department in preventing trespass, encroachment, grazing, fire, poaching, theft or damage but (they) hardly enjoy the power to "punish" or to decide the nature of punishment for those caught indulging in any of these prohibited activities.' (Arora *op cit.*: 694). Further, the committees are expected to assist the FD in the execution of work, selection and distribution of species etc., which reduces the spirit of participation of the people to a subservient institution of the Government. Thus, 'Foresters are intent on preserving their control through silviculture, a knowledge that through manuals and working plans is claimed as their exclusive preserve. Given the participatory framework, this leaves the awkward question of what should be conceded to the domain of local knowledge, where under the rules of JFM villagers are skilled practitioners. The answer, jointly provided by environmentalists and development specialists, is the knowledge of NTFP (Non-timber Forest Produce) collection and processing' (Sivaramakrishnan, quoted in Sundar *op cit.*). Even where the Department concedes to the local demands as to which species should be planted, it may not be in a position to deliver the goods, as the supply very much depends on the targets and availability of the species in the nurseries of the Department. Another bizarre outcome of the programme is that in many cases the major threat to forest land for JFM comes from commercial interests and large-scale development projects, to which the Government is prone to succumb to keep its impoverished economy going.

JFM, therefore, is conceived elsewhere and imposed on the people in much the same way as earlier 'top down' development programmes, like, Community Development, Integrated Rural Development Programme, Integrated Tribal Development Programme, Tribal Sub-Plan etc. 'Joint' in JFM is nothing more than a populist rhetoric as people continue to remain at the receiving end only, putting into jeopardy their prospect of deriving empowerment, autonomy and utilization of rich local knowledge for local area development. Even if it is claimed that JFM programme is a success in West Bengal, a recent survey in the village Krishna Rakshit Chak has proved that the programme is disastrous, as it does not assess the survival needs of the poorest of the poor before being implemented. This ends up in illegal felling of the trees, patronization of culprits by the influential members of the committee, premature winding up of the project, emergence of divisive forces within the village community, thus shattering the integrity of the village and doubting the credibility of JFM in this West Bengal village (Mukherjee 1995: 3130-3132). The question, therefore, is that whose interest does JFM serve? In an ill-conceived JFM, neither the state gains nor the poor, except promoting the interests of a high-handed bureaucracy or giving a feeling of spurious satisfaction to a donor international NGO.

Despite all its shortcomings, JFM has sought to involve local population in forest regeneration and management. There was a hope in some circles that village forests could be used as a modified form of JFM in future. But the proposed forest Bill goes to the extent of withdrawing whatever incentive was theoretically given to the forest communities by empowering the state to take back the management of village forests from the local bodies, if they deemed unable to manage the forest according to the prescribed plans of management prepared earlier. This certainly gives complete control to the FD to decide the fate of the forest communities as per its own conviction, as its officers are sufficiently shielded by law. Further, the Bill states that no beneficiary of a village forest shall be eligible to claim rights to any reserved or protected forest (Chhatre *op cit.*: 1085), as he has to live or die with his village forest alone, whatever its practical utility may be to mitigate his survival needs.

CONCLUSION

From the point of view of the forest communities in India, there is hardly any perceptible difference between the first Indian Forest Act of 1865 and the currently drafted forest Bill, except that the latter has become more stringent in withdrawing customary rights over access, control and management of natural resources. Commercialization and centralization of forest resources have clashed with the basic subsistence needs of the forest communities. Because of this, they have registered their dissent in no uncertain terms during the British Raj and in post-independence era. But redress has not yet been forthcoming. Even the latest attempt of people's participation in JFM has proved to be an eye-wash, because it is imposed on them, leaving little room for them to participate freely and fairly. So long as the development programmes contradict with people's values and they do not benefit from these efforts, no welfare state can claim to have achieved its goal.

REFERENCES

Arnold, David (1982), Rebellious Hillmen: The Gudem-Rampa Risings 1839-1924, in Ranjit Guha (Ed.) *Subaltern Studies I: Writings on South Asian History and Society*, Delhi: Oxford University Press, 88-142.

Arora, Dolly (1994), From State Regulation to People's Participation: Case of Forest Management in India, *Economic and Political Weekly*, March 19, 691-697.

Atkinson, E.T. (1882), *Himalayan Gazetteer*, Vol III, Allahabad: Government Press.

Behura, N.K. and K.K.Misra (1987), Position and Problems of the Working-class Tribal Women in Urban and Industrial Settings, *Vision*, 7 (1 & 2), 70-80.

Bird-David, N. (1992a), Beyond the Hunting and Gathering Mode of Subsistence: Observations on Nayaka and other Modern Hunter-Gatherers, *Man* (N.S), 27 (1), 19-45.

Bird-David, N. (1992b), Beyond the Original Affluent Society: A Culturalist Reformulation, *Current Anthropology*, 33, 25-47.

Chhatre, Ashwini (1996), A Socio-Ecological Basis for Natural Resource Management: Forest Bill Debate, *Economic and Political Weekly*, May 4, 1084-1090.

Elwin, Verrier (1945), Saora Fituris, *Man in India*, 25.

Furer-Haimendorf, C. von (1943), *The Chenchus: Jungle Folk of the Deccan*, London: Macmillan and Co.

Furer-Haimendorf, C. von (1967), *Morals and Merit: A Study of Values and Social Controls in South Asian Societies*, London: Weidenfeld and Nicolson.

Gadgil, M. and M.D.S. Chandran (1992), Sacred Groves, in Geeti Sen (Ed.) *Indigenous Vision: Peoples of India—Attitudes to the Environment*, New Delhi: Sage.

Gadgil, M. and R.Guha (1992), State Forestry and Social Conflict in British India, in David Hardiman (Ed.) *Peasant Resistance in India, 1858-1914*, Delhi: Oxford University Press.

Guha, R. (1983), Forestry in British and Post-British India: A Historical Analysis, *Economic and Political Weekly*, 18 (44, 45 & 46), 1882-1896 and 1940-1947.

Guha, R. (1989), *The Unquiet Woods: Ecological Change and Peasant Resistance in the Himalaya*, Delhi: Oxford University Press.

Misra, K.K. (1986), From Millenarianism to Jharkhand: The Changing Nature of Social Movements in Tribal Chotanagpur, *Journal of Asian and African Studies*, 21 (3 & 4), 226-236.

Misra, K.K. (1988), Shifting Cultivation in Orissa: A Rethinking, *Man in Society*, 3, 43-49.

Mukherjee, Neela (1995). Forest Management and Survival Needs: Community Experience in West Bengal, *Economic and Political Weekly*, 30 (49), 3130-3132.

Pouchepadass, J. (1995), Colonialism and Environment in India: Comparative Perspective, *Economic and Political Weekly*, 30 (33), 2059-2069.

Rangarajan, Mahesh (1996), The Politics of Ecology: the Debate on Wildlife and People in India, 1970-95, *Economic and Political Weekly*, 31 (35, 36 & 37), 2391-2409.

Sahlins, M.D. (1971), *Stone Age Economics*, Chicago: University of Chicago Press.

Singh, K.S. (Ed.) (1972), *Tribal Situation in India*, Shimla: Indian Institute of Advanced Study.

Shiva, Vandana (1989), *Staying Alive: Women, Ecology and Development*, London: Zed Books.

Stebbing, E.P. (1982), *The Forests of India* (reprint), New Delhi: A.J.Reprints Agency.

Sundar, Nandini (1997), The Construction and Destruction of Indigenous Knowledge in India's Joint Forest Management Programme, paper presented at the East-West Environmental Linkages Workshop, Canterbury.

7

FOREST ECOLOGY AND SUSTAINABLE TRIBAL DEVELOPMENT IN INDIA

R. R. Prasad

INTRODUCTION

Forests, which are considered as the soul of the country, are also the backbone of the tribal economy. Therefore, sustainability of forests ensure sustainability of the life styles of the tribes inhabiting them. The life style of a tribal family or village mostly depends upon the productivity from forests and the availability of Minor Forest Produce (hereafter called MFP), which include edible forest products like roots, tubers, fruits, flowers etc. as well as a variety of other items for sale. *Beedi* or *tendu* leaves, gums, resins, brooms, *adda* leaves etc. are exclusively collected by the tribes for sale to outsiders or to appropriate government agencies.

The forestry sector with 23 per cent of geographical area of India provides employment equivalent to 2.3 million man years, which is much less compared to many other countries. The fact that of the total employment of 2.3 million man years generated from the forestry sector, employment of 1.6 million man years is available from the MFP, which explains that the role played by MFP in this regard is very significant. Forest Department (FD) has generally viewed the MFP as secondary in importance after timber, and to the extent that these have been realized as commercially viable, there is a growing lobby in India and other countries to change the terminology into Non-Timber Forest Products (NTFP), Non-Wood Forest Products (NWFP), Multi-use Forest Products (MFP), Major Plant Products (MPP) etc. from the conventional Minor Forest Produce.

The benefits accruing to the tribals from forests are various and derived in a variety of ways. The tribals are so accustomed to these benefits that they have become a part of their daily routine. It is estimated that 4.13 crores of tribals and other forest dwellers depend on MFP for their subsistence. Out of this, an estimated 60 per cent of production consisting of edible items is consumed by these communities either as main food or as supplementary diet. Several researches conducted on forests and tribals in India have revealed that the magnitude of dependence of tribals on food and income derived from the sale of MFP is enormous. In fact, MFP is a major source of income and livelihood for the forest dependent tribal communities. Their very sustenance hinges on fruits, fibres, tubers, roots etc. from the forest. Thus, any change in the forest policy affects the tribals more than any other section of the population.

MFP is an important source of supplementary income for tribals and other forest communities. It has been aptly observed by the National Commission on Agriculture: 'Minor Forest Products have the potential for bringing about an economic revolution for the tribals of the country'. Such revolution, however, should be based on painstaking grass-root level investigations and planning. The revolution cannot also be fully achieved, if the tribals remain contented as collectors of MFP; they must assume the role of collectors-cum-processors-cum-manufacturers of finished goods with MFP as raw materials. They ought to be involved in the marketing of these finished/processed products as well. The state also has to assume the role of an enabling agent, and has to take the responsibility of identifying the resource potential, available skills, and sharpening the skills through village or block level institutions. Besides, the Non-Governmental Organizations (NGOs) should also take up the role of organizing the MFP collectors into people's co-operatives, making them aware about their rights on wages received, prices realized, and helping them in skill upgradation, value addition, processing, marketing etc.

At the national level, over 50 per cent of the forest revenue and 70 per cent of the export income from forest products come from the MFP (Campbell 1988). Of the total wage employment in the forestry sector, MFP have accounted for more than 70 per cent (Gupta and Guleria 1982). In spite of all these impressive statistics, potential production and use of MFP, and eventual strengthening of the tribal economy, still remains under the veil till recent times (Mathur 1994). To bring the MFP related tribal economy to a full bloom, the following factors need to be considered with all seriousness.

Tribal Ownership over MFP

It is felt by many that if the tribal people are given full right over the MFP, much of their economic problems could be solved. Moreover, this will give a feeling to the tribals that forests belong to them and they are partners in their management. The present position is that the government is the owner and the tribals are only wage labourers for collection like many other marginal communities living in the vicinity of the forest. In spite of various resolutions passed at high-level Ministerial Conferences, there has been no substantial change in the government policy in this regard and the revenue angle of MFP continues to dominate. The rights presently claimed by the government on MFP even with reference to the provisions of the Indian Forest Act are not legal, and royalty levied thereon is unethical (Government of India 1987-89). Recognizing the tribal people as the owners of the MFP would mean that the state no more should impose any royalty on these items, and the marketing of MFP should be organized in such a way that the tribal gets full market price of the collected commodities.

When the right to collect MFP by the forest communities had been accepted at the time of reservation of forest itself, then this claim of the state governments that they have the right over it and hence, they can levy royalty cannot be considered to be correct even under the present law. This right of the state is a right asserted under duress. Therefore, the people have a right to assert over the MFP under the present law, and it is the duty of the state governments that they should accept the claim of the tribals and make suitable arrangements, so that they can get the full price for the MFP they collect. If the state governments drag their feet on this question, it becomes the duty of the central government to issue directions to the states to honour the legitimate right of the tribal people (ibid). If the tribal people are accorded the status of the owners instead of mere collectors of the MFP, it would be the first revolutionary and most important step to end the historical injustice to them.

The role and importance of MFP in sustainable forest management and improvement of socio-economic conditions of the forest dwellers is now well understood. The attention of the Government of India was drawn towards this important issue and after a series of meetings of the Forest Ministers of the states and the Central Board of Forestry, it was proposed that the right of ownership of the MFP should be conferred on the tribals on account of their traditional dependence on such produce. In the mean time, the provisions of the Panchayats (Extension to the Scheduled Areas) Act of 1996 which *inter-alia* empowers the Gram Sabhas and Gram Panchayats in the Scheduled Areas to safeguard and preserve the traditions and customs of the people, their cultural identity, community resources, and customary methods of dispute settlement, and more specifically to provide for endowing the Panchayats at the appropriate level with the ownership of MFP, has come into effect. It is believed that if this provision is effectively implemented, the tribal Panchayats would become the richest Panchayats in the country in terms of financial resources, as the revenue which presently accrues to the state governments by way of royalty, sales and purchase tax etc. would be collected by the Panchayats in the Scheduled Areas.

Exemption from the Payment of Royalty

Almost all the states have the system of levying royalty on

procurement of MFP, if they are meant for trade. The prevailing trend of imposition of royalty has adversely affected the commercial viability and trade of these items, which in turn affects the earning of the tribals on the one hand, and the prospect of promoting trade on the other. There seems to be no criteria for the imposition of royalty. Further, royalty is an ever increasing phenomenon without having any linkage with the market scenario. The imposition of royalty has resulted in unequal price realization to the tribals, and it also poses a multitude of problems in marketing the MFP.

Due to the imposition of royalty, the State Forest Development Corporations and Tribal Development Co-operative Corporations are not in a position to pass on a still higher collection charges to the tribals. Imposition of royalty on the MFP, therefore, goes against the interest of the tribals, who are among the poorest sections of the society, and make out their existence under most adverse circumstances. Abolition of royalty will definitely make the price of the MFP more competitive in the international markets (NCUI 1990), and ensure payment of higher collection charges to the poor tribals.

Exemption from Purchase and Sales Tax

Under the present arrangements, the Forest Development Corporations (FDC) and Tribal Development Co-operative Corporations (TDCC) have to pay purchase tax in addition to sales tax to the respective state governments at the point of sale. Because of the payment of purchase and sales taxes, the capabilities of these corporations to pass on higher collection charges to the tribals is jeopardized. Though the sales tax paid is collected from the buyers by the corporations, it affects the selling rate of the products, and thereby, the profitability. In this connection, it is pertinent to mention that the Girijan Co-operative Corporation (GCC) in Andhra Pradesh has been fully exempted from the payment of purchase tax, sales tax or other commercial taxes by the Government of Andhra Pradesh. Other state governments should also exempt the FDCs and TDCCs from the payment of commercial taxes for the MFP handled by these corporations.

Overheads on Marketing and Establishment

The FDCs and TDCCs have big establishments in tribal areas. The financial burdens of these establishments ultimately fall on the consolidated fund of the state or the union. The overheads of marketing, besides transportation charges, are also quite heavy, because of the sparse population and general inaccessibility of the tribal areas as a whole. If the residents of the hills and forests have to bear the higher cost of marketing because of their inaccessible habitat, what is the difference between the trader and the government? It is the duty of the government to attend to the problems, which arise because of the difficult situation in the tribal areas. It is regretted that in the present marketing system, on the one hand, the tribal is shouldered with the responsibility of establishment of marketing, with the result that he does not get even full benefit of his own collection. On the other hand, huge expenditure is made on development and administration in the name of serving the tribal interest. From every point of view, be it policy, practice, justice or constitutional propriety, it is evident that the entire expenditure on marketing and establishment costs of the Corporations should be borne by the respective state governments or the central government (Government of India 1987-89).

Establishment of MFP Tribal Co-operatives

Marketing of MFP with a view to securing for them remunerative return is one of the cardinal objectives of LAMPS (Large-sized Multi-purpose Societies). Many FDCs and TDCCs, therefore, have been employing LAMPS as the agent for procuring MFP from the tribals at a fixed procurement price, with an intention of eliminating the middlemen in the process. However, research results have revealed that the LAMPS, particularly in the state of Bihar, have not really succeeded in eliminating the middlemen. The contrary, however, is often the case. In several places former middlemen have become *de facto* agents of the FDC and TDCC. As a result, exploitation still continues unabated. The same middlemen, who till recently were exploiting them as moneylenders-cum-merchants, today continue their work in the garb of the agents of FDC/TDCC or LAMPS (Fernandes *et al* 1988).

There are instances where the tribals have either not been paid MFP collection charges or paid lower than the fixed procurement price. LAMPS have also been indulging in smuggling of the MFP, thereby causing loss to the FDC or the TDCC.

The problems of the poor tribals are rooted in exploitation, injustice and lack of organization. Because of the last factor mentioned, the MFP collectors are unable to exert pressure on these agencies. Although rare, there are however some good cases to show how the tribals, particularly the tribal women, have been able to eliminate middlemen in MFP trade and taking it of by themselves by organizing their own co-operative societies. Mention may be made of the 'Kotra Co-operative' and 'Pratapgarh Co-operative' in Udaipur and Chittorgarh districts of Rajasthan, through which the women *beedi* leaf collectors have organized themselves into struggle committees to demand higher wages for collection, and then have formed *tendu* leaf collectors' co-operative to manage the *beedi* leaf trade themselves. This has been a very successful experiment and this model needs to be appropriately replicated in other states of the country. This, however, requires active involvement of the reputed voluntary organizations dedicated to the cause of tribal upliftment.

Another successful model of people's organization in managing the procurement and marketing of the MFP is the 'Paharia Gram Sabha' (PGS) in the Santhal Pargana area of Bihar. It is believed that the PGS model may be easily replicated in other states. For this, there is a need to organize commodity-wise co-operatives like *tendu* leaf collectors' co-operative, gum collectors' co-operative, sal (*Shorea robusta)* seed collectors' co-operative etc. Members of these co-operatives should be only the actual collectors of a particular MFP commodity for which the co-operative society has been constituted. Such co-operatives should be given working capital as per the requirement at 4 per cent annual interest to meet the expenditure on payment of collection charges, packing and forwarding etc. Such co-operative societies should also be given free hand to sell the collected MFP by inviting tenders. The profits made in this trade handled by the MFP co-operatives should be shared among the members in the form of bonus.

Decentralization of MFP

Nationalization of MFP in various states effected at different times between 1960 and 1970 with an intention of helping the poor, has contrarily, affected the interest of the collectors. *Tendu* leaves as one of the most important MFP is a case in point. In Madhya Pradesh the collection of *tendu* leaves fell from 5.10 million bags in 1981-82 to 3.9 million bags in 1985-86. In Orissa, despite nationalization, while collection of *tendu* leaves between 1967-73 was 36,000 Mts, it was 35,200 Mts between 1979-85, thus indicating stagnation in collection.

After nationalization, collection of *sal* seeds fell in India from 2 lakh tonnes in 1979 to only 60,000 tonnes in 1987. Production of lac, another nationalized MFP, had gone down from an average of 32,000 tonnes per year during 1961-70 to 16,000 tonnes during 1981-86 (Government of India, 1988).

While some states have nationalized many MFP commodities, others acquired monopoly rights on them. The objective was to make the tribals sell their produce exclusively to the FD or its formally or informally appointed agents like FDC, TDCC or LAMPS. The businessmen making high profits at the cost of the forest communities has almost been taken for granted. What one fails to understand is the fact that the public sector institutions like FDC, GCC, TDCC have an equally strong profit orientation and are earning revenue for the state at the cost of the poor tribals. In fact, the most profitable MFP seems to have been nationalized and their monopoly procurement is given to these institutions (Fernandes *et al* 1988). In the state of Bihar, there are instances, where the government agencies have not purchased certain nationalized MFP from the tribals, nor can these commodities be purchased by the private parties with the result that the poor tribal has to suffer from severe hardship.

One of the declared objectives of commercialization and nationalization of the MFP was to integrate the tribals into the national mainstream by working through the FDC and the TDCC. But, unfortunately, these agencies have integrated the tribals through the worst form of capitalism. They have been kept poor and subordinate through subsistence wages, while all the profit goes to the state and the middlemen. The tribals are thus forced to integrate themselves into this system as exploited wage earners living below the poverty line.

The very principle on which commercialization and the pricing pattern of the FDC, the TDCC and other agencies is based, can be questioned. The forest is considered to be the property of the state as per the forest legislation. The tribals are, therefore, offered only wages for the collection of MFP like the *tendu* leaf. In the case of many other produce, the price offered is equivalent to the minimum wage for the time the collectors are supposed to be spending to collect a given quantity of the MFP. Therefore, all the profits go to the state exchequer or to the middlemen, and those who work to make these profits are given only minimum wage and sometimes even less.

The tribals seem to lose out because of nationalization everywhere and because of the commercialization of the obsolete National Forest Policy, which should be dynamic enough to aim at the welfare of the people living within or in the vicinity of the forest for generations. Given the complicated procedures of the state after the nationalization of the MFP, a large bureaucracy has to be maintained from the MFP revenues to enforce the rules. Since the state does not want to suffer any reduction in its revenue, the additional amount required to maintain the bureaucracy has to be obtained by raising the price paid by the final consumer (the *beedi* manufacturer in the case of *tendu* leaf), or by reducing the price paid to the producer, i.e., the tribal collector, or by combining the two. But in practice, given the distribution of power, the state cannot put as much pressure on the final consumer as on the poor producer. Eventually, the state-run organizations have by and large opted not to charge from the final consumer much more than what he used to pay earlier. Hence, the producer, who does not have much of power or political clout, gets a low price (Fernandes *et al* 1988).

In spite of all good intentions, Chambers *et al* (1989) argue that nationalization has become a disincentive to MFP gatherers/collectors, when they say, 'Nationalization reduces the number of legal buyers, chokes the free flow of goods, and delays payments to gatherers, as government agencies find it difficult to make prompt payment. This results in contractors entering from the back door, but they must now operate with higher margins required to cover uncertain and delayed payments by government agencies, as well as to make police and other authorities ignore their illegal activities. This all reduces tribals' collection and incomes.'

Due to nationalization of the MFP, the price the tribals get for their produce is very low, compared to the price in the neighbouring market. In Bihar, for example, the state agencies procured *sal* seeds at Rs. 1.30 per Kg. and *mohua* at Rs. 5.75 per Kg., while the sales prices of these items were Rs. 3.20 and Rs. 7.00 per Kg. respectively. The Parliamentary Committee on Welfare of Scheduled Castes and Scheduled Tribes (1992-93) enquired as to why the state government agencies are exploiting the tribals by not paying them remunerative price for the MFP and keeping to themselves a substantively high margin. Due to nationalization of the MFP and the monopoly procurement right of the agencies like FDC, TDCC, LAMPS etc., there exists a vast difference between the procurement and the sale prices of these commodities. These public sector institutions have very strong profit orientation and are earning high revenue for the state at the cost of the poor MFP collector. The major factor one needs to understand is the very thought behind the setting up of these organizations. Though their declared intention is tribal welfare, they are formed to commercialize forest products. In this system, those who function as the agents of business and industry have all the bargaining power they need, while the forest dwellers for whom the sale of MFP is a means of survival, are powerless. While the former have many other options available for them to earn profit, the latter have nothing but to helplessly surrender as the MFP is the major source of their survival.

In this unequal relationship, a solution may not be found through better implementation of the present policies, as is often advocated. However sincere the officials may be, the present marketing pattern is geared to integrating the forest dwellers within the existing commercial-industrial system in a position of weakness, i.e., as cheap labour without any bargaining power. Alternatives to the present state of powerlessness have to be found in order to make the benefits accessible to the tribals.

To what extent and in what form is government intervention needed in the MFP business? The role of marketing co-operatives and forest corporations should be reexamined to maximize benefits to MFP collectors and producers. Instead of nationalizing the MFP, the government through FDC could provide price support to the MFP. The support price offered should be adequate and competitive, otherwise the middlemen would siphon out the MFP by offering a marginally higher price. Further, in the present liberalized market policy of the government, which is heading towards privatization of market economy, there should be competitive MFP procurement and marketing by the public, co-operative and private agencies. This should generate healthy competition. However, the reverse seems to be happening. Government agencies like to deal only with those MFP commodities where they have a monopoly and a high profit margin is assured. Where the government alone does marketing, it is inefficient, and where it is left to private trade, it is exploitative.

MFP Processing and Value Addition

The prospects for MFP processing industries in tribal areas are exceedingly bright. But, unfortunately, a large part of the MFP are exported from tribal areas in raw form. Wherever, therefore, there is an availability of raw material (MFP) locally, the principle should be that this has to be processed before it is exported outside the tribal areas. It would be more economical to sell forest products in processed or value added form. Establishment of processed units at suitable places might help in achieving this objective.

Apart from merely considering the tribals as gatherers of MFP, the inequality is being compounded by lack of any effort for value addition to the produce. Various oilseeds like *sal, karanj, kusum,* niger, castor, *mohua* etc. are being sold out of the tribal areas, without conversion into respective oils. Lac, gums and resins are hardly graded and treated. Even deseeding of certain produce like tamarind is more of an exception than a rule. Rolling of *tendu* leaves into *beedis* (country cigarette) is a rather simple affair. Yet, *tendu* leaves are plucked and sent out as such. Similarly, reeling of *tasar* and even weaving of clothes can be easily done by the tribals before exporting outside, which guarantee high return to them.

There is a dire need of first grading, processing of MFP through co-operatives of primary collectors for ensuring value addition. The requisite skill for this job should be imparted to them. Although some good work in this direction have been attempted in isolated pockets, there is a need for intensification as well as expansion into other areas. In Andhra Pradesh, the Integrated Tribal Development Agency (ITDA) at Parvatipuram has proposed to organize training programmes for tribal women who collect *tendu* leaves to roll *beedis*. The ITDA has also made a tie-up arrangement with two reputed *beedi* manufacturing companies located at Warangal and Mangalore to lift 80 per cent of the *beedi* manufactured by the tribal women, after affixing their trademark and quality checking. This is a very significant effort in the direction of converting the tribal collectors into the status of manufacturers of the finished goods. Value addition to the MFP will not only generate gainful employment in the endemically employment-starved tribal regions, but also provide the much needed additional source of income.

Another noteworthy effort in the direction of value addition has been made by the ITDA, Bhadrachalam in Khammam district of Andhra Pradesh. The ITDA has helped the tribals to form '*Kattha* Manufacturing Co-operative Society'. The members of the society who were earlier selling *kattha* (used in *Pan* or betel leaf) in the raw form, are now selling it in the processed form, after getting required training arranged by the ITDA. This arrangement for value addition has generated additional employment in *kattha* collector tribal families, which has also become a source of earning an additional income.

Yet another successful case of value addition has been championed by an NGO, PRADAN, working in Godda district of Bihar. This has helped the local tribals to grow host plants of *tasar* silk worms, rear *tasar* cocoons, reeling of *tasar* cocoons, and weaving *tasar* yarn into fabrics. Similarly CARE in Bihar has been helping the tribal women in Khunti block of Ranchi district to take up bee-keeping with Italian bees. The organization has imparted training to the tribal women in modern bee-keeping techniques, providing bee-hive colonies, and processing of honey. The GCC in Andhra

Pradesh is also quite active in promoting bee-keeping among the tribes of the state. All these efforts have yielded higher income and more employment for the tribal families.

The objective behind this process of value addition, however, should be that whatever processing method is employed, the tribals must be the primary beneficiaries. The responsibility of the state should be to provide the much needed logistical support in this venture.

One of the prerequisites of improving MFP-based tribal economy is to determine if any value addition is possible to a particular commodity before its export. Analysis of the MFP product profile shows that for some products processing at primary level is possible. For some others, however, processing is possible only at some intermediate level beyond the primary level, and/or at a final point. Yet another group of MFP require processing outside the area of availability of the raw material. Nevertheless, these have to be so arranged and the marketing so planned that the increased value of the product does not go to private parties, but to the government agencies that deal with the product, so that the benefit could ultimately percolate down to the primary collector of the product. In the MFP trade, particular attention has to be given to the question of equitable access to resources and to opportunities for obtaining greatest benefit at the stages of collecting, processing and marketing.

The time is now set to project the tribal as the manufacturer of the MFP-based finished products, especially those that do not require heavy machinery or sophisticated technology. Certainly, these requirements the tribal at present cannot absorb, except the tasks that could be handled by cottage or village industries or by tribal co-operatives. Since it is already established that MFP can make a significant contribution to the state and the national economy, it is high time that the tribal should be motivated to exploit the potential of MFP-based processing and marketing activities. For this, he should march or should be made to march from being the mere collector of the MFP to the manufacturer of MFP-based consumer products.

Marketing Channels

Marketing margins of the MFP vary significantly from channel to channel. The price spread is maximum in the case of a channel like, collector → village merchant → primary wholesaler → secondary wholesaler → consumer; and minimum in collector → village merchant → consumer. Several studies have indicated that higher marketing margin and marketing cost are largely on account of handling losses, high transportation charges, weighing, loading-unloading, and high margin of the intermediaries. It is further proved that the producer's share and marketing margins are directly and significantly associated with the length of the channel. The smallest is the channel, the lower is the marketing margin and higher producer's share in the consumer's rupee and vice versa (Mishra *et al* 1988). Presently, the producers/collectors of the MFP are not getting reasonable share in the consumer's rupee. This may be due to the restriction in marketing of some products by the FD. The other problem is that the tribals shy away from marketing the produce themselves. Therefore, in order to promote efficient MFP trade, ensure optimal distribution and reasonable collector's share in consumer's rupee, the government policy must be rationally modified and clearly spelt out in facilitating the forest dwellers to market their produce through the smallest marketing channels. How by cutting or reducing marketing channels, the income of the MFP collectors increases substantially, has been ably demonstrated by the Tribal *Tendu* Leaf Collectors' Co-operative Ltd., Kotra in Udaipur district of Rajasthan. Further, strengthening of market intelligence and marketing extension should be effective in better disposal of the forest products. Easy availability of marketing finance would help the tribals to free themselves from the clutches of the moneylenders, contractors etc.

Pricing Policy

Much before the collection season of particular MFP, uniform price policy should be publicized and implemented. Price should be determined by market forces and not by any administrative decree. Tribal collectors should be paid the prevailing market price without any deduction whatsoever and all the incidentals should be reimbursed by the government after subtracting the profits earned on account of sale of the produce. These incidentals may include fluctuations, hire charges etc.

Price Fluctuation Fund

This fund should be created at the national level for all the MFP. Presently, TRIFED has this only for the tree borne oilseeds. It is suggested that all the TDCC, FDC, and MFP Development Corporations (MFPDC) should have TRIFED's representation in their respective Board of Directors for better coordination and interaction.

Infrastructure and Single Window Concept

Adequate funds should be allocated for setting up warehouses and cold storage in far flung areas at suitable locations throughout the country. Further, adequate funds should be allocated to operationalize the single window concept, where the collectors of the MFP can obtain essential items at reasonable rates, and where they can sell their produce at remunerative prices. This will help in confidence building in the long run between the government and the forest dwellers.

The MFP Demand Survey and Collection

At present not much information is available on the demand of different types of MFP. A comprehensive survey would help in identifying the products and their likely demand. This is necessary to regulate the process of collection of the MFP. Currently, the methods followed for the collection of MFP are the traditional ones. Very little attention is paid to the quality aspect while plucking/picking. Further, the season of collection has a direct bearing on the maturity and availability of the product. Indiscriminate collection may lead to total destruction of the resource base, particularly in case of medicinal herbs, as with the case of *sarpagandha.*

Regulation

In majority of the markets, the MFP has not been notified for the purpose of regulation. In general, there is little interest in notifying the MFP in view of the uncertainty in the quantum of arrival. Further, the importance of the MFP varies from state to state. But to bring about an overall improvement in the marketing system, it is imperative that the MFP are regulated in consumer markets as well.

Standardization and Grading

Grading of the MFP at the producers' level prior to selling would go a long way to realize the price that commensurate with the quality of the product. To facilitate grading, standards should be laid down for the MFP. The market committees and co-operatives/corporations should provide infrastructure in terms of equipment, laboratories, and graders to facilitate grading at the primary level.

Training

Training of personnel involved in the collection of the MFP, and those engaged in the co-operatives/corporations and marketing committees, would help streamlining the marketing of the MFP. Training programmes should be arranged at the grass-root level, preferably in forest areas/tribal villages.

Programmes for MFP Regeneration

Though the MFP play a significant role in tribal economy, regeneration of the MFP has attracted only a token effort. There has been a little or no place for the MFP in social forestry. For example, the Seventh Plan target for the MFP planting was only 9 million hectares for five years. While planning for the social forestry activity, the basic thrust has been on wood production. But the non-wood forest products, such as, gum, resin, medicinal plants, aromatic products, leaves, oilseeds, tans and dyes, grasses, seeds, canes, bamboo etc., which have great potential to earn revenue and enhance employment for the tribals, have received scant attention under the social forestry programmes. Since the MFP offer an opportunity to sustain tribals' economic interest on a long term basis, emphasis should be made on raising the MFP plantation in concentrated blocks to facilitate collection and marketing.

Panchayats and Management of the MFP Trade

After the 73rd Amendment of the Constitution, Panchyati Raj institutions have to play a very important role in planning and implementing programmes for economic development and ensuring social justice. Twenty-nine items of development have been clubbed together with the Panchayati Raj institutions in the Eleventh Schedule of the Constitution. One of these twenty-nine items is the MFP. Therefore, these institutions should now be actively involved in the cultivation and propagation of the MFP species, organizing collection, and processing and marketing of the MFP. These institutions have to ensure best returns to the local people in their role as collectors of the MFP by eliminating large profit margins pocketed by the middlemen, and by passing the benefits to the tribal people with better wages and working conditions.

REFERENCES

Campbell, J.Y. (1988), Putting People's Products First: Multiple Use Management for NWPs. Unpublished Paper.

Chambers, Robert *et al* (1988), *To the Hands of the Poor: Water and Trees,* New Delhi: Oxford Publishing House.

Fernandes, W. *et al* (1988), *Forests, Environment and Tribal Economy: Deforestation, Impoverishment and Marginalisation in Orissa,* New Delhi: Indian Social Institute.

Govt. of India (1987-89), *Report of the Commissioner for Scheduled Castes and Scheduled Tribes,* New Delhi.

Govt. of India (1988), *Commodity Studies* (6 Volumes), Ministry of Welfare, New Delhi.

Gupta, T. and A. Guleria (1982), *Non-Wood Forest Products in India,* New Delhi: Oxford and IBH Publishing Co.

Mathur, P. (1994), Constraints of MFP Marketing and Trade, *MFP News,* 4(1).

Mishra, P.K. *et al* (1988), Marketing Margins of Cuddapah Almond (Chirongi) in Chindwara District of Madhya Pradesh, *Indian Journal of Agricultural Economics,* 43(3).

NCUI (1990), Proceedings of the National Workshop on Export of MFP - Role of the Co-operatives, New Delhi, 16 April.

8

Mohua Plantation and its Socio-Economic Importance in Tribal Ecosystem

S.B. Ota and *S.K. Mishra*

INTRODUCTION

India is a land of more than 400 tribal groups, who still live on traditional agriculture like shifting and terrace cultivation on the hill slopes, supplemented by hunting of small games and gathering of seasonal fruits, roots and tubers from the forest. Because of their dependence on nature, they have developed an intense and intimate relationship with their surrounding ecosystem, which is different from the non-tribal ecosystem. With their experimentation for centuries, tribal people know for certain many plant and animal species that have a potential food value for them. These species have been preserved in the tribal ecosystem most often as sacred objects, with the perception that any damage to them invites severe supernatural wrath. One such species is Mohua (*Madhuca indica*), which is very jealously guarded by the tribals of Central and South-Eastern India even today. In fact, in many parts of India, Mohua trees grow wild in the forest and play a very important role in the economic as well as socio-cultural life of the local tribal communities. In this article an attempt is made to understand Mohua plantations in the tribal pockets of India and their bearing on the society, economy, culture and behaviour pattern of the local tribal communities.

Mohua plays such a vital role in the subsistence economy, division of labour and social organization of several tribal groups of Central and South-Eastern India, without considering its importance no ethnographic account on the tribal life of these regions will ever be complete. In order to have an indepth account of this aspect, a bigger research project was taken up in one of the tribal dominated districts of Orissa, named Phulbani (formerly known as Boudh-Khondmal), inhabited by the Kondh, a well known tribe of Central India, of which the present paper forms a small part.

Mohua Ecology and Botany

Mohua, the most popular and widely found tree of tribal dominated tracts of Phulbani in Orissa, belongs to a wild variety of Central Indian flora which is commonly known as *Madhuca indica* to Indian botanists. Several other varieties of this species, identified as *Madhuca longifolia, Bassia longifolia, Bassia latifolia* are also seen in these tracts, which are commonly known to the tribal population as 'Mohwa' or 'Mohua' without any significant dialectical differentiation (Gopalan *et al* 1982: 167).

Mohua is a species forming part of dry and mixed deciduous forest of India that grows wild throughout the sub-continent, particularly in the states of Uttar Pradesh, Gujarat, Maharashtra, Madhya Pradesh and Orissa. It is not uncommon to notice these trees in the monsoon forests of Western Ghats from Konkan southwards, usually along the banks of rivers and hill streams. But the Mohua trees are generally endemic in dry deciduous forests, very often in rocky and sandy soils up to an altitude of 1,200 metres above sea level. Hence, it is mostly seen in association with Sal (*Shorea robusta*) forests of Orissa and Madhya Pradesh. As a matter of fact, Mohua trees grow in all sorts of habitats and typographical zones excluding slopes and foothills. In tribal dominated areas these trees are mostly seen in the village forests, wastelands, and the outskirts of reserve forests as well as scattered in the interior and relatively inaccessible forest areas. Sometimes they are also grown as avenue trees along the roadside and in village groves. Previous studies have estimated that the total number of Mohua trees in the country at 94 lakhs only. Orissa occupies a significant place in the use of Mohua products in the country and Phulbani acts as its centre-spread (TDCC Market Study Report-4 1997: 2).

In general, the mature tree of Mohua grows up to a height of 12 to 15 metres and the shape of its crown is pyramidal. The trunk is thick, stout and grows up to a maximum of 75 cm in diameter and very rarely it grows laterally. The branches from the trunk give rise to sub-branches and the sub-branches to a number of smaller stems, which yield leaves and flowers. The stems are devoid of thorn and are easily climbed by the people. Mohua wood is not considered good for furniture and occasionally used for fuel by the local tribes. The crown of the tree gives a deep shade from rainy season onwards till the coming up of summer. The matured leaves are stiff and measure about 20 cm in length. Mohua flowers, which are the most popular edible portion of this tree, are cream coloured, very soft, juicy and succulent. The complete flower is eaten as it is and looks like a plum with the likes of a big size grape. The size of the flowers varies from 1.5 to 2.0 cm in diameter with maximum of 2 cm in length and weighing about 7 to 8 gm in general. When Mohua flower blooms, it drops down from the tree.

Under favourable soil and climatic conditions Mohua trees begin to bear fruit within 8 to 10 years that continues for another 50 to 60 years. Its fruits are egg shaped, pulpy enclosing one to five (more commonly four) tenacious seeds of shiny brown colour. The skin of the green fruits is dark green in colour that contains fibres and becomes stronger when it ripens. The green fruit contains sap, which is white in colour, very thick and sticky. The size of the matured fruit, weighing about 70 gm becomes 5-6 cm in diameter. Mohua seed shell is not very hard as these are decorticated by simple stone grinders or in a mortar with a pestle. The kernel constitutes about 75 per cent of the weight of the seed and usually two kernels are found in a seed which are brown in colour and concave in shape. In general these kernels are about 2.5 to 4.0 cm long and 1.0 to 1.5 cm broad.

Seasonality and Behaviour of Mohua Plantation

The seasonal behaviour of Mohua is very interesting. Except the summer four months i.e. from mid-February to mid-June Mohua trees remain evergreen and provide deep shade. Each tree remains leafless for a period of about two months in summer. Some of them start shedding leaves early, some others late, during this period. The mature leaves ripe and begin to fall down, and the trees become completely barren within a fortnight. Shedding of leaves in other trees in the forest during summer is generally a gradual process. As a result of this process, appearance of new leaves can be seen alongside the falling of leaves. But as the shedding pattern of leaves in Mohua trees is different from others during summer, these can be easily distinguished in the forest from a distance.

Once the tree becomes completely devoid of leaves buds start coming out from all the tips of small branches. And within five to eight days these buds blossom. Once they bloom they start falling on the ground. Mohua trees start yielding flowers by the end of the February and continue up to the first half of May in a few cases. But the average pick period of flowers is from mid-March to mid-April. To be very precise, the yielding of flowers on Mohua trees is for a period of about twenty days, of which the middle ten days is the highest yielding period. During this period flowers start falling gradually with an increased quantity daily till the tenth day. Slowly this phenomenon recedes and finally stops after a period of ten days. In certain areas the second flowering of the trees is occasionally noticed very late in the season, but does not continue for a longer duration (TDCC Market Study Report-4, 1997:2).

It is very interesting to note that Mohua flowers require a particular temperature to drop down from the branches during the peak season. It does not fall during daytime when the temperature becomes high. Even the uncommon cold weather is unfavourable for the flowers to drop during nights. Mohua trees drop flowers for a very short spell which starts at about 4 a.m. and continue throughout the dawn to stop before sunrise. During this time it is very enchanting to enjoy Mohua groves as all around on the ground a thin bed of flowers is created with a sweet fragrance, and flowers continue to drop on the ground as if flowers are raining from the sky.

As soon as the flowering period is over, tender leaves of pink colour start coming out from the smaller branches, and within a fortnight, trees become green once again. Like the flowers, the fruits also start coming and ripening as early as May and continue till the end of July in some cases. The peak season to collect ripe fruits is between the second half of May and the end of July.

The Mohua Products

The annual yielding capacity of Mohua trees in respect of both flowers and fruits is very high. However, this varies from area to area according to the growth of the tress, soil conditions and other climatic factors. Variation in rainfall affects the yielding capacity considerably. Usually the yield per tree in terms of dry flowers ranges from 75 to 150 kg at an average of 112 kg per tree. The calculated yield of fresh flowers varies from 250 kg to 500 kg per tree and at an average of 375 kg. The yield of dry Mohua flowers from a fairly mature tree in a good flowering season is about 135 kg, which is roughly 500 kg in fresh weight. In certain cases it has also been noticed that the yield of flowers is much higher and can go up to 250 to 300 kg in dry weight with an equivalent of 1,000 kg fresh weight. The yield of Mohua seeds is about 50 to 55 kg per tree and some times it may go up depending upon the seasonal variation.

As per the TDCC Market Study Report-4 (1997:2), the following table gives an approximate estimate of the average annual yield of Mohua products per tree:

Table 8.1: Average Annual Yield of Mohua Products

S. No.	*Mohua products*	*Average annual yield/ tree in Kg*	*Remarks*
1.	Flowers	250-500	Weight of fresh flower has been calculated from the dry weight at the ratio of 1 Kg of dry flower equal to 3 Kg of fresh flower.
2.	Seeds	50-55	
3.	Kernels	38-42	Estimated from the yielding capacity of seeds, as it constitutes 75% of the weight of the seeds.
4.	Oil from kernels	8-12 in	20-30% of the weight of the kernel.
		13-15 in expellers	24-37% of the weight of the kernel.
		16-17 in solvents	40-43% of the weight of the kernel.

(*Source*: TDCC Market Study Report, 1997)

However, the data for yield of fresh Mohua flowers per tree is not available to date. So it has been calculated from the dry weight of Mohua flowers only. The tribal people weigh it in a local unit of measure called *mano* which roughly states that about 10 *manos* of fresh flowers become 3 *manos* after being dried up. The above calculation is based on the local assumption only. The yield of kernels has been estimated from the yield of seeds with the ratio mentioned in the report, as the kernel forms 75 per cent of the weight of the seed. The yield of edible oil from the kernel differs with different ways of extraction. Under normal conditions yield of oil is 20-30 per cent of the weight of kernels when crushed in local oil mills (called *ghana*), 34-37 per cent in expellers, and 40-43 per cent when extracted by solvents. So the yield of oil given in the above table has been calculated accordingly using these estimations.

The People at Work

In a tribal society where food collection and gathering is a collective effort, although it can be done individually, a lot of local variations are seen in formation of groups to do the said job. It, however, depends on the role of a plant in a food gathering society in terms of its economic value and yielding capacity. One such example can be seen in Kungs at mongongo work (Lee 1979:192-201). Like that of mongongo, Mohua plays a vital role in the tribal economy of the study area because of its high yields, and also forms a major part of the subsistence economy. The nature and variability of work involved in Mohua economy requires a group effort, which is either restricted to one particular Kondh family or certain members of the family, depending upon their age and sex. To make the work more systematic and effective, the distribution of labour in Mohua work is remarkable where one finds a clear-cut division of labour and organized effort in a very structured manner at every stage of work. A detailed account of this is discussed below.

Clearing of Ground

The work for Mohua begins with the shedding of leaves, one can see a thick layer of dried leaves covering the ground below the trees. Within a week's time the flowers begin to drop down from the trees. During this intervening period of one week the dried leaves are collected at one place under each tree and burnt in order to clear the ground. Then the surrounding of the tree is cleared, grasses and small bushes are cut up to the range of the spreading branches to keep the ground clear when the flowers drop down. This helps to collect them neatly and quickly. The children of either sex do this job under the guidance of their parents. The trees that are owned by the villagers or are situated in the vicinity of the villages are prepared in this way. The rest in the jungles are left as they are.

Collecting Methods of Mohua Flowers

The collection commences with the dropping of flowers and continues till the collection of seeds is over. As mentioned earlier, the collection work requires total family involvement. The participation of friends and neighbours are often sought, as and when required. Mostly the female members of the community take a very active interest in these activities, very often helped by their children in their work. Although no special technique or intensive labour is required for this work, patience and perseverance play a very vital role. Boys above the age of 10 to 12 years are often engaged in other tedious works and seldom accompany their mothers in this mission.

Collection technique of Mohua flowers is very simple. For each tree at least one person is earmarked and in a group not more than 10 to 12 people are fanned out to all sides to start the work simultaneously. The collection posture begins with bending gracefully from the waist with knees slightly bent or sometimes by sitting on the ground. This depends on the concentration of fallen flowers and the nature the topsoil. At one point they collect all the flowers within their reach and then take the next step forward. Different persons from different angles repeat the process and then the whole ground is cleared within a stipulated time before proceeding to the next patch. While picking up, they carry a small bamboo basket along with them, and sometimes it is tied up with a rope to hang from one side of the body. When they collect a handful of flowers then only they put it inside the basket. When individual baskets are full, they gather at one place to transfer it to a larger basket. Again they come back to the same place from where they have left and repeat the process once again. Once one area is completed they move to the next area. Women and adolescent girls collect flowers at the fastest rate of 50 per minute in average, and if collected in a uniform speed it becomes a kilogram after 5 minutes. But it all depends on the concentration of flowers on the ground. The women and children hardly take any rest during the collection of flowers and sometimes they sing certain folk songs in between to get some relaxation. Most of the women and children carry head-load of flowers back to their homes after the day's work. But if the collection is huge enough to be carried back by them then the men using yokes on their shoulders carry them home. The men hardly carry it on their heads. It has been often seen that in the evening hours this process takes a long time during the peak seasons. The collection work, which starts at the early dawn, comes to a close before noon. Again when the fruit season comes, both the raw green variety and the ripe ones are plucked by men climbing up the Mohua trees, to which the natives are easily used to, due to the branching pattern. Both the adult male and female members of the tribal groups are adept climbers but generally the males do the plucking when women and children collect the fruits on the ground.

The duration of collecting Mohua seeds is short and in the absence of organized harvesting a considerable proportion of the crop is lost during the monsoon months. Unlike the collection mode of flowers and fruits, seed collection is not an organized effort. This may be due to two reasons: one, due to its limited use as the Mohua seed is not edible; and second, the higher market price of flowers and fruits than the seeds. Usually the ripe fruits are collected from the ground and brought back to homes where the seeds are separated from the fruit by pressing it lightly. Then they are dried up and shelled out to get the kernel. When collection of flowers and fruits demands the engagement of all members of the household, collection of seeds as well as extraction of kernels remain restricted to women only.

Protection Measures

As Mohua flowers form the major part of the local economy, a lot of care is taken for its protection against monkeys, cattle and sometimes men from the neighbouring places during harvesting seasons. The tribal people often divide themselves into smaller groups to keep a watch on these trees during peak seasons. But sometimes, male members also do it individually for the trees, which either they own or are situated near the vicinity of the village. During daytime all other members of the family do help them in this work. But for the trees which are in forest areas and not owned by any single family, whosoever reaches the tree first can collect the flowers form it for that day only. The only enemies whom the tribal people cannot keep away are the monkeys in large flocks who are also very fond of these flowers as human beings. Sometimes, it is seen that despite all efforts to safeguard the trees and its flowers they do take their share without much difficulty. The smaller children are often seen in taking up the responsibility of protecting Mohua flowers from the monkeys by chasing them, when the elders collect them safely. The whole village gets together at times if the monkeys come in large numbers to destroy these flowers during the peak season and chase them away to deeper jungles.

Preservation Techniques

Both Mohua flowers and seeds are preserved for use as food during lean seasons of the year. However, flowers are stored more in quantity as these can also be fed to the livestock as well as to make liquor out of it. From the seeds they extract oil and sometimes these are used for a 'Dal' like preparation. As flowers are more delicate than seeds, care is taken to preserve them in a better way. For preserving the flowers, which are juicy as well as fleshy, it takes long time, as they are dried under the sun just after its collection for a minimum of six to seven days. Once it becomes dry it is beaten up with the help of a soft hammer to remove its dried stigma and stamen which helps the flowers to be preserved for a longer duration. Then they are stored in a special kind of a basket prepared out of date-palm leaves inside which an inner lining of tendu leaves are given for maintaining a suitable temperature to preserve the flowers. The seeds after being sun-dried do not require any further processing and are stored in baskets made out of bamboo strips. Women do the bulk of the work for preserving the flowers and seeds, except of course, making of the special kind of baskets needed for this job.

Domestic Usage and Economic Importance of Mohua Products

Mohua products play a very vital role in the tribal economy of this region, both for food and market economy, which concern the tribal and the non-tribal population equally. The consumption pattern as well as its market demand make Mohua products the most sought after items during the peak seasons. Although its concentration, mode of collection and preservation differ widely from area to area no tribal life cycle is complete without the use of Mohua in its day to day life. The tribals, of course, depend much on Mohua as they have got very limited occupations like the non-tribal groups. It has been noticed that while tribals utilize Mohua, both for food and market, the non-tribals solely use it for market. Most of the Mohua traders, belonging to the local trading castes, regularly exploit the tribals. When for day to day expenditures the tribal people sell the Mohua products in the local market, the traders usually purchase them cheaply to sell them later at a higher price. The profit margin is always enjoyed by the resellers who even act as brokers at some stages to procure Mohua for the wealthy tribals for preparing liquor. As food, drink or cash, tribal people depend on Mohua for more than six months in a year, which attracts the anthropologists to study the ethnic groups and their dependence on Mohua species.

National data on Mohua Products

Sufficient data on the potentiality of production and collection of Mohua flowers is not available for the whole country, which sometimes create problems for policy makers and planners to develop a suitable strategy for its inclusion in the planning process. The total potentiality can only be estimated if the earlier physical counts based upon the method adopted by K.M.Tiwari is relied upon, which estimates the total number of Mohua trees at 94 lakhs for the whole country. Applying standard calculations, the total yielding of Mohua flowers will be nearly 35,06,200 tonnes in fresh flower weight and 10,52,800 in dry weight. However, data concerning the potential production and actual collection of Mohua seeds are available from different sources as given below:

Table 8.2: Potential Production and Actual Collection of Mohua Seeds

Sources	*Estimated Potential Production of seeds (tonnes)*	*Estimated Collection of seeds (tonnes)*
Indian Central Oil Seeds Committee	1,16,868	—
Directorate of Non-edible oils and Soap Industry, Industries Commission, Bombay	4,90,000	71,428
Oil Seeds Development Council, Government of India	2,18,000	42,000
K.M.Tiwari, Conservator of Forests, R&D Circle, Uttar Pradesh	2,18,000	50,000
Panel on Soap Industry of the Planning Commission	—	50,000

(*Source*: TDCC Market Study Report, 1977)

The table showing data on production potential and collection estimated by different agencies vary greatly except, of course, the last three which may be taken as authentic in this regard.

The concentration and production potential of Mohua trees in the district of Phulbani is not properly established as yet, and whatever data is there in the Forest Department of Orissa has been included here on the basis of divisional pattern, followed by the department. Estimates in tonnes of potential, collection, domestic retention and marketable surplus of Mohua flowers and seeds in Orissa as well as the district of Phulbani are as follows:

Table 8.3: Collection, Retention and Surplus of Mohua Flowers and Seeds

Category	*Flowers (in Tonnes)*		*Seed(tonne)*	
	Orissa	*Phulbani*	*Orissa*	*Phulbani*
Potential	7,25,000	35,000	1,40,000	8,500
Collection	5,50,000	26,000	64,500	3,500
Domestic Storage	1,22,000	6,000	—	—
Marketable Surplus	4,28,000	20,000	—	—

(*Source*: TDCC Market Survey Report, 1977)

Mohua Products in Daily Life

Both tribal and non-tribal populations do utilize Mohua flowers, fruits (both green and ripe), seeds and oil from kernels in a number of ways. But the tribal way of its utilization adds a variety to it, which is very interesting to observe and fascinating to taste. The best of all are the Mohua flowers, which are taken raw during the harvesting season and in dried form during the lean periods. While collecting, the fresh flowers are eaten raw as they are succulent and afterwards being fried or baked into cakes to be taken as a regular dish. But more often they are boiled for a few hours and left to simmer until the water evaporates completely, so that the characteristic odour of Mohua flowers disappears as a result of long cooking, and the material becomes soft and juicy. It is eaten with rice, tamarind, sal seeds, and food grains as a sweetmeat. On the whole, during the flowering season, Mohua flowers constitute a major part of the daily diets of the local tribes. In the lean season, dried Mohua flowers are eaten after boiling it and then it is cooked. Well-dried Mohua flowers are sometimes mixed with niger seeds, gingelli seeds or perched rice and powdered to be made into small balls. These are often kept preserved to be used during the lean periods. The non-tribal groups living in the plains also use Mohua flowers as feed for livestock when the tribal people largely use the dried flowers to prepare liquor throughout the year. Most of the men are engaged in this work and use the out-still system to make liquor. This practice is widely in vogue throughout the tribal areas. But in plains hardly people make liquor on their own and always prefer to sell it to the liquor preparing agencies that distill it in a large scale.

The tender green fruits of Mohua are consumed after cooking and preparing curry out of it. These green fruits contain a thick sticky milky substance, which is not edible. So after peeling the unripe fruits these are cut and washed in water to remove the milky substance before cooking. The ripe fruits are consumed raw that tastes slightly sweet. Just like mangoes it contains a lot of fibres and it is only chewed to suck the juicy portion. However, the consumption of ripe fruits is much less in comparison with the tender green variety.

Nutritive Value of Mohua Products

In the context of extensive use of Mohua products, it can be said that both the flowers and fruits are enriched with nutrients. Out of these two, flowers contain more edible portion at about 89 per cent and in respect of calorie contents it has 311 K.Cals. whereas in fruits it is only 111 K.Cals. So on the whole flowers are more nutritious than fruits which is very clearly shown in the Table 8.5, prepared by Dr. Sarath Gopalan, the then Director General of National Institute of Nutrition (NIN) of Hyderabad.

Extraction of Oil from the Seeds

The local tribes mainly retain the Mohua seeds and crush it to extract oil from it. Both the tribal and non-tribal groups use the oil for cooking purpose, which is known as *Tola tel* in native language. The local *Ghanas* (oil mills) are used to do this job, which during the harvesting seasons accrue good profits. Fresh Mohua oil from properly stored seeds is thick and pale yellow in colour with not so unpleasant taste. In winter, the oil further condenses like margarine and sometimes being used for illumination. The kernels in lean periods are often used as 'Dal', after crushing them into a paste and cooking like pulses. For all these purposes Mohua seeds are stored in large quantities at homes and used for domestic purpose only. Mohua oil is hardly sold in the local market.

Mohua Market and its Socio-Economic Importance

Broadly speaking there are three types of markets in Orissa for Mohua flowers and seeds namely, (i) Primary (ii) Secondary and (iii) Tertiary or terminal market.

Primary markets are usually weekly village markets, where mainly the collectors assemble both flowers and seeds during the harvesting seasons.

Secondary markets are mostly operated by the wholesale dealers and commission agents where the stock is kept awaiting despatch either to terminal markets to be sold to distillers and oil extractors, or to tertiary markets again to be sold to the consumers through resellers in other areas or states.

Terminal or Tertiary markets are not operated all the year round and mostly depend on the stock despatch from the secondary markets. During lean periods they do other businesses as well.

The market season of both Mohua flowers and kernels (of market surplus) starts in February and continues till September during which the natives keep themselves busy in collecting, processing and selling of Mohua products. The following table shows the market season for both of them:

Table 8.4: Marketing Seasons for Mohua Flowers and Seeds

MOHUA FLOWERS		*MOHUA SEEDS (KERNELS)*	
Month	*Percentage of market surplus*	*Month*	*Percentage of market surplus*
February	10	April	5
March	30	May	20
April	40	June	40
May	15	July	20
June	7	August	10
July	5	September	5

It has been confirmed from field investigations that the liquor manufacturers, both within and outside the state handle 60 to 70 per cent of market surplus, which is rather very significant. In comparison with other minor oilseeds like Neem, Karanj, Sal etc. Mohua seeds have considerable market utility. Despite being used by the tribals for their daily consumption, this oil is sometimes used as an adulterant for Vanaspati Ghee, and for this purpose it is clarified with buttermilk to mask the odour. Mohua oil is also extensively used for manufacture of soaps, particularly for cleaning of the clothes. Several other important uses include candle manufacturing, batch oil in jute industry, etc. By refining and hydrogenating Mohua oil can be used for manufacture of lubricating greases and fatty acids. The medicinal properties of this oil have made it a valuable constituent in the preparation of medicines for skin diseases, rheumatism etc., and for this reason it is often termed as an all-purpose tribal medicine.

Quality Determination

The buyers usually test the quality of Mohua flowers by taking a handful of Mohua flowers, pressing and releasing the same once or twice. If after releasing the pressure the flowers assume their original shape the quality is guaranteed. As far as seeds are concerned the well-dried variety is always preferred. Fruits that are fully ripe and shed from the trees with least effort usually contain seeds of good quality and the oil content is naturally high. Fruits that are plucked by shaking the branches are not fully mature and yield seeds, which are relatively immature and dull in colour. The broken percentage is high in the process of decorticating and the yield of kernel is also less. The buyers and oil mills usually test seeds by breaking the same and if the cross-section shows reddish colour it is classed as good quality kernel.

Socio-economic Importance of Mohua Products

Among all other available wild plant food resources in this region, Mohua products have got maximum economic importance. Apart from domestic consumption for food, both the tribals and non-tribals make a lot of money by selling the Mohua products to purchase all other items of daily use. So during peak seasons Mohua products do generate a great deal of market demand. During the last decade Mohua business has become more profitable also.

The most interesting feature among the tribal groups, specially of the Kuttia Kondh of Belghar in this district is that they express their yearly life cycles in terms of Mohua seasons due to their close rapport with this very natural phenomenon. Even the old records of 1951 census report for the district shows that the crop failure in both Balliguda and Khondmal subdivisions caused serious distress to the people in 1907-08 and among them Mohua was mentioned as one of the staple foods for the dominant tribal population of the area. During the last couple of years it has been observed that though some pockets of the state have undergone continuous deforestation activity for bringing the forest land under regular cultivation, one can not find any tree other than Mohua in the cultivated fields that have been left untouched. Both the tribals and non-tribals are always against the cutting down of these trees and they always narrate some of its mythological importance linking it to several benefits. Tribal people even have several social taboos to cut any Mohua tree and the non-tribal groups have also started to plant Mohua trees in their own fields. Due to this the tribal people have also started now to do it mainly in fallow land. So many ritualistic customs are inter-linked with Mohua tree that sometimes the anthropologists term it as 'Mohua culture'. No tribal socio-economic study of this region is ever possible without the mention of Mohua in it. The social dimension of tribal ecosystem is always directly related and regulated by the Mohua factor and in all respects this has become the trademark of the tribal cultures of this region.

Table 8.5: NUTRITIVE VALUE OF MOHUA FLOWERS AND RIPE FRUITS

EDIBLE PARTS		*MOHUA FLOWERS*	*MOHUA FRUITS (RIPE)*
1.	Edible portion	89%	—
2.	Moisture	185	736
3.	Protein (gm)	4.4	1.4
4.	Fat (gm)	0.6	0.6
5.	Minerals (gm)	2.7	0.7
6.	Fibre	1.7	—
7.	Carbohydrate (gm)	72.0	22.7
8.	Energy (K.Cal.)	311	111
9.	Calcium (mg.)	140	45
10.	Phosphorous (mg.)	140	22
11.	Iron (mg.)	15	1.1
12.	Carotene (μg.)	23	307
13.	Thiamine (mg.)	0.03	—
14.	Riboflavin (mg.)	0.83	—
15.	Niacin (mg.)	5.2	—
16.	Vitamin C (mg.)	7	40

Source: Dr. Sarath Gopalan

REFERENCES

Gopalan, C., B.V. Rama Sastri and S.C.Balsubramanium (1982), *Nutritive Value of Indian Foods*, Hyderabad: National Institute of Nutrition.

Lee, Richard (1979), *Kung San: Men, Women, Children at Work*, Cambridge: Cambridge University Press.

TDCC (1977), *TDCC Market Study Report-4*, Bhubaneswar: Tribal Development Co-operative Corporation of Orissa Limited.

9

People and Environment in Himachal Himalaya: A Socio-Economic Perspective

Gopal S. Singh

INTRODUCTION

The Himalayas extending over 2,500 km. in length from Nanga Parbat in the North West to Namche Barwa peak in the North East cover fully or partly eight developing countries of Asia. This zone is characterized by sharp variations in altitude, slope, rainfall, thermal regime, soil type and accessibility. The Himalayas spread over a geographical area of about 590,000 sq.km. wherein about 51 million people live. Geographically, the entire region is divided into Eastern, Central and Western Himalayas, each one of these having rich cultural diversity. The Western Himalayas is about 1.7 per cent of the country's area and about 11 per cent of the Himalayan landmass, harbouring 92.4 per cent people in villages characterized by subsistence farming livelihood. The Himachal Himalaya (33°22′ - 33° 10′ N latitude and 75° 46′ - 70° E longitude) occupies 55,673 sq.km. in the Western Himalayas. The river Tons separates Himachal Himalaya from Uttar Pradesh in the southeast, Jammu & Kashmir in the north and Punjab in the west and southwest. Beginning from the foothills of Siwaliks (300 m.) it extends up to the high hills (7,000 m.) covered with snow.

Altitudinally it can be divided into 5 zones, i.e. outer Himalaya, lower Himalaya, lesser Himalaya, greater Himalaya, and trans-Himalaya. Administratively it includes 12 districts, namely, Sirmur, Solan, Shimla, Kinnaur, Bilaspur, Una, Mandi, Kullu, Lahaul and Spiti, Hamirpur, Kangra and Chamba.

With vast variation in altitude and topography, the region enjoys different climatic conditions, and has large variety of flora and fauna and cultures. The region broadly provides life support to majority of the people who inhabit it. The valley areas support traditional agricultural practices. Introduction of fruit-bearing trees in some pockets of the region is very recent. The traditional agriculture has inseparable linkages with forest and livestock resources. Socio-cultural diversity coupled with environmental complexity has resulted in the development of many traditional techniques and technologies for long term social and ecological sustainability. This paper discusses about the social, cultural and economic dimensions of the traditional societies in the Himachal Himalaya and their interaction with the environment since many generations.

History and People

The traditions of the people of the Himachal Himalaya date back to the dawn of the human civilization. Prehistorically the Aryans settled down in the lower hills following the fertile valley of the higher Himalaya. Gradually they fused with the indigenous population already inhabiting this region. In the cold desert of Lahaul, Spiti, Kinnaur and Pooh, settlers came from Tibet, who were primarily of Mongoloid origin. At the upper hills, they merged with the local inhabitants and eventually adopted the area as their own by harmonious use of a variety of locally available resources.

The people and culture of this region are specifically identified by the collective term, *pahari* (of the mountains). The people are short in stature and dark in complexion, representing the Scheduled Castes, Khasas (Aryan origin), Rajaputs, Muslims and Brahmins. Subsistence agriculture supplemented by livestock rearing, and trading forest commodities are the main occupations of these people. Some of them are artisans and work as cobblers, basket makers, blacksmiths, goldsmiths, tailors and weavers. Although majority of the population believes in Hinduism, believers of Buddhism, Jainism, Sikhism, Islam and Christianity also have respectable places in this region. In general, the religious and ethnic spectra of the Western Himalayas are characterized by peaceful coexistence and mutual tolerance.

Except for a few towns, the people mostly live in villages consisting of isolated hamlets to conglomerated hamlets. Normally, a few hamlets are found to be dotted over the agricultural fields. In the lower hills houses are usually single storied, while in upper regions there are 2-4 storied houses, cemented with stones, timber and mud with slate roofs. The ground floor or basement of the multistoried houses is used for keeping cattle.

Land Use Pattern

Patterns of land use of Himachal Himalaya for the years 1980-81 and 1990-91 is given in Table 9.1. Area under cultivation has increased considerably during this period in this region. The increase in the area under cultivation might have been due to the conversion of cultivable waste land lying close to the settlements. The cultivable waste land which was not utilized so far, has been utilized now. This is because of the increase in population in the region which naturally demanded more area under food and fruit cultivation. Moreover, the area under fruit cultivation has increased considerably in the region. A considerable part of cultivated area is sown more than once. Waste land and other uncultivable areas are exclusively used for the purpose of grazing.

Table 9.1: Himachal Himalaya at a Glance

Features & land categories (ha.)	*1980-81*	*1990-91*
Total population	4280818	5170877
Literacy rate	42.5	63.9
Geographical area (Professional Record)	5567300	5567300
Geographical area (Revenue Record)	2985200	3367600
Forest area	806800	103900
Area not available for cultivation	303300	377000
Culturable waste	1249000	1308700
Waste land	54000	60100
Net sown area	572100	582800
Gross cropped area	946400	983600
Horticulture plantation	108676	400800
Land cultivated more than once	374300	400800

(*Source*: Statistical Outline, Himachal Pradesh, 1994)

Geo-climatic and Socio-economic features

Geo-climatic and socio-economic features of the Himachal Himalaya/Himachal Pradesh are presented in Table 9.2 on page 160. Altitudinal changes are the root cause of flexibility of climate.

It experiences a wide variation in receiving rainfall; Lahaul, Spiti and Pooh areas are almost rainless. The entire area is characterized by well defined seasons, *viz.*, summer (mid-April-June), monsoon/rainy (July-September), autumn (late September-early October), winter (late November-mid March) and spring season (Mid March-mid April). The average maximum temperature is the state ranges from 28° C to 32° C. Snowfall is very common in tracts lying above an elevation of 2200m. AMSL. The temperature in winter season remains below the freezing point in many parts of the higher Himalayas.

Four major land uses—land cover types, e.g. valley, forest, pasture/alpine lands are categorically noticed here. Cultivated lands are privately owned, where as forest and pastures/grazing land are owned by the Forest Department of the state of Himachal Pradesh. Valley lands are cultivated and are generally distributed across the river belt; these lands have moderate natural irrigation based on traditional designs. Terraced lands are merely rainfed and spread on gentle/moderate slopes (5-10°) to steep slopes (> 10°- 45°). Paddy and wheat are the major cultivated crops in the valley regions characterizing low crop diversity. Wheat, barley, maize, pulses, finger millets, amaranths, and buckwheat are the major harvested crops from the terraced fields indicating high agro-biodiversity. Introduction of cash crops in some parts of the Himachal Himalaya is a recent phenomenon. Forest, grassland and alpine meadows are other distinct land use types. From these areas one can bring fuel wood, fodder and other minor forest produce for daily use; even one can bring timber for the house construction. Usually, alpine pastures are used for rearing of livestock and medicinal plant collection. The overall human and livestock population is moderate; sheep and goat rearing at higher elevations is not uncommon. Erosion of soil is relatively high at higher elevations; avalanches at higher elevations result in heavy landslides and soil erosion. At higher elevations fuel, fodder, timber,

Table 9.2: Geo-climatic and Socio-economic Features of Himachal Himalaya

Features	*Sub-montane (sub-tropical)*	*Mid-hills (sub-humid)*	*High-hills (wet temperate)*	*High-hills (dry temperate)*
	1	2	3	4
Altitudinal range (m.)	Foot hills and valley (up to 800m.)	Lower hill terraces (800-1600m.)	Moderate hill terraces (1600-2200m.)	High hill terraces (2300-2700m.)
Climate	Sub-tropical	Mid-temperate	Humid-temperate	Dry-temperate
Annual rainfall	About 150cm.	170cm., least snow fall	100-150cm., moderate snowfall	< 20cm., high snowfall
Physical area	35%	32%	25%	8%
Cultivated area	33%	53%	11%	3%
Soil erosion susceptibility	Low	Moderate	High	Moderate to high
Soil type	Sandy loam with scattered loamy patches	Sandy loam to loam	Clayey loam to loam	Parent material (granite) with sandy loam
Agriculture system	Rainfed on terraces, valley moderately irrigated	Rainfed on terraces, in patches valley irrigated	Terraced land rainfed, valley with moderate natural irrigation	Rainfed along with natural irrigation

{Cont.}..

	1	2	3	4
Traditional crops (major)	Wheat, maize, rice, pulses, oilseeds, sugarcane	Rice, wheat, maize, mustard, pulses	Wheat, barley, maize, pulses, fingermillet, amaranths	Buckwheat, barley, wheat
Cash crops (modern/introduced)	Vegetables, pulses, groundnut, ginger	Vegetables, ginger, pulses	Vegetables, apples, plum, pear, almond etc.	Potato, pea, hops
Forest type	Broad leafed deciduous	Mixed and sub-tropical	Mixed and moist-temperate	Coniferous dry-temperate
Alpine and pastures	—	Moderate	Least occurrence	Frequent occurrence
Human and live-stock population	Thick	Thick	Moderate	Low
Sheep and goat rearing	—	Moderate rearing on hilly areas	Common rearing on hilly areas	Rearing is given priority
Constraints of the people	Shortage of fuel, fodder, soil and water conservation	Acute shortage of fuel, fodder and water conservation	Shortage of fuel, fodder, fruit packing material, transport, water conservation	Acute shortage of fuel, fodder, wood, fruit packing material, water conservation

(Modified, based on R.N. Sehgal and V. Chauhan 1989)

fruit packing materials, electricity, irrigation provision, soil and water conservation and transportation etc. are the major constraints for the people to lead a comfortable life (Singh *et al.* 1997b).

Traditional Systems of Farming

Hill agriculture system in the Himachal Himalaya is traditional. It exhibits a great deal of variability in crop diversity, crop composition, crop rotation and cropping pattern (Singh 1996). Large variations in altitude, topography, land size, slope direction, slopping pattern, landraces, temperature, humidity, rainfall/precipitation, climate, edaphic factors, livestock population, use of composts, forest resources and irrigation facility together with social, cultural and economic factors, resulted in a variety of land use-land cover types in the region. The heterogeneity becomes apparent when ecological conditions are superimposed on this. Constraints like inaccessibility, marginality, ecological fragility, environmental heterogeneity, and marginal socio-economic conditions favour evolution of complex farming systems in different landscapes. The traditional agriculture production system is, therefore, a complex product of traditional landraces, livestock, forest resources and domestic inter-linked subsystems.

Three broad categories of basic farming systems could be found in the Himachal Himalaya. All these systems are livestock and forest based, and form a spectrum of economic activity ranging from nomadic, semi-nomadic (transhumance) to settled agriculture. Settled agriculture is predominant over a broad range of altitudes. Monocropping is usually practiced in valley/plain area, the width of which is less than 5 km., and in some places even less than half a km. But mixed cropping is the characteristic feature of terraced land, the size of terraces varying between 0.01ha. and 0.1ha. Apart from the narrow strip of Bhabar in the foothills of Siwaliks where extensive and intensive agriculture is practiced on flat land under irrigated conditions, in the rest of the mountain terrain it is practiced under irrigated conditions and based on traditional lines. Majority of the farmers is marginal and have less than 1ha. of farming land, sometimes in scattered form. Since the land holdings are very small as well as scattered, the livestock supplements the income, and the latter is considered as the capital asset. Farmers are aware of a number of ways and means for optimal utilization of locally available resources. Organic manure derived from animal's dung, urine and local resources are the major inputs for the indigenous land races. Farmers even leave substantial amount of harvested stubble and weeds, which are recycled and reused for subsequent cropping. The traditional agriculture practices are significant for controlling weeds and pests, and are effective for the recycling of biomass (Altieri 1995). Use of bullocks as draught power and humans for labour are important inputs into the system. Sharing of human labour on an exchange basis, which is in existence since generations, is a way of long term sustainability of the system. Locally designed tools and implements (Singh *et al.* 1996) are being used by the farmers, which help in maintaining the stability of the system.

Agro-biodiversity and Cropping Patterns

Variations in altitude and climate have led to the evolution of high agricultural diversity and cropping patterns in the region (Singh *et al.* 1997a; 1997b). Existing natural diversity has, indeed, been utilized by the marginal farmers for their sustenance through developing diverse food production systems. This diversity is maintained through diverse farming systems, farming situations, cropping systems, crop diversity and genetic variability within the species. Such systems favour the use of locally available organic manure. Kharif and rabi are the two main crops harvested in early winter and summer respectively. In high altitudes of Lahaul, Spiti and Kinnaur areas winter crops are absolutely lacking due to perpetual snow cover. The sowing and harvesting seasons are entirely different in the lower areas. In high mountains kharif sowing takes place from March to July and harvesting is done from September to November. Similarly, rabi crops are sown from mid-September to mid-December and are harvested in April to mid-July. Early sowing and harvesting take place in valley areas. The duration of sowing and harvesting varies even within the same region. In Sangla valley of Kinnaur district the rabi crop is a kharif crop, sown in April-May and harvested in September-October. In Pattan, Chandra and Bhage valley of Lahaul region, barley is sown at the end of March and is harvested in early July, followed by buckwheat or mustard which ripens in September.

Table 9.3: Major Crops in Himachal Himalaya

BOTANICAL NAME	*COMMON NAME*	*LOCAL NAME*
1	2	3
Local varieties		
Amaranthus spp.	Amaranths	Sariyara
Brassica compestris	Mustard	Sarso/yungar*
Chenopodium album	White goosefoot	Bathua
Dolichos uniflorus	Horsebean	Kloth
Echinochloa frumentacea	Sanwamillet	Chini
Eleusine coracana	Fingermillet	Kodra
Fagopyrum debotrys	Buckwheat	Besha
F. esculentum	Buckwheat	Kathu/braphoo*/ogla
F. tataricum	Buckwheat	Gangri/phulado*/phapra
Glycine max	Soybean	Lobia
Hordeum himalayense	Barley	Jai/thaungjad*
Hordeum vulgare	Barley	Jau
Oryza sativa	Rice/Paddy	Jatu, dhan
Phascolus mungo	Blackbean	Mash
Psium sativum	Pea	Matar/nyarcha*
Setaria italica	Foxtailmillet	Kauni
Solanum tuberosum	Potato	Alu/adu*
Triticum aestivum	Wheat	Ganam/chava*
Vigna mungo	Greengram	Moong
V.sinensis	Frenchbean	Rajmash
Zea mays	Maize	Chhali/makki
High yielding varieties		
Humulus lupulus	Hops	Hops
Oryza sativa	Paddy	Dhan
Pisum sativum	Pea	Matar/nyarcha*
Solanum tuberosum	Potato	Alu/adu*
Triticum aestivum	Wheat	Ganam/chava*
Wild plants		
Banium cylindricum	Janli cuminum	Singu/ghanyorog*
Banium persicum	Cuminum	Kalajera*
Inula racemosa	Mano	Mano*
Saussurca lappa	Kuth	Kuth*

* Indicates Lahaul Valley.

As many as 17 food crops are being harvested in Kulu valley (Singh *et al.* 1997a), 7 in Lahaul valley (Singh *et al.* 1997b), 10 in Sangla valley of Kinnaur district and about 6 in Bhabar areas of the Siwaliks. Almost all crops are local breeds except wheat, rice, pea, potato and hops, as may be seen in Table 10.3. Rice is confined to the lower elevations of valley areas; hops in Lahaul and Spiti is preferred in plain/valley land. Wheat, rice, barley, mustard, pea, groundnut and potato are generally grown as monoculture, whereas crops like, amaranths, buckwheat, fingermillet, maize, and a variety of pulses are grown intermixed. Out of 17, 12 crops are, in general, cultivated as mixed crops in rainy season in Kullu valley, the number of crops constituting the mixture ranges from 2 to 5 (Singh 1996). Mixed cropping is usually practiced in the uplands where crops are susceptible to environmental risks. The traditional agricultural practices favour to cope up with food security in uncertain environmental conditions. Monoculture is practiced in dry temperate areas of Lahaul, Spiti and Kinnaur. In Bhabar area, apart from wheat and rice cultivation, sugarcane and groundnut are also cultivated. Similarly, crops like ginger and capsicum are usually confined to the lower elevations. Some of the wild cash crops like *kuth, mano, kalajera* and *singu* are cultivated in or around the farm fields in Lahaul and Spiti (Singh *et al.* 1997b). *Kuth* is also cultivated in some parts of Kinnaur district. These plants are exclusively used as spices and for medicinal purposes. On the whole, the crop diversity and cropping pattern of the Himachal Himalaya are entirely different from other Himalayan regions (Pandey and Singh 1984; Ramakrishnan 1992; Maikhuri *et al.* 1996; Semwal and Maikhuri 1996). Even within a region, one may notice significant diversity in cropping pattern as well (Sharma and Minhas 1993; Singh *et al.* 1997a, 1997b). This diversity is more pronounced in other mountainous regions than in the Himachal Himalaya (Sarmiento *et al.* 1993; Dougherty 1994).

Harcourt (1872) noted that rice, opium, tea, tobacco, wheat, maize, barley and amaranths in Kullu valley, and wheat, barley and buckwheat in Lahaul valley were once major food crops. But, in mid-1950s great revolutions took place in some areas where farmers started shifting from the indigenous farming practices to horticultural practices. Huge agricultural lands were converted into orchards in different agro-climatic zones. With the advancement of agro-technologies many new high yielding varieties of food and fruit crops were introduced according to their suitability to the ecological conditions and needs of the farmers. But now these new inventions are in a 'transitional phase' (Singh and Ram 1997; Singh 1998) and the system has become unsustainable. The traditional varieties of food crops have gradually disappeared from the area (Singh *et al.* 1996; Singh *et al.* 1997b). Therefore, there is an urgent need to recognize agriculture as an ecological system, besides being considered as a production system (Ramakrishnan 1992; Singh and Ram 1997). Fortunately there has been a renewed interest in traditional systems of farming throughout the world (Loomis 1984; Ewel 1986). Mixed cropping, a characteristic feature of traditional societies all over the world is also common in Himachal Himalaya, and it is receiving more attention so as to increase productivity per unit area.

Traditional Animal Husbandry

Traditional rearing of livestock is an integral part of agricultural system in Himachal Himalaya and acts as a major source of livelihood. Cows, bullocks, buffaloes, sheep, goats, mules, ponies and yaks are kept in the villages by majority of the marginal people to ensure livelihood security. Cattle are usually kept for their drought power, organic manure for crops, and milk and milk products for daily consumption. Sheep and goats provide wool, meat, milk and drought power. These animals are usually local breeds having advantages over introduced ones (Singh *et al.* 1996, 1997b). At lower elevations, cross-breeds of cows and buffaloes are also being reared.

Yak is a native breed of Tibet and is domesticated in the districts of Lahaul and Spiti, and Kinnaur. Its well-known ability to withstand low temperature and snowy condition, and to survive on coarse fodder is unique. Depending on the size of the village and population of cattle, majority of the villages has one or more male yaks for breeding purpose. Some people privately also own yaks. According to local belief, it is worshipped as a god of animals in the area. Different breeds of yaks for Lahaul and Sangla valley are given in Table 9.4. The original yak is exclusively segregated in the fifth generation after crossing cow with yak. Different breeds are locally named differently.

Table 9.4: Different Offsprings of Yak

Cross with	*Offsprings*
Lahaul Valley	
Yak X Cow	Churu* and Bong!
Yak X Churu	Gari* and Garu!
Yak X Gari	Lari* and Laru!
Yak X Lari	Bree* and Jee!
Yak X Bree	Bree* and Yak ^
Sangla Valley	
Yak X Cow	Jomo* and Job!
Yak X Jomo	Gare* and Gara!
Yak X Gare	Gire* and Gira!
Yak X Gire	Bume* and Buma!
Yak X Bume	Breme* and Yak ^

(*female offsprings fetching milk; ! male offsprings sterile and for drought power: ^ original yak for breeding and drought power)

Indigenous Knowledge on Wild Tree Species

In Himachal Himalaya fodder tree species are found to be properly maintained on agricultural bunds and nearby forest areas (Ram and Singh 1997). The leaves of coniferous species are mostly used for preparing organic manure. Depending on the availability of these resources, subsistence farmers use them for different purposes (see Table 9.5).

Fruits/seeds/flowers of a number of wild plants are used as edible. Similarly variety of plants are exclusively used as traditional medicines (Dobriyal *et al.* 1997). The frequency of usage of these species and their parts vary depending upon the species and the nature of the ailment. Traditional techniques regarding the preparation of herbal medicine for various diseases is very well known to the local people. Older persons have faith and love for the use of locally available herbal medicines and are enthusiastic to share this knowledge with the younger generation. Wild edibles are known for their high nutritive value. It is generally believed that these improve the quality of milk among the cattle, goats and sheep.

Indigenous Knowledge of Men and Women

Participation of men and women in different levels of work/ activities is distinct, as may be seen in Table 10.6, characterized by the level of expertise for different purposes. For example, for agriculture, both men and women claim expertise, while for horticulture related activities men are more involved. Sedentary activities involved in agricultural activities like harvesting, weeding, field watching to save the crops from birds and animals are also preferred by women since generations. Men usually perform arduous work, particularly, pre-sowing land preparation, ploughing, irrigation, cattle rearing in forest, carrying harvested crop/grains and their marketing etc. Collection of non-timber forest produce like medicinal plants and wild fruits are exclusively taken care of by the women. Except some non-technical work required for livestock husbandry, most of the work is attended by the women. Traditionally, women are more skilled for domestic chores.

Customs and Manners

Festivals and fairs are an indispensable part of the cultural life of the people of Himachal Himalaya. Every fair and festival has a legendary origin. It has educational, social as well as religious character. It fulfils the need of social equity from both economic and cultural points of view. What is more interesting is that every season has its own appropriate festival(s), as may be seen in Table 10.7. The arrival of winter is celebrated with the festival of bonfire and the summer is welcomed with the festival of flowers. Each season is marked by an appropriate festival, which is influenced by the climatic needs or other characteristics of the season. Some festivals are related to moon, agricultural cycle, and to gods and goddesses. Festivals are the occasions for mass feasting, drinking and dancing.

Table 9.8 lists some of the important fairs in Himachal Himalaya. The concept of fair is quite different from what it is in other parts of the country. The local gods and their devotees create the atmosphere of a fair. The gods/goddesses and their devotees participate in these fairs. The fairs help the people for a get-together, a custom unique to the hill people. These are the occasions

Table 9.5: Wild Plants in Himachal Himalaya

Plants	*Fodder*	*Fuel*	*Bedding/manure*	*Edible*	*Medicinal value*
1	2	3	4	5	6
Abies pindrow	—	high	high	—	—
Acacia catechu	—	low	—	—	high
Aconitum heterophyllum	—	—	—	—	high
Aesculus indica	high	low	—	high	—
Angelica glauca	—	—	—	—	low
Berberis lycium	—	—	—	—	medium
Cedrus deodara	—	high	low	—	—
Celtis australis	high	low	—	—	—
Fragaria vesca	low	—	—	high	—
Juglans regia	high	low	—	high	high
Jurinea macrocephala	—	—	—	—	high
Morus himalayana	high	low	—	—	—
Morchella esculenta	—	—	—	high	medium
Picea morinda	—	medium	low	—	—
Picrorrhiza kurrooa	—	—	—	—	high

{Cont.}...

1	2	3	4	5	6
Pinus wallichiana	—	medium	high	—	—
P. roxburghii	—	medium	high	—	—
Podophyllum emodi	—	—	—	—	low
Prunus armeniaca		low	—	high	—
P. pashia	low	low	—	high	—
P. parsica	low	low	—	high	—
Quercus dilatata	low	medium	—	—	—
Q. leucotrichoflora	high	medium	—	—	—
Robinia psedocasia	medium	low	—	—	—
Saussurea lappa	—	—	—	—	medium

for mass recreation as well. Fairs may be seasonal, mythical and religious, trade and agricultural etc. All groups/classes of men, women and children take part by singing and dancing in their traditional styles during these fairs. Fairs like Nalwari, Jhothe-ka-mela and Sari are meant for the cattle. Fairs also have a commercial importance, during which local agricultural and bamboo products, forest products, medicinal products and items of handicraft are bought and sold.

Table 9.6: Indigenous Work Participation of Men and Women

Activities/works	*Men*	*Women*
1	2	3
On-farm based		
Terrace/bund preparation	++	-
Ploughing and harrowing	++	-
Breaking of clods/pods	+	++
Hauling and spreading manure	-	++
Application of agro-chemicals	++	+
Sowing grains	++	+
Planting seedlings	-	++
Weeding and tilling	-	++
Crop irrigation	++	-
Harvesting of crops	+	++
Carrying harvested crops	++	+
Thrashing crops	+	++
Storing food grains	++	+
Grafting and pruning fruit plants	++	-
Pesticide spraying	++	-
Fruit plucking and carrying	+	++
Fruit grading, packing and loading	++	-
Forest based		
Litter collection for bedding materials	-	++
Lopping/pruning of fodder and collection	+	++
Fuel wood collection	+	++
Timber collection and processing	++	-
Collection of wild fruits and medicinal plants	++	+
Forest based resource management	++	-
Livestock based		
Stall feeding of cattle	-	++
Animal rearing	+	++

(Cont.)....

1	2	3
Milk extraction	+	++
Manure/dung replacement	-	++
Wool shearing	++	-
Sale/purchase decision of livestock	++	+
Domestic chores based		
Food preparation	+	++
Water collection	-	++
Washing of clothes	-	++
Washing of utensils	-	++
Child rearing/care	+	++
Household goods/commodities marketing	+	++
Bamboo items preparation	++	+
Woollen items preparation	-	++
Fibre processing and value addition	+	++
House construction and repairing	++	-

(*Source*: Singh *et al.* 1996)

Himachal Himalaya is also characterized by a number of traditional and informal village institutions/committees, which are formed by the local inhabitants (Singh 1997a; Shabab 1996). The village committee looks after the management of common resources, forest resources, road repairing and resolution of social conflict in the village. The *deota*/deity committee of the village takes care of all the affairs relating to the village deities. This task becomes imperative because of the local belief that the local deities protect the village residents directly or indirectly from all natural and man-made calamities. These institutions not only help in the perpetuation of the traditions, but also in the management and conservation of biological diversity in and around the village (Singh 1997b).

Himachal Himalaya is rich in traditional techniques of handicrafts, as may be seen in Table 9.9. These techniques are often associated closely with different caste occupations in this region. Men are generally more skilled in pottery, basketry, metal and wood works etc. that provide livelihood to them. Weaving and embroidery, knitting of woollen garments are the fields of expertise of the women cross-cutting caste and class boundaries.

Table 9.7: Important Festivals in Himachal Himalaya

Name of the festival	*Month/period*	*Remarks*
Baisakhi/bissu/bisha/bisowa/bishoo	1st day of Baisakh (the 13th April)	Bathing in river, stream or lake; prayers, dancing and singing.
Chet/dholru/chatrali/chatra	1st day of the month of Chet (March)	Playing with dancing.
Chrewal/badranjo/pathoruru	1st day of the month of Bhadon (August)	Worship of Lord Shiva, feasting and dancing.
Diwali	Kartik Amavasya	Lighting of homes with small earthen lamps.
Dussehra	October	Gathering of gods/goddesses at Kullu town.
Haryali/rhyali/dakhram/shegtsum	1st day of the month of Sawan	Sowing, animal care, pests burnt with cow dung, praying, feasting and dancing.
Jagra	End of Bhadon (September)	Praying to deities.
Lohri/maghi	1st day of the month of Magh (January)	Bonfire, feasting and dancing.
Navratra/Durga ashtami	Eight days of Navaratra	Praying Goddess Durga.
Phulech/U-khyang	September	Flower show, garlands offering to local deities.
Rakhpunya/rakhi/salunu	1st full moon of Sawan (August)	Sacred thread tied to brothers' wrists by sisters.
Sair	1st day of the month of Asadh (September)	Feasting and dancing.
Shivratri	Phalgun (February)	Shiva worship.

These items prepared by the women find their way into the local market. Although knitting of woollen garments is a craft performed by all sections of women, the lower income group among them depend more on the marketing of these items.

Table 9.8: Important Fairs of Himachal Himalaya

Name of fair	*Place/district*	*Period*
Dungri	Manali/Kullu	May
Sarhi jatra	Nagar/Kullu	May
Bajnar mela	Bajnar/Kullu	May-June
Kullu dashehra	Kullu town/Kullu	October
Jhothe-ka-mela	Kufri-Koti-Mashobra/Shimla	September
Sipi fair	Mashobra/Shimla	May
Pather-ka-khel	Halog/Shimla	October-November
Rohru jatar	Rohru/Shimla	April
Rampuri jatar	Rampuri/Shimla	July
Solan fair	Solan/Solan	June
Sari fair	Solan/Solan	July
Triliknath fair	Triloknath/Lahaul-Spiti	February
Brahmaur jatra	Brahmaur/Chamba	August
Chhitrari jatra	Chittrari/Chamba	September
Sui fair	Chamba town/Chamba	April
Phul jatra	Kilar-pangi/Chamba	October
Jawalamukhi fair	Jawalamukhi temple/Kangra	October
Dal fair	Dharamshala/Dharamshala	August
Nalwari fair	Bhangrotu-Sundarnagar/Mandi	March
Shivratri fair	Mandi/Mandi	March
Markandya fair	Markandya shrine/Bilaspur	April
Naina devi fair	Nainadevi temple/Bilaspur	August
Lavi	Rampur-Bushahr/Kinnaur	November
Rainka fair	Rainka lake/Sirmaur	November

The tradition of fraternal polyandry among the hill people of the Himachal Himalaya is still retained in villages. This institution provides stability to the society. Usually the division of conjugal right between the brothers is through mutual understanding. The custom of polyandry prevents overpopulation and division of the property, where agricultural land is not sufficient to support large population in rugged hilly terrain. It also helps to maintain the unity of family by the common parents of all the children. Traditionally, the eldest brother represents the family and is the controller of all younger siblings in the matters of marriage and conjugal life. Now it is practiced among the lower sections of the hill society. It is not strange to find polygony, if a cultivator possesses a large land-holding and needs more working hands for agricultural operations.

Table 9.9: Handicrafts in Himachal Himalaya

Skill	*Common objects/articles/items and usage*
1	2
Pottery	Ghara (pitcher) — to carry/store water, grains, milk and butter. Chillam/hukka — for tobacco smoking. Bowls — to store grains and vegetables etc. Earthen lamps — for lightening purpose.
Basketry	Kilta (conical basket) — to carry water-filled pitcher, manure, wood, apple etc. Tokri (semi-circle basket) — to keep horticultural and agricultural produce. Shoopa/soop/odi — for winnowing grains. Karandu/kardu — for keeping vegetables, eatables. Peru/pechholi (huge basket) — for storing grains. Chatera/chhikri/jhabera (cup-like small basket) — for covering the mouth of the cattle while threshing wheat, paddy etc. Majri/mandri/chatai — used as mat. Pullah — to make fibre shoes. Leather items — excellent containers and sandals.
Weaving	Pattu, dohru, pattis — as a body wrapper in winter. Shuktu — shawls for women. Kharcha/chuktu/chugdan — rough carpets. Zomba/pichaya — woollen shoes
Embroidery	Designed on handkerchieves, purses, bed sheets, pillow covers and shawls.
Metal craft	Gold, brass and iron items in the form of jewellery, religious objects, musical instruments, agricultural implements etc.
Wood work	Wood carving on doors, windows. Kunla — a wooden bowl. Kosi — a milk pot. Ongri — to store grains etc. Takli — a spinning wheel.

CONCLUSION

The traditional customs and culture of the Himachal Himalaya that one may find today is an outcome of ages of experience of the people in this region. These experiences have resulted in the development of a multitude of traditional knowledge to design a variety of value added objects and products. Accumulation of field knowledge has subsequently helped in the domestication of wild plants and animals and for the harmonious use of natural resources. High agro-biodiversity in this region is the result of complex production systems with livestock-forest interlinkage. Cultural diversities and their manifestations through a number of fairs and festivals are the mechanisms for the adaptation of the people to such a harsh and inhospitable environmental condition. Such traditional systems need to be protected for the long-term sustainability of the system and the society. There is an urgent need to revive the efficacy of traditional knowledge based on the empirical knowledge of the local people. Eco-environmental and socio-economic changes have recently started taking place in some pockets of the region (Singh 1998); but the gaps arising out of these changes could be adequately bridged by proper landscape planning of the region (Singh and Ram 1997).

REFERENCES

Altieri, M. (1995), Agroecology puts Synergy to Work to create Self-Sustaining Agro-ecosystem, *Ceres FAO Review*, 154, 27, 15-23.

Dobriyal, R.M. *et al.* (1997), Medicinal Plant Resources in Chhakinal Watershed in the North Western Himalaya, *Journal of Herbs, Spices and Medicinal Plants*, 5, 15-27.

Dougherty, W.W. (1994), Linking Between Energy, Environment and Society in the High Atlas Mountains of Morocco, *Mountain Research and Development*, 14, 119-135.

Ewel, J.J. (1986), Designing Agricultural Ecosystem for the Humid Tropics, *Ann. Rev. Ecol. Syst.*, 17, 245-271.

Harcourt, A.F.P. (1870), *The Himalayan Districts of Koolo, Lahaoul and Spiti* (Reprinted 1972), Delhi: Vivek Publishing House.

Loomis, R.S. (1984), Traditional Agriculture in America, *Ann. Rev. Ecol. Syst.*, 15, 449-478.

Maikhuri, R.K., K.S. Rao and K.G. Saxena (1996), Traditional Crop Diversity for Sustainable Development of Central Himalayan Agroecosystems, *Int. Jou. Sustain. Dev. World Ecol.*, 3, 8-31.

Pandey, U. and J.S. Singh (1984), Energetics of Hill Agroecosystems: A Case Study from Central Himalaya, *Agricultural Systems*, 13, 83-95.

Ram, S.C. and G.S. Singh (1997), *Grewia oppositifolia* — Time for Revival in Himalaya, *Agroforestry Today*, 9, 14-15.

Ramakrishnan, P.S. (1992), *Shifting Agriculture and Sustainable Development: An Interdisciplinary Study from North Eastern India*, MAB Series, Vol. 10, UNESCO-Paris and Carnforth: Parthenon Publishing Group.

Sarmiento, L., M. Monasterio and M.Montilla (1993), Ecological Bases, Sustainability and Current Trends in Traditional Agriculture in the Venezuelan High Andes, *Mountain Research and Development*, 13, 167-176.

Sehgal, R.N. and V. Chauhan (1989) Dynamics of Land Use Patterns and Socio-economy of Himachal Pradesh, In S.K.Chadha (ed.) *Environmental Holocaust in Himalaya*, New Delhi: Ashish Publishing House.

Semwal, R.L. and R.K. Maikhuri (1996), Structure and Functioning of Traditional Hill Agro-ecosystems of Garhwal Himalaya, *Biological Agriculture and Horticulture*, 13, 267-289.

Shabab, D. (1996), *Kullu: Himalayan Abode of the Divine*, New Delhi: Indus Publishing Co.

Sharma, P.D. and R.S. Minhas (1993), Land Use and the Biophysical Environment of Kinnaur District, Himachal Pradesh, India, *Mountain Research and Development*, 13, 41-60.

Singh, G.S. (1996), Changing Traditional Land Use Pattern in Himachal Himalaya at Kullu, Himachal Pradesh, In P.S.Pathak and B.Gopal (eds.) *Studies in Indian Agroecosystems*, 1-13.

Singh, G.S. (1997a), Sacred Groves in Western Himalaya: An Eco-cultural Imperative, *Man in India*, 77, 247-257.

Singh, G.S. (1997b), Socio-cultural Evaluation of Sacred Groves for Biodiversity Conservation in North Western Himalaya, *Journal of Hill Research*, 10, 43-50.

Singh, G.S. (1998), Environmental, Ecological and Socio-economic Impact of Introduced Crops in Western Himalaya, *Journal of Human Ecology*, 9, 63-72.

Singh, G.S. and S.C.Ram (1997), Prospects of Sustainable Development of Kullu Valley in North Western Himalaya, *Journal of Rural Development*, 16, 359-368.

Singh, G.S., K.S. Raφ and K.G. Saxena (1997a), Energy and Economic Efficiency of the Mountain Farming System: A Case Study in the North-Western Himalaya, *Journal of Sustainable Agriculture*, 9, 25-47.

Singh, G.S., S.C. Ram and J.C. Kuniyal (1997b), Changing Traditional Land Use Patterns in the Great Himalayas: A Case Study of Lahaul Valley, *Journal of Environmental Systems*, 25, 195-211.

Singh, G.S., K.G. Saxena, K.S. Rao and S.C. Ram (1996), Traditional Knowledge and Threat of its Extinction in Chhakinal Watershed in North Western Himalaya, *Man in India*, 76, 1-17.

10

Ethnoecological Systems of the Gond: Approaches and Methods

Ajay K. Awasthi

Concept of Ethnoecology

Over centuries, people who have retreated into the forest and hilly tracts and have preserved their simple and distinctive way of life have come to be known as tribes. Tribes have been conventionally described as *Adivasis* or dwellers from the very beginning, our contemporary ancestors, inhabitants of unpolluted and harmless world, a race possessing the most profitable natural properties or resources, those who are most lively and vigorous, sun burnt Indians that have no other wealth but peace and pleasure, the first created 'Adam' and 'Eve' etc.

The tribal people may be hunters, gatherers, shifting cultivators, herders or simple farmers. They have a contained ethnic system living either inside the forests or in the fringe of the forests. Therefore, tribal communities have a close relationship with forests; their customs, religious practices, social fabric and folklore have been greatly influenced by forest. Tribals depend on the forest for their food, medicine, material for housing, fuel, fodder etc. At the time of food shortage in particular, they depend mostly on forest for their sustenance. In normal times, the roots, tubers, fruits and flowers collected from the forest substantially supplement the tribal diet. Tribals enjoy various privileges in cultivating, grazing, collection of fuel wood and minor forest produce (MFP) from forest.

India has over 68 million tribal population consisting about 8.08 per cent of the total Indian population, as per the Census of 1991. Madhya Pradesh is the home of many tribal communities, where 23 per cent of the State population is that of the tribals. In fact, it has the largest concentration of tribal population in the country.

Tribal knowledge of plants and animals have been recorded under various titles like, ethnobotany, ethnozoology, ethnomedicine, ethnobiology etc. from time to time. The term ethnobotany is one of the earliest expressions of relating tribal knowledge with their environment, and was first used by Harshberger in 1895 with an aim to recording plants used by the aborigines. De (1968) defined the term ethnobotany 'as the study of interrelationship between primitive people and plants'. According to him, primitive peoples refer to the people who are devoid of any written language, but retain their traditions by verbal means.

Ethnoecology is now emerging as an important inter-disciplinary science, which concerns with ecological studies on 'ethnoecosystems' of specific ethnic groups. Ethnoecology is the holistic study of specific ethnic communities in their natural environment and can be defined as the study of environmental system of that community. Such a system has an ecological structure of its own and also characteristic functions.

In an ethnoecological system, the focal component is the ethnic community. Communities are important components of ethnoenvironmental systems, as they possess ecological structure and characteristic functions. Not much has been done in terms of ethnoecological studies, and the bulk of the literature revolves round ethnobotanical and ethnozoological exercises. The study of the role of plants and animals in tribal culture and their values, and the nexus of relationship between culture and environment are the prime focuses of ethnoecological studies.

Ethnoecological System

An ethnoecological system has two important components:

1. The ethnic group.
2. Interacting environmental system.

The ethnic group together with the interacting resources system (agriculture, forest, animals etc.) constitute the biotic resource component of the ethnoecosystem. Physical system together with urban resource system constitutes the abiotic resource component.

Thus, the ethnic population system interacting with the resources system forms an ethnoecosystem, which essentially possesses (i) structure (ii) energy and material relations and (iii) homeostasis mechanism. The interacting resource system is flexible and can be substituted as and when required.

Aspects of Study

The aspects of studying an ethnoecological system may include the following:

(i) Review of historical background and record.

(ii) Structural characteristics of specific ethnoecological system, such as:
   a. animal and plant diversity;
   b. edaphic conditions;
   c. land use patterns; and
   d. resource quality.

(iii) Demographic structure of the ethnic group, such as:
   a. age profile;
   b. sex ratio;
   c. vulnerable populations;
   d. morbidity;
   e. chronic diseases;
   f. venereal diseases;
   g. disability; and

h. population dynamics — migration and its causes.

(iv) Culture and traditions of the ethnic group.

(v) Aspects of energy flow and material cycle.

(vi) Environmental dependence and affected components of the environment.

(vii) Analysis of the present status and future development projects in the area and management recommendations.

Gond Ethnic System: A Case Study

The present study was conducted in six Gond tribal villages in Sidhi district of Madhya Pradesh, namely, Sahaja, Satnara, Kathas, Hanumangarh, Barigama and Akori. The villages Sahaja and Satnara have been identified as agricultural villages, as majority of families practice agriculture. Villages Hanumangarh and Kathas are forest villages, because forest is the major source of income for the villagers. Barigama and Akori are identified as urban for the dependence of their population on urban centres. A questionnaire based survey was conducted in all these six tribal villages selected for the present study. Finally, an analysis of human component, domestic animals, socio-economic status, sex ratio, educational status, utilization of forest and animal resources, and resource dependence have been done.

Human Component Analysis

The data on human component analysis, as presented in Table 10.1, reveals that a state of imbalance in the sex ratio has been noticed in all the six villages under study. The sex ratio of 842 and 781 females/1000 males in villages Sahaja and Satnara, 738 and 772 females/1000 males in villages Hanumangarh and Kathas, and 898 and 791 females/1000 males in villages Barigama and Akori reveal the numerical dominance of males over the females in all these villages. The situation can be explained as follows:

(i) The imbalance in the sex ratio due to less number of females makes the communities vulnerable to gene flow from other communities in the form of accepting brides from other neighbouring groups. The urban societies are more vulnerable to this flow than agricultural and forest based societies.

Table 10.1: Human Component Analysis

Name of village	*Population*		*Sex Ratio*	*Literacy %*	*Man animal Ratio*	*Occupation*					
	M	*F*				*Agril.*	*Agril. Lab.*	*Contr. act*	*Multi occu*	*Serv- ice*	*Beg- ger*
Agriculture village:											
Sahaja	57	48	842	4.76	1:0.84	65	8	6	30	-	-
Satnara	55	43	781	5.10	1:1.45	60	4	-	34	-	-
Forest village:											
Kathas	57	44	772	2.97	1:1.29	25	10	6	60	-	-
Hanumangarh	84	62	738	1.36	1:0.77	30	42	9	65	-	-
Urban village:											
Barigama	79	71	898	5.33	1:1.01	25	27	30	68	-	-
Akori	91	72	791	4.29	1:1.30	18	38	60	35	10	2

(ii) Low rate of literacy among all sections of the society indicates less percolation of socio-economic benefits to the communities granted through the welfare programmes of the Government and NGOs.

(iii) The occupational analysis reveals that Gonds face economic stress; only agricultural societies having some semblence of economic stability. The forest people depend upon natural resources (various forest produces) and on periodical jobs as labourers. The urban societies have no other alternative except to work as labourers.

(iv) The man-animal ratio in these Gond villages ranges between 1:1 and 1:1.5, meaning thereby that for every single person there is one animal at least. While the agricultural societies can and do feed their animals the agricultural waste, the forest and urban societies put an additional stress on the surrounding resource system and on their economy through their livestock. The poultry, of course, provides some economic gain, but not to compensate the burden created by other animals.

Forest Utilization Analysis

The relevant process and factors responsible for the forest utilization in the study area have been identified as well as quantified in order to have an idea of their impact on ethnic system and the exploitation pressure on the forest resource system (see Fig. 10.1). Forest utilization has been discussed under two categories:

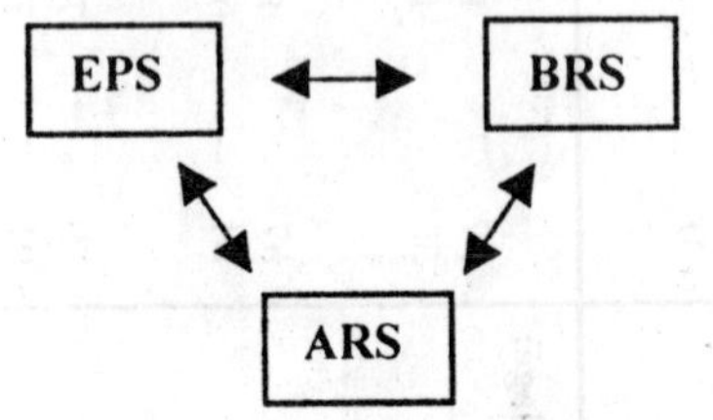

EPS: Ethnic Population System
BRS: Biotic Resource System
ARS: Abiotic Resource System

Fig. 10.1: Interacting Ethnoecosystem Components

Table 10.2: Forest Resource Utilization

Name of village	*Population*	*Fire wood (kg.)*	*Fruit (kg.)*	*Tendu leaves (kg.)*	*Other leaves (kg.)*	*Gum resins (kg.)*	*Mohua flower (kg.)*	*Total (Rs.)*	*Per capita (Rs.)*
Agriculture									
Sahaja	105	43420 (43420)	290 (5220)	9351 (23377)	70 (28)	115 (230)	3720 (10229)	82504	785.75
Satnara	98	34910 (34910)	290 (5220)	7475 (18687)	160 (64)	150 (300)	2960 (8140)	67321	686.95
Forest									
Kathas	101	46610 (46610)	595 (19710)	10370 (25925)	1030 (412)	195 (390)	3780 (10385)	103432	1024.07
Hanuman-garh	146	72550 (72550)	690 (12410)	13340 (33350)	580 (232)	345 (690)	4420 (12163)	131405	900.03
Urban									
Barigama	150	15358 (15358)	225 (4050)	12120 (30300)	130 (52)	80 (160)	2770 (7617)	57537	383.58
Akori	163	27788 (27788)	205 (3690)	10470 (26175)	296 (116)	60 (120)	3500 (9625)	67514	414.19

(Values presented in parenthesis are in Rupees)

a) *General forest utilization.* This is directed towards the utilization of different species, such as, fire wood, timber for housing, fruit, gum, bark and resin collections.

b) *Specific forest utilization.* This is directed towards specific plant species like collection of leaves from *Diospyros melanoxylon* (tendu), *Butea monosperma* (palas), *Bauhinia vahili* and flowers of *Mudhuca indica* (mahua) etc.

The overall average collection rates of different forest produce have been calculated for the Gond ethnic system taking into account total collection of different forest produce and population in all the six villages studied. This gives us an integrated picture of the average collection rates of different forest produce by the Gond, which is discussed below:

(i) Fire wood collection rate comes to 0.81 kg/person/day.
(ii) Timber collection rate is 53.04 kg/person/year that ensures a saving of Rs. 106.08p/person/year when this free collection from forest is valued in terms of rupees.
(iii) Fruit collection rate for gum, bark, resin etc. is 1.30 kg/person/year.
(iv) The overall collection rate of tendu leaves is 83.95 kg/person/year.
(v) The overall collection rate of palas leaves is 3.19 kg/person/year.
(vi) The mahua flower collection rate is 28.88 kg/person/year.

All the above items are gathered without any economic investment by the ethnic population from the surrounding forest. If we calculate the market price of each of the collections, we can very well say that these items collected free of charge definitely contribute to the saving of the ethnic population.

Resource Dependence Analysis

Resource dependence analysis in the present investigation has been done in order to know per capita material, energy and economic gain or savings on account of various resource inputs. Table 10.3 presents required data on resource dependence. The

Table 10.3: Urban Resource Dependence

Name of village	*Population*	*Grains (kg.)*	*K.oil (kg.)*	*Edible oil (kg.)*	*Bamboo and other wood*	*Cloth (Rs.)*	*Condiments (Rs.)*	*Mis (Rs.)*	*Total (Rs.)*	*Per capita (Rs.)*
Agriculture										
Sahaja	105	5900 (23600)	297 (891)	204 (6732)	2880 (4320)	7840	1570	3220	48173	458.8
Satnara	98	5890 (23560)	305 (915)	180 (5940)	2500 (3750)	7480	1220	4810	47675	486.5
Forest										
Kathas	101	5610 (22440)	411 (1233)	250 (8250)	5000 (7500)	8770	1910	5110	55213	546.7
Hanuman-garh	146	10000 (40000)	1030 (3030)	421 (13893)	5800 (8700)	13940	2750	9050	91363	625.8
Urban										
Barigama	150	15710 (63840)	505 (1725)	605 (19965)	6400 (9600)	16000	3510	13460	128100	854.0
Akori	163	20730 (82920)	1303 (3909)	470 (15510)	10100 (15150)	19940	3890	14670	155989	956.9

(Values in parenthesis are in Rupees)

relevant resource system that is considered for resource dependence analysis includes forest, agriculture, animal and urban resource systems.

It is very clear from the overall resource dependence analysis that forest and agricultural resource systems mainly provide economic support to the ethnic population. Animal resource system provides very little economic support, and is rather a liability on the economy of the ethnic population. The role of forest resource system is much more vital because of free forest inputs without any investment. This is also free from any harassment by the forest officials as the tribals have been given the right over the forest insofar as their demand for basic 'Nistar' is concerned. The agricultural system requires some of the basic inputs like seeds, ploughing, agricultural implements etc., thus requiring a basic economic investment. It is, therefore, obvious that forest system dominates over agricultural system in providing economic support to the ethnic population.

The urban resources available in the nearby urban markets and periodical village markets significantly play a role in improving life style of the ethnic population. The purchase of urban items results in money outflow from the ethnic system. The attraction towards urban produce and life style naturally increases the demand for more money which obviously put exploitation pressure on easily available forest resource system or the life supporting resource system of the Gond.

It is concluded from the present investigation that the Sidhi Gond tribal system is facing a great economic crisis and it is of utmost importance that the ethnic population should immediately be provided with the means of economic stability in terms of agricultural land and farming facilities in forest periphery regions to avoid forest land for agriculture. The ethnic population together with the animal population is not a static system; it changes with time and may exert pressure on surrounding natural environmental system. The surrounding environmental system is also changing, and such forces would certainly bring about changes at a fast rate. The ethnic population shows a drift towards urban system due to its attraction towards urban produce and life style.

This would increase demand for more and more money with every passing year out of the life supporting forest system, thus increasing utilization and exploitative pressure on the forest system. It is finally concluded that the forest ethnic system shows a drift towards breaking down due to economic instability and also accelerating forest diversity devastation (Mishra 1986) on account of increased utilization pressure and thus, ecological as well as economic crisis to the ethnic population.

It is evident that an ethnoecological study is not only useful from the point of view of evolving management guidelines for ethnoecosystems of the tribals, but also gives a deep insight into the understanding of most fundamental ethnoecological aspects like biological (population structure and dynamics, density, sex ratio, age-class etc.), cultural (art and religion), socio-economical (educational status, occupational status, per capita income, dependence on natural and urban produce etc.) and ecological (material and energy relations).

REFERENCES

Awasthi, A.K. (1993), Ethnoecology: An Ecological Strategy for Managing the Ethnoecosystem, *Indian J. App. Pure. Biol.*, 8 , 103-106.

Awasthi, A.K. et. al (1993), Ethnoecological Studies on Baiga Ethnic System, *Proc.Acad. Environ. Biol.*, 2, 175-178.

Awasthi, A.K. and K.M.L. Shukla (1992), Ethnoecology of Kol Ethnic System, *Ecobalance*, 1, 19-24.

Khatoon, S. (1991), Ethnoecological Study on Kondar Ethnic System, M.Phil. Thesis, APS Univ. Rewa (M.P.).

Mishra, S. (1988), Ethnobiology of Tribals of Sidhi District, Ph.D. Thesis, APS University, Rewa (M.P.).

Singh, M. (1988), Ethnobiology of Tribal Communities of Kanger Forest of Bastar with Special Reference to Plants, Ph.D. Thesis, APS Univ., Rewa (M.P.).

Singh, R. (1992), Ethnoecology of Tribals with Special Reference to Gond Ethnic System, Ph.D. Thesis, APS Univ., Rewa (M.P.).

11

THE PARADOX OF HARMONY: FOREST, TRIBAL AND DEVELOPMENT NEXUS IN ANDHRA PRADESH

P. Venkata Rao

INTRODUCTION

Appropriately referred to as *Vanyajati* (forest community) and *Girijan* (people of the hills), tribals are known for their association with forests and hills. The tribes in Andhra Pradesh variously claim themselves as *adivi rajulu* (kings of the forest) or *adivi talli pillalu* (children of the mother forest). The age old dependency and association with forest are reflected in all aspects of tribal culture. Honorific titles, *viz.*, *Manne Dora* (lords of the jungle), *Konda Dora* (lords of the hills) reflect their proud identification with forests and hills. Of the thirty-three Scheduled Tribes of Andhra Pradesh, thirty inhabit hilly and forest regions. Gond, Kolam, Koya, Konda Dora, Konda Reddi, Savara and Jatapu are among the principal tribes inhabiting hilly and forest areas. Andhra Pradesh has 42 lakhs Scheduled Tribes, as per the 1991 census. The largest concentration of tribal population is found in

Khammam district (5.59 lakhs), followed by Visakhapatnam district (4.69 lakhs). The state has 21.3 per cent of its total area under forest cover. But, in areas of tribal concentration, where Tribal Sub-Plans are being implemented through Integrated Tribal Development Agencies (ITDA), forest constitutes 62.43 per cent of the total geographical area. The tribal economy of the state can be characterised as agro-forest based. According to the 1991 census, 90.4 per cent of the tribal workers in the state is in the primary sector, whereas only 4.79 per cent and 4.81 per cent are in secondary and tertiary sectors respectively. The tribal population of Andhra Pradesh increased from 16.6 lakhs to 42 lakhs between 1971 and 1991. This increase is partly due to the inclusion of the Banjara community into the list of Scheduled Tribes. While the tribal population increased, the area under Forest Department (FD) control has not changed much, as may be seen in Table 11.1. According to the above figures, the area under forests came down. But the area under Reserve Forest shows an increase. It is the unclassified land, which are normally accessible to tribals, that have disappeared rapidly. The proportion of Reserve Forest to the total forest area increased, which means that more forest area is inaccessible to tribals. The above figure do not realistically reveal the situation as land under the control of FD does not mean that forest actually exists. Actual area under forest is much less according to the remote sensing pictures.

Table 11.1: Forest Area in Andhra Pradesh (in sq. km.)

Year	*Reserve Forest*	*Protected Forest*	*Unclassified*	*Total*
1967	41714	19014	5778	66506
1977	48081	14716	1576	64373
1986-87	50099	12245	1431	63775
1990-91	49929	12363	1487	63779
1993	50478	12365	969	63813

(*Source*: Statistical Abstracts, Bureau of Economics & Statistics, Govt. of A.P.)

Changing Land Ownership in Tribal Areas

In Andhra Pradesh, for a long period in history, there was not much pressure on forest. The rulers retained minimal interest in the control over forest. State intervention was confined to preservation of royal and public hunting grounds, and protection of pastures for feeding horses and elephants. The British, after realizing the commercial value of forest, started making inroads into these areas. They appointed committees to examine the proprietary rights over forest. Forest legislations in India date back to 1865, when Indian Forest Act was enacted and 'scientific forestry' began. The then Madras Presidency formulated its own Act, Act V of 1822, under which forest became the public property to be owned and managed by the state. The traditional collective ownership of forest by the tribals was neither claimed nor recognized. As a result, the interests of the tribals became subordinate to the interests of the larger society. Demarcation of forest boundaries started as early as 1864 and is continuing till today. It is to this demarcation process much of the discontent of the tribals, *viz.* the Adilabad Gonds, has been traced to (Furer-Haimendorf 1979: 546-549). In the 19th century, attempts were made to augment revenue by encouraging the non-tribals to settle down in tribal areas by clearing and cultivating forest land. The Nizam rulers in Telengana granted large tracts of land in the forest zone to the soldiers discharged from service for cultivation (Khader 1984). Forest was under the control of the Revenue Department until 1867, when a separate Forest Department (FD) started functioning. Though FD came into existence in 1867, its functioning was very much limited. The Hyderabad Forest Act, Act of 1355 *fasili* was mainly intended to levy and collect duties on the forest produce like timber. This had the provision of converting forest land into agricultural land, subject to keeping minimum required land under forest. This was the beginning of the large-scale destruction of forest. After the formation of Andhra Pradesh as a state of the Indian Union, consolidated A.P. Forest Act, Act No. 1 of 1967 came into existence. The intentions of the Act were clear from its Preamble which stated:

> *The first necessity is to provide for the constitution of the more important forests as state reserves, and either to clear them under arrangements for due compensation of private rights which militate against forest conservancy, or to ascertain and define such rights so that future extension of them and fresh encroachments are impossible* (Jagannadha Rao 198: 2).

Over a period of time, pressure on forest land increased with population growth and influx of non-tribals into the tribal areas. Cultivation of forest land under *Siwai-I-jamabandi* (without *patta*) has become a common feature and many such lands were given *pattas* later. Large areas were brought under cultivation during 1938 to 1940. Laying of railway tracks in the state and outside had its toll on the forest. The railway lines passing through the tribal areas further accelerated the reduction of forest cover. The Hyderabad-Palwoncha railway line (1874) leading to the coal reserves in Khammam district, Kazipet-Balarsha line (1929) opening up Adilabad district, and the relatively recent D.B.K. railway line passing through Visakhapatnam district are the glaring examples of this.

Tribal Land Alienation and Displacement

As the population grew, influx of non-tribals into the tribal areas started. Tribal land was encroached by the non-tribals by various means. The realisation of the problem of non-tribal encroachment into the tribal areas led to a number of protective legislations for the tribals. Even after enacting a series of them, the extent of land remaining under the control of the non-tribals has been substantial. In fact, land under the possession of the non-tribals in the Scheduled Areas of the state under nine districts is to the tune of 753435.66 acres, which is 48.29 per cent of the total land in these areas (Mohana Rao 1990: 16). 12951 cases were pending under Land Transfer Regulation in Andhra Pradesh, involving 37405.81 acres of land (Eighth Five Year Plan, Tribal Areas Sub Plan—A.P. : 125). According to a relatively recent figure, there are 7666 cases involving an area of 107582.95 acres of land, which are pending for disposal (Tribal Sub Plan 1997: 98). The percentage of land under the control of the non-tribals is much higher than the state average of 48.29 per cent in the extremist dominated districts of Warangal (71.64 per cent), Khammam (52.79 per cent), and Adilabad (60.69 per cent). The problems with regard to land and forest, exploitation of tribals by various elements, coupled with growing aspirations of the tribal population formed the basis of various tribal movements in Andhra Pradesh.

In addition to land alienation, various national needs like

irrigation projects, mining and industrial complexes, wild life parks etc. have led to the reduction of forest and tribal land. Machkund and Sileru hydro-electric projects displaced many tribal villages in Visakhapatnam district. Nagarjuna Sagar and Srisailam projects led to submergence of large areas of forest. The Inchampally project is going to affect tribals of Adilabad district. The Polavaram barrage to be taken up on the Godavari river will be affecting a large number of Konda Doras, Koyas and Konda Reddis. Coal mining started in Yellandu area in 1889 and Singareni Collieries Company Limited came into existence in 1929 at Kothagudem of Khammam district. Attempts are being made for mining bauxite deposits in Visakhapatnam district. A number of industries came up around the coal mines of Kothagudem over a period of time. Singareni collieries, Kothagudem and Ramagundam Thermal Power Plants, Palowancha Sponge Iron Factory, Heavy Water Plant at Manuguru are foremost among the industries established in tribal dominated regions. Apart from these, there are industries which depend on bamboo and wood from the forest. Rayon Factory at Ethurnagaram, Andhra Paper Mills, Bhadrachalam Paper Board, Rayalseema Paper Mills, Kagajnagar Paper Mills, Plywood Factories at Rampa Chodavaram are some of them. The Sriharikota Rocket Launching Station displaced the Yanadis living in the vicinity for centuries. Similarly, Quawal (Adilabad district), Ethurnagaram (Warangal district), Papikonda (Khammam, East and West Godavari districts), Kinnerasani (Khammam district), Nagarjunasagar-Srisailam (Mahaboobnagar, Guntur, Prakasam, Nalgonda and Kurnool districts) wild life sanctuaries and Tiger Reserves have affected largest number of tribal families in the recent past.

These projects have deprived tribals of their land, their major resource base, without giving them proportional benefits. These have caused environmental problems through deforestation and pollution. Fewer benefits percolate down to the tribals, as industries and irrigation dams are established in tribal areas for boosting agriculture and development in non-tribal areas. According to a study on displacement and rehabilitation of tribals in Andhra Pradesh, of the 23 instances of displacement involving tribals, compensation has been paid to the tribals only in 5 cases. For the rest of the cases, either information is not available or payment is to be taken up at a later date. Only in two instances, tribals are employed in the industry. In rest of the cases, tribals are not employed or information is not available. The Eighth Five Year Plan for the Tribal Sub Plan areas of Andhra Pradesh gives the figures in Table 11.2 with regard to the number of tribals displaced in the state.

The figures in Table 11.2 do not reflect the magnitude of the plight of the tribals in terms of the effects of these projects on the people in the hinterland, where these might have triggered off migration and pressure on existing resources. It is well known that displacement has cumulative effect on the uprooted families.

Table 11.2: Displaced Tribals in Andhra Pradesh

Project	*No. of STs displaced*
Industries	187
Irrigation and Power Projects	119328
Wild Life Sanctuaries	85802
Total	205317

Though displacement is going on in the state for a long time, consolidated instructions for rehabilitation of displaced tribals were issued through G.O.M.S. No. 64 (S W) T dated 18.4.90. The G.O. has the provision for providing rehabilitation to those who have been displaced already. When well conceived rehabilitation measures are running through bad weather, successful rehabilitation of the people who were uprooted and already dispersed is a doubtful proposition. The way in which the G.O. unfolds, makes an interesting reading. First it lays down that there should be no displacement. Then it stipulates that Tribal Welfare Department's permission is needed for projects causing displacement. It suggests that no new irrigation project is to be taken up which may displace tribals, and recommends for smaller irrigation projects. For industries and mining, a comprehensive rehabilitation plan, the cost of which is built into the project cost, becomes a must for clearance by the government. The G.O. maintains that rehabilitation has to be on land to land basis. If no land can be provided, employment has to be provided. If no employment can be provided, the tribals have to be absorbed in the sister projects. Training may be provided to the tribals. Tribal entrepreneurs are to be trained and raw materials to be provided to them. Monetary compensation, wherever provided, needs to be kept in a Bank on long-term basis. The guidelines also mention about assistance to the tribals for setting up ancillaries, encouraging agro-based industries, and giving petty works to the tribal contractors.

The above provisions offer high amount of flexibility and freedom to the concerned authorities to prepare and implement rehabilitation schemes. It is well known that compensation fixed by the government has never been adequate to buy another piece of land. Social costs of displacement are difficult to calculate. Calculations on costs of rehabilitation generally do not consider the incremental costs of displacement.

Tribes and Agricultural Development

Although tribal economies are by and large agro-forest based, the emphasis has been on intensification of agriculture. In tribal areas there is not much scope for expansion of land under cultivation, because of the presence of forest and forest legislations. 62.43 per cent of the total land under ITDA areas is under forest. The cultivable area is therefore less, and at many places the terrain is not suitable for intensive cultivation. At the all-India level, the trend is that in tribal areas land-holdings are becoming smaller. In Andhra Pradesh, the majority of tribal cultivators (43.76 per cent) has marginal holdings (less than one acre of land), followed by small farmers (23.07 per cent) having 1-2 acres of land. Accurate figures on shifting cultivation are not available. But, it is a known fact that the marginal farmers and other cultivators generally resort to shifting cultivation or *podu* to supplement their meagre income. According to a survey, the area under shifting cultivation in Andhra Pradesh has increased from 17,493 hectares to 49,038 hectares between 1974 and 1984. Substantial part of this expansion is an encroachment into the Reserve Forest. Citing the above figures, the Seventh Plan document for Sub Plan areas of Andhra Pradesh (1985) mentions that 49,771 families are depending on *podu*, cultivating 49,038 hectares of land. The Eighth Five Year Plan document (1990) shows an increase with 62,504 families cultivating 62,948 hectares under *podu* cultivation. It is important to note that all this land is not *podu* land, as forest land cleared for permanent cultivation is also being shown under *podu.* The reason given for this is that the operation involved is the same, *i.e.* felling of trees and clearing the forest. The objection against *podu* is that it results in the loss of valuable forest and soil erosion leading to silting of reservoirs. But, these reservoirs of hydro-electric projects have uprooted the tribals, who were forced to resort to shifting cultivation for the sake of survival (Krishna Murthy 1990). Increase in the area under *podu* indicates a trend of shrinking land-holdings of the tribals. Shifting cultivation has been a contentious issue in the tribal areas. No viable alternative has been suggested to shifting cultivation. Even where there is a semblance of viable alternative, faulty implementation has led to failures. Large number of marginal farmers, shifting cultivators and agricultural labourers benefit less because of agricultural innovations popularized under tribal development programmes.

Only 13.35 per cent of the total cultivated land in the tribal areas of Andhra Pradesh has access to irrigation, most of it being partial. Thus, the thrust on agriculture has its drawbacks in the absence of suitable irrigated land for wet cultivation. Wet crops received priority in the wake of the measures taken for green revolution. The report of the Working Group on Tribal Development for the Eighth Five Year Plan recognized this problem, and recommended the improvement of dry and partially irrigated agriculture. It also envisaged establishment of research centres for agro-forestry, horticulture and mixed crops.

Despite its limitations, settled agriculture continues to be the source of livelihood and hope for a secure future. According to the 1991 census, of the 2130981 main workers among the Scheduled Tribes in Andhra Pradesh, 877806 (41.19 per cent) and 992358 (46.56 per cent) are engaged in agriculture and agricultural labour respectively. The trend towards marginalisation can be seen from the decline in the percentage of cultivators from 43.21 per cent in 1981 to 41.19 per cent in 1991, and the rise of the percentage of agricultural labourers from 43.72 per cent in 1981 to 46.56 per cent in 1991. The tribals need land and they cannot afford to think about the consequences of deforestation.

The process of deforestation can be explained through a case study of a tribal village in Tadawai mandal in Warangal district, where the author conducted a study. The village under study was established about 25 years ago, when scattered Koya families were settled at a single place by availing the incentives for house construction. Some land was available near the village. As the village grew, there was expansion of cultivation by encroaching into the Reserve Forest. The successful entry of groundnut crop into the area and the growing prosperity of the non-tribals in nearby villages made the tribals to realize the importance of land. Encroachments increased rapidly, once the grip of FD was weakened after the rise of Naxalite influence in the area. The villagers have no subsidiary occupation to earn a regular income. Then, a cottage industry was started in the village, in which large amount of money was spent without success. Similar process of deforestation is going on in many villages. Therefore, it is felt that the tribals could be allowed to expand cultivation only in a limited scale. There should be compensatory forest cover in non-tribal areas. Funds for this could be raised by imposing taxes on the industries using raw materials from the forests.

Forest Development Vrs. Tribal Development

ITDA projects have been functioning in the tribal areas of Andhra Pradesh from the Fifth Five Year Plan period onwards. For the purpose of balanced development of natural and human resources in the project areas, Sub Plans have been prepared with built-in financial, organizational and programme integration (Pratap 1978). This integrated development remained partial in not being able to plan for the effective utilization of natural resources available in large areas of forest in the Sub Plan areas. Forest regulations and the way in which these are interpreted locally, does not stop at depriving the tribal right over life sustaining resources. There are several instances where these came on the way of the developmental programmes. At many places, housing colonies in the tribal areas ran into rough weather due to lack of coordination between forest officials and development functionaries. It is the tribals who are the victims in this process. Carpentry training centres planned as an employment generating programme could not pick up because of the procedural problems in obtaining wood (Rao 1988: 54-56). Restrictions on the utilization of bamboo affected traditional crafts of the tribals. Even basket making as a source of income was made difficult to pursue. An I.A.S. officer narrates interesting instances from Khammam district of how the rigid attitude of the forest officials affects tribal welfare activities (Vidya Sagar 1993). There are revenue villages in Warangal district, which remained untouched by development functionaries, as these are surrounded by Reserve Forest and hence, road could not be laid there. It is a known fact that an unapproachable village remains untouched by development.

Minor Forest Produce (MFP) plays an important role in the tribal economy. The coastal districts of Andhra Pradesh have a variety of useful items, which augment the meager tribal income. Though less number of items are available in Rayalseema and Telengana districts, items like *tuniki* leaf and *gumkarya* are economically more valuable. In forest development activities, FD does not undertake steps to grow and protect these items, which satisfy the monetary needs of the tribals. In fact, for FD, wood and charcoal form the major forest produce, while items like bamboo and *tuniki* leaf are considered as MFP. FD would have earned the respect and appreciation of the tribals, had it planted MFP producing trees, keeping in mind the needs of the local tribals.

The employment opportunities available in FD activities like afforestation, conservation, protection etc. are very limited when compared to the landless tribals in the lookout for employment. In this context, it is interesting to see the way in which Sri Lankan repatriates were brought to the Visakhapatnam agency. Coffee plantations were made in large scale from 1961 onwards in the Eastern Ghats. These came handy for the rehabilitation of these repatriates during 1972-78. Though the scheme was to take only 83 families, many families of relatives and friends joined them. The justification for bringing the Sri Lankan repatriates to these plantations was given as 'the seasonal nature of the attendance of tribals, and community approach towards sharing the work'. This has prevented the emergence of a permanent cadre of coffee workers among the tribals. Only after a prolonged labour unrest among these repatriates for the implementation of the Plantation

Labour Act, the forest officials realized the advantage of employing the local tribals. Recently, a plea has been made to shift the Sri Lankan repatriates saying that coffee cultivation is a welfare measure for the tribals. This kind of experience notwithstanding, it has been again suggested to settle ex-service persons in the trouble-prone district of Adilabad for the purpose of afforestation. The justification given is similar to the one mentioned earlier in case of the Sri Lankan repatriates that outside labourers settle down and work seriously, whereas the local tribals work only seasonally. It is also said that being ex-service persons, they can also deal with the Naxalites effectively (Mukherjee 1987). It may be recalled that much of deforestation in Telengana districts occurred when the Nizam's administration asked its soldiers to settle there by allotting them forest land for cultivation.

Despite the suggestions of various authorities and recommendations by different committees and commissions, not much progress has been achieved in establishing small-scale and cottage industries in the tribal areas of Andhra Pradesh. The performance of the existing units is dismal. Successive census reports show that a very small percentage of tribals are engaged in household sectors, i.e. manufacturing, processing, servicing and repairing. According to 1991 census, only 2.16 per cent of ST workers were engaged in this sector. The percentage of workers engaged in these activities outside household sector was 1.6 per cent only. The High Power Committee appointed by the Government of Andhra Pradesh in its report on 'Tribal Industrialization in Andhra Pradesh' has suggested a detailed list of industries that can be set up in each district of the state. The Committee also suggested that steps should be taken to ensure proper training, institutional finance, necessary incentives and marketing facilities. The establishment of industries should be related to: (1) the goals of providing productive and gainful employment to the tribals, (2) utilization of locally available raw material, and (3) encouragement to the tribal entrepreneurs. The Working Group of the Planning Commission for the Seventh Five Year Plan also identified a number of forest based small-scale industries for the state. It recommended for reserving ancillaries for the tribals to enable them to start small units. One of the recommendations of the Working Group also was to set up a separate cell for industrialization of the tribal areas of the state.

Attempts have been made in this direction in tribal areas of Andhra Pradesh by establishing production-cum-training centres to impart training in vocational crafts. Tribal entrepreneurs are being encouraged to start their own ventures. Some Industrial Training Institutes, Polytechnics and Training Centres are established for this purpose. Despite subsidies, incentives and loans to the tribal entrepreneurs, they find it difficult to compete with their non-tribal counterparts. Usually, non-availability of required raw materials and lack of guidance affect them (Rao *op cit.* 54-56). There are vary few opportunities for the technical trainees and little demand for their skills. The training programmes are formulated with a built-in bias towards middle class urban needs, and not on local needs. Because of lack of employment opportunities, the trainees do not stick to the vocations in which they receive training, resulting in the wastage of large amount of money spent on training.

Although considerable potential exists in the tribal areas in terms of raw material, person power etc., these areas lag behind in small-scale and cottage industries. For example, in Visakhapatnam region, units using forest produce have been established in non-tribal areas. Honey processing units at Narsipatnam and soap making units at Vijaynagaram are best examples. By and large, the tribals remain as procurers of raw materials for processing and manufacturing in non-tribal areas. Utilization of forest based raw materials locally would have helped providing more employment opportunities to tribals, for which they might have developed a positive outlook towards forest resources.

Tribal Rights in Forest

The age old dependency of tribals on forest is well recognized by the policy makers, thus providing them with several concessions in the utilization of forest resources. Various committees recommended the involvement and participation of tribals in conservation and development of forests. The expectations in the early phases of planned development were very high, which is conspicuous from the following quotation:

> *The Indian Forest Act will be eventually replaced by a new regulation in order to promote the philosophies and aims of community development, Panchayat Raj, and the cooperative movement. Any comment or criticism of the existing legislation is hardly called for, because the relationship of the government to people has been changed due to the new objectives of a welfare state, the concept of planned development and the will of the government to improve the economic conditions of the poorest sections of the society (Mehta 1968: 189).*

The Renuka Roy Committee suggested that steps should be taken to introduce a system of guided management whereby tribals or their representatives or their representative bodies would be progressively associated with the management and exploitation of forests (1959: 138). Elwin Committee argued for assuring the tribals that 'their rights in forest should be respected and that an entirely new attitude should be taken towards them by forest authorities throughout India' (1960: 62). The same Committee also suggested that there should be a Forest Extension Officer in each block to act as a liaison between the tribals and the government. It further suggested that some share of the profits earned from the forests should be given back to tribals to convince them that their interests were linked with that of the forest (1960: 65, 66). The Commission led by U.N. Dhebar recommended that FD should deemed to be charged as part of the government with the responsibility of participating in the betterment of tribals. If there is any change in the forest policy leading to any curtailment of tribal rights, they should be given satisfaction in other ways. It would be still better, if the FD was integrated with economic betterment of tribals (1961: 141). A people oriented forestry was proposed by B.D. Sharma (1979), which advocated participatory management of the forests by the tribals. The report of the Committee on Forests and Tribals in India (1982) recommended that in forest rich regions (with forest area of 30 percent or more), forestry oriented development programmes should be taken up linking forest development with tribal development. It suggested for taking up agro-forestry instead of cultivation in marginal and sub-marginal areas. It was felt that through the selection of suitable technology and production pattern, about a hectare of land could make a family economically viable. All landless tribals were to be employed in forest activities or forest based industries. Some of the cottage, small and medium forest based industries should be locally established to generate employment. It was also recommended that beneficiary oriented programmes in forestry should be executed under Integrated Rural Development (IRDP), National Rural Employment Programme (NREP), Drought-Prone Area Programme (DPAP), Hill Area Development Plan, Tribal Sub Plan etc.

The attitudes of recognizing tribals' rights over forest and their needs, and taking them into confidence have not been followed fully in the successive forest policies in India. Compared to the British forest policy, the post-independence policies have put more restrictions on the use of forest by tribals. The age old rights of the tribals have been withdrawn through various forest legislations. With the depletion of the forest cover, more and more stringent measures are being adopted. The tribal emerges as the incorrigible criminal violating laws of the state every day. These aborigines and lords of the forest have become encroachers of their own land. Whenever need arose, they are being evicted from the forest, which has been the abode of their forefathers. The tribal becomes dispensable constituting only 6.3 per cent of the total population of Andhra Pradesh, which is neither an organized vote bank nor a politically powerful community. The customary rights of the tribals are not comparable to the civil codes of the minority communities.

The Fifth and Sixth Schedules of the Constitution of India provide various protective and anti-exploitative measures to suit the interests of the tribals. Article 29.1 of the Constitution recognizes the right to conserve one's own distinct culture. Though tribal cultures and forest are intricately intertwined, no explicit recognition has been given to the rights of tribals either in different Articles or in the Fifth Schedule of the Constitution. While their rights are not recognized, legislations come in the way of their development. Examining the Forest Conservation Act of 1980, the Working Group of the Planning Commission for the Eighth Five Year Plan felt that the Act came in the way of the development of a large number of tribals depriving them of basic infrastructural facilities like roads, dispensaries, schools etc. Those things for which land requirement is very small, powers need to be delegated to local authorities for permitting the use of forest land. It was also pointed out that by not recognizing medicinal plants, horticultural species and oil seeds as of forest use, the Act prevented state FD from planting them for the benefit of the tribals. The Working Group warned that provision for the imprisonment of the encroachers for fifteen days under Section 3-A of the Act would create serious consequences in tribal areas (pp. 41-42). There are instances in Andhra Pradesh, where encroachments into government *poromboke* land have been regularized. It is ironical that at a time when the government is regularizing encroachments in non-tribal areas, the original inhabitants are being alienated from their habitats.

Efforts are on to replace the Indian Forest Act of 1927 to provide absolute power to Forest Settlement Officer (FSO), who will be an employee of FD, to declare any area as Reserve Forest by issuing a notification. FSO or an officer authorized by him assumes the power of the civil court in trial suits. Experience shows that the manner in which forest regulations are enforced, generates a negative attitude by tribals towards forest. This author has witnessed how tribals in Visakhapatnam district burnt down FD plantations after their numerous visits to meet the FSO proved futile.

Tribes and Joint Forest Management

The 1988 Forest Policy envisaged the participation of people in the protection and regeneration of forest in India. The good experience of Joint Forest Management (JFM) from West Bengal made the government to extend JFM to the entire country (Malhotra and Poffenberger 1989). In June 1990, the Government of India issued instructions to various states to set up JFM committees to become the interface between FD and the local people. Under JFM, plantations are being taken up, keeping in mind the economic interests of the tribals, which will be managed with their participation. Growing of forests of high commercial value around tribal villages is envisaged under this programme. For the first time the tribals became a party in the selection of the species for plantation through JFM. But, assessment of JFM needs to be done in terms of people's participation, autonomy, utilization of people's knowledge and experience etc. without being bogged down by vested interests.

In Andhra Pradesh, Vana Samrakshana Samithis (VSS) have been formed under A.P. Forest Project for the protection of forest by tribals, who now became entitled to not only MFP, but also a share in the sale proceeds of major forest produce. The G.O. issued by the Government of Andhra Pradesh (GOMS No. 224 EF S & T dt. 11.11.93) lays down that ITDAs of the Tribal Welfare Department are to be associated with JFM. It mentions that FD officials should act as nodal agencies. The two departments having different goals and approaches have been made to come together and coordinate under this scheme.

JFM appears to be meant more for the protection and development of degraded forest than for empowering tribals. Participation is only on the fringe, as jointly managed forest is restricted to be within 500 metres from the village boundary. The guidelines prescribe micro-planning for forest regeneration. Though priorities of the villagers are considered, FD has the final say in species selection, with the plea that the officials there are technical experts. Availability of the species is controlled by FD, as the nurseries are under their control. As per the guidelines, VSSs will have usufruct right, provided these institutions discharge their duties and responsibilities properly. This keeps the people and their institutions at the mercy of the FD, as the former do not have any legal right in the jointly managed forest. The tribals are worried, whether FD will allow them to use the forest after the scheme is over. Another apprehension is that if the forest regeneration is good, it will be taken over by FD to be declared as reserve. In many villages, the survival rate of the saplings planted under JFM is found to be poor and the officials blame the tribals for not taking adequate care of the saplings.

CONCLUSION

The course of history has drawn the weak and less organized tribal societies into the economic processes of dominant non-tribal societies. State intervention has deprived the tribals of free access to forest land, the abode of their forefathers and their only dependable asset. Large-scale influx of non-tribals into the tribal areas followed by land alienation further restricted their resource base. Tribal development programmes drifted away from forest development activities, further widening the artificially created gulf between tribals and forest. Compelled by the motive to survive and urge to do well in a changing situation, the tribal now cuts forest without any hesitation, as it no more belongs to him. For the well being of both the forest and the tribals, which are inseparably intertwined, the tribal must be assured of his right over forest. The need is to make the tribals develop more interest in the protection of forest, which becomes a possibility, only when tribals realize their stakes in forest and forest development. This inevitably necessitates linking forest development with tribal development, allowing a sense of security and feeling of participation to tribals. All these are possible when the Forest Acts and Policies explicitly recognize the rights of tribals.

REFERENCES

Bhowmick, P.K. (1981), Forestry, Tribe and the Forest Policy in India, in L.P. Vidyarthi (Ed.) *Tribal Development and its Administration*, New Delhi: Concept Publishing Co.

Furer-Haimendorf, C. von and E.Haimendorf (1979), *The Gonds of Andhra Pradesh*, New Delhi: Vikas Publications.

Govt. of Andhra Pradesh (1985), Seventh Five Year Plan (1985-90) — Tribal Areas Sub Plan, Hyderabad: Department of Tribal Welfare.

Govt. of Andhra Pradesh (1990), Eighth Five Year Plan (1990-95) — Tribal Areas Sub Plan, Hyderabad: Department of Tribal Welfare.

Govt. of Andhra Pradesh (1993), Facts and Figures (Issued by the Principal Chief Conservator of Forests), Hyderabad: Forest Department.

Govt. of Andhra Pradesh (1997), Tribal Sub Plan, Draft Ninth Five Year Plan (1997-2002) and Annual Plan (1997-98), Hyderabad: Department of Tribal Welfare.

Govt. of India (1959), Report of the Study Team on Social Welfare and Welfare of Backward Classes (Renuka Roy Committee Report), New Delhi.

Govt. of India (1960), Report of the Committee on Special Multi-purpose Tribal Blocks (Elwin Committee Report), New Delhi.

Govt. of India (1961), Report of the Scheduled Areas and Scheduled Tribes Commission, Vol. I (Dhebar Committee Report), New Delhi.

Govt. of India (1982), Report of the Committee on Forests and Tribals in India, Ministry of Home Affairs, New Delhi.

Jagannadha Rao, V. (1981), *Forest Laws in Andhra Pradesh*, Hyderabad: Asia Law House.

Khader Shaik Abdul (1984), The Impact of Nizams Forest Policy on Selected Tribes of Telengana, Unpublished M.Phil. dissertation, University of Hyderabad.

Krishna Murthy, A.V.R.G. (1990), Forest Destruction and Tribal Displacement, Paper presented at the Seminar on Displacement and Rehabilitation of Tribals, T.C.R. & T.I., Hyderabad.

Malhotra, K.C. and M.Pofferberger (1989), Forest Regeneration through Community Participation: The West Bengal Experience, Proceedings of the Workshop on Forest Protection Committees, Calcutta.

Mehta, B.H. (1968), Forestry and Tensions in Tribal Areas, in L.P.Vidyarthi (Ed.) *Applied Anthropology in India*, Allahabad: Kitab Mahal.

Mohana Rao, K. (1990), Basic Dimensions of Displacement and Rehabilitation as a Mode of Adjustment and Loss of Command over Resources, Proceedings of the Seminar on Displacement and Rehabilitation of Tribals, T.C.R. & T.I., Hyderabad.

Mohana Rao, K. (1993), *Socio-Cultural Profile of Tribes of Andhra Pradesh*, Hyderabad: T.C.R. & T.I.

Mukherjee, S.D. (1987), Tribal and Forest, Proceedings of the Seminar on Forest Policy and Tribal Development, Hyderabad.

Pratap, D.R. (1978), Planning for Tribal Development, in *Occasional Papers on Tribal Development*, New Delhi: Ministry of Home Affairs, Govt. of India.

Rao, P.V. (1988), *Institutional Framework for Tribal Development*, New Delhi: Inter-India Publishers.

Rao, S.K. (n.d.), Problems in Coffee Projects and Solutions (mimeo), Office of the Chief Conservator of Forests, Govt. of A.P., Hyderabad.

Sharma, B.D. (1978), *Tribal Development — The Concept and The Frame*, New Delhi: Prachi Prakashan.

Vidya Sagar, A. (1993), *Bhadrachalam-Mannem Kathalu* (Telugu), Hyderabad: Goutami Publications.

12

Will the Paradise Lost be Regained? A Study of Changing Forest-Tribal Relationship

V.N.V.K. Sastry

INTRODUCTION

The forest-tribal relationship has undergone a perceptible change over the last 100 years. Until the British declared the forest policy more than 100 years ago, forest was under total ownership and tribal community management. From the British Forest Act of 1865 till the Forest Policy of 1988, the Forest Department (FD) was the absolute owner of forests for conservation and development purposes. The Joint Forest Management concept came into existence as a policy of the Government which provided for the participation of people for protection and management of forests. The 73rd Amendment to the Constitution of India and its extension to Scheduled Areas gave rise to conditions of absolute ownership and management of forests by the tribal communities through the elected members of Gram Panchayat. An attempt is made in this paper to trace the history and development of tribal-forest relationship by taking Andhra Pradesh as a case.

Forests and Tribals

There are 41.99 lakh Scheduled Tribe population in Andhra Pradesh as per 1991 census, and majority of them (60 per cent) live in forests and hilly areas. Out of 33 Scheduled Tribe communities, 30 live in forests and hilly areas, while a sizable among the remaining also live in such areas.

In the state as a whole, there are 63,779 sq.km. of forests, of which 66 per cent is located in predominantly tribal areas. The tribal concentrated regions in the districts of Srikakulum, Vizianagaram, Visakhapatnam, East Godavari, West Godavari, Khammam, Warangal, Adilabad and Mahboobnagar are declared as Scheduled Areas, under the provisions of the Constitution of India, for providing special protection and for overall development of the Scheduled Tribes living in these areas. Most of the forests within the Scheduled Areas are declared as Reserve Forests for their protection. While these are the administrative statuses of the Reserved Forests and Scheduled Areas, the tribal-forest interface in the socio-economic context of the tribals is characterized by their dependence on forests for food, wood, subsistence etc. There are also several totemic associations with the animal and tree species.

The Interface

The Scheduled Tribes have been divided by the Government of India in 1975 for the purpose of development as: (1) tribes living in areas of concentration, and (2) dispersed tribal groups. Within the tribes living in areas of concentration, there are eight tribes who are very backward and are declared as Primitive Tribal Groups (PTGs). The tribes like the Savara, Khond, Poraja, Konda Reddi, Kolam etc., who fall in this category, depend mostly on forests for livelihood by way of slash and burn agriculture on hill slopes, collection and sale of Minor Forest Produce (MFP), and hunting and gathering of food. It is in these areas, the tribals still have a well-knit social organization for exploitation of natural resources in the benefit of the entire community. The concepts of village territory, common property resources etc. are still in vogue and traditionally practiced in these areas. Further, the tribals still establish mythical relationship with trees, animals, hillocks etc., and most of their clans are named after them. Their water sources are named after animals, such as *Puli Madugu* (pool frequented by tiger), *Chintaguda* (a settlement with a neem tree) and the like.

Each tribal village has its own clearly defined territory, which is locally known as *haddu* or *polimera*, and is recognized by each and every village. It is also respected by the residents of adjoining villages. Within the village boundary, forests (natural growth) are treated as common property, while trees owned by individuals in their private gardens are treated as individual property. Hill slopes suitable for shifting cultivation are also treated as common property with usufruct right of individual farmers as long as they cultivate, while the flat lands in the villages or in the valleys are generally owned individually. Forest resources like trees, fruits, small game etc. are also parts of the common property. In recent times, with the introduction of market economy, even the trees yielding MFP with commercial value are being treated as individual property. Similarly, with the possibility of converting shifting cultivation areas into horticultural fields, the concept of individual property has come into being. Many such hill slopes in the Godavari basin outside the designated Reserved Forests have already been given legal titles by the Government of Andhra Pradesh in recent years. For the tribes like, the Gond, Koya, Jatapu etc., who are settled agriculturists, the dependence on forests is partial, mostly for timber for construction and domestic use.

Reserve Forests

In the state of Andhra Pradesh, there is 63779.22 sq.km. of forest areas, out of which 78 per cent is classified as Reserve Forest (RF). The remaining areas are declared as Protected Forests. As already pointed out, 66 per cent of forest areas is in tribal concentrated regions. This also shows that forests still remain mostly in tribal areas only. It may be pertinent to briefly review the history of forest policy to understand the changes that have come about in the tribal social and economic pursuits.

The British Period

The process of transfer of ownership of forest from village communities to the state began in the early 1800 with the survey of the availability of teak in Malabar forests. In the year, 1855, Lord Dalhousie, the Governor General of India, proclaimed in the forest policy that timber standing in state forests was the state property. This was followed by the enactment of the Forest Act of 1865, creation of FD of India in 1866. In the year 1878, the customary rights of the rural communities to manage forests were also curtailed. The forest policy statement of 1894 further consolidated the position of the state by enabling it to forcibly take over all forests, including private and community forests. The Forest Act of 1927 did not recognize the rights of the people over the forest produce, 'simply because they were domiciled there'.

The Forest Acts and Policies during the British period aimed at increasing the hold of the state on forests while failing to recognize the rights of the village communities over forests. In this process, the customary management practices also got relegated to an insignificant place. From immediate control and management by the people, there was a shift to remote control by the state. The priorities of management also naturally started changing because of the vested interests of industries and politically powerful people living far away from the forest. In other words, priorities of people nearer to the centre of power dominated over the daily subsistence needs of the local people.

Tribal communities in several parts of Andhra Pradesh, like their counterparts in other parts of the country, revolted against the British as well as the Nizam's administration. The forest related issues dominated during the tribal movements like the Rampa Rebellion in Godavari Agency (1873) and the Babi-Jhari Rebellion in Adilabad district (1940) etc.

The Post-independence Scenario

After India attained independence, and especially after the Constitution of India came into existence, priority has been given to the protection and promotion of developmental avenues of the tribes. Various laws have been enacted in achieving these objectives. The National Forest Policy of 1952 and the reports of various committees and commissions also discussed in detail the problems of the tribes due to the stringent forest policy of the British. As Dhebar Commission (1960) pointed out in its report, certain concessions to the tribes were given in independent India, after the British took away their basic rights. The concessions as per the A.P. Forest Act in 1967 include free collection of wood for domestic use like construction of houses, manufacture of agricultural implements etc.

Government of Andhra Pradesh has also utilized the provisions under the Vth Schedule of the Constitution of India to regulate the trade of notified MFPs and *beedi* (country cigarette) leaves. By two separate regulations, the trade of these items were monopolized. The Girijan Cooperative Corporation (GCC), which is a state-owned organization, is vested with the monopoly in trade of selected MFPs, while the FD through its Forest Development Corporation (FDC) regulates the trade of *beedi* leaves in Scheduled Areas. This is done mainly to eliminate private traders and also to ensure good price to the GCC for the sale of MFPs, collected by the tribals. Government of Andhra Pradesh is also fully subsidizing staff cost, so that it will not add to overheads in fixing procurement price. It also provides a formula by which the open market price minus the transport cost has to the procurement price of a commodity. The MFPs are purchased from the traditional tribal weekly markets. To support these operations, a network of Daily Requirement Depots to cater to the needs of all tribal families are started, through which essential commodities and other domestic requirements are being sold. In case of *beedi* leaves, the FD opened collection centres (called *kallam*), to be operated by the local tribals in the summer season.

Although these protectionist measures for the tribals in Andhra Pradesh between 1964 and 1970 began to yield positive results, two other important Acts, namely, Wild Life (Protection) Act of 1972 and Forest (Conservation) Act of 1980, imposed several restrictions on them. Under Wild Life (Protection) Act of 1972, several areas were declared as sanctuaries, the most important and largest of which is located near Srisailam with an area of about

3,500 sq.km. It almost coincides with the habitat of the Chenchus, who are recognized as a PTG by Government of India, because of their extremely low level of literacy, low technological level, endemic state of malnutrition, and a very high rate of infant mortality. In 1973, this Act was extended to the whole of Andhra Pradesh to providing protection to wild animals and endangered species of birds etc. By this Act, even hunting of small game, which had been practiced by the tribals for centuries, was prohibited. Using of even traps, snares, bows and arrows was an offence under this Act. Even though at the official level, the Act is not strictly implemented in letter and spirit as far as tribals are concerned, restrictions have been imposed on the movement of domesticated animals belonging to the tribals. There is no scope for taking up construction of school buildings, permanent houses, roads etc., and for taking up any developmental programmes involving infrastructure development in the jurisdiction of these sanctuaries.

The Forest (Conservation) Act of 1980 puts a blanket ban on conversion of any forest land or any part thereof for non-forest purposes. This has created a lot of problems for the tribals, who are cultivating land in the forest areas traditionally. There have been several law and order problems in Adilabad, Warangal, and Mahaboobnagar districts, because of unending disputes regarding forest and revenue boundaries. After detailed reviews, Government of Andhra Pradesh in the year 1987, gave instructions to the FD not to evict the tribals from the possession of Reserved Forest land occupied prior to 1980, i.e. from the year in which Forest (Conservation) Act of 1980 came into force. In spite of this, the tribes living in or near the Reserve Forest face a number of problems. In the year 1995, a committee headed by this author, on the instructions of the then Commissioner of Tribal Welfare, enumerated the problems arising due to the implementation of these two Acts, which are discussed below:

1. Problems for hunter-gatherers, shifting cultivators in pursuing their livelihoods;
2. Problems of depletion of MFP and lack of programmes to replinish them;
3. Problem of non-tribals migrating and collecting *beedi* leaves by force;

4. Depletion of medicinal plants, roots and tubers, and small games due to clearance of bushes for commercial forestry;
5. Restrictions imposed on shifting cultivation;
6. Threat to shifting of habitations;
7. Cumbersome rules in the payment of compensation;
8. Denial of fishing rights in water sources located in sanctuary areas;
9. Boundary disputes for land under agriculture;
10. Non-declaration of forest enclosures in Chenchu areas as Revenue Villages, thus denying the basic facilities, funds for development, and sometimes even the right to vote in elections;
11. Problems in collection of wood for construction, grazing of animals and collection of fire wood; and
12. Restrictions imposed on extending infrastructure, like roads, electrification, drinking water, school, health centres etc.

Not only in Andhra Pradesh, but also throughout the country, there are protests and agitation against these Acts, resulting in the change in the policy by the Government of India. The National Forest Policy of 1988 offered several concessions, but not without prescribing lengthy procedures for availing these concessions. The salient features of the Forest Policy of 1988 are:

1. Meeting the basic needs of the people, especially fire wood, fodder and small timber, for the rural and tribal people;
2. Maintaining the intrinsic relationship between forests and tribals and the poor people living in and around forests by protecting their customary rights over the forest; and
3. Involving people for the protection and regeneration of forests.

Impact of the New Policy

The important aspect to be noted here is that the tribals who lost their rights over forest after the British Act of 1878, more than a hundred years ago, have now been officially recognized as partners in progress. Their intrinsic relationship with forest has been ultimately recognized. But by this time, enough destruction has already been done to forests. Depletion of natural resources has its adverse impact on the tribal economy, as well as on the national economy. The worst sufferers are the MFP gatherers, as MFP yielding trees have gradually vanished from the forest.

As a follow up of the Forest Policy of 1988, Government of Andhra Pradesh evolved a policy of Joint Forest Management (JFM) through village-level associations, called Vana Samrakshna Samithi (VSS). The VSS consists wholly of Scheduled Tribes in Scheduled Areas. Two most important aspects of this policy are: (1) the tribals have 100 per cent share in MFP; and (2) 50 per cent share in the forest produce protected and grown by the VSS concerned. This policy gave larger scope for participation of tribals in the forestry related activities for their present as well as future benefit. However, the forest officials (especially those at the cutting edge) are yet to change their 'mind set' that they are the *de facto* owners of the forest. Their job is to protect the forest, but not to develop it for the people. Another important aspect that needed change is the attitude of mutual suspicion between the people and FD. While the forest officials apprehend that tribals are the main destroyers of the forest, the tribals do not trust the foresters for harassing them and denying them their customary right over forest. At this juncture, a lot of interaction to convince the people and training sessions to change the 'mind set' of the forest officials is imperative. For the creation of infrastructure for human resource development, several procedures have reviewed and delays cut down.

The most important development that occurred in the recent years is the 73rd Amendment to the Constitution of India and its extension to the Scheduled Areas. Elections to Gram Panchayats are yet to be held in Andhra Pradesh. However, the Amendment has the provision for ownership rights and powers to manage natural resources, marketing etc. by the Gram Panchayats. Tribals need a lot of education and training to use this powerful tool to their advantage. Hence, only future would tell whether tribes in Scheduled Areas would regain the 'paradise lost'.

REFERENCES

Furer-Haimendorf, C. von (1945), Aboriginal Rebellions in the Deccan, *Man in India*, 25(4).

Govt. of A.P. (1992), A.P. Forests, Facts and Figures — 1992, Hyderabad: Forest Department.

Govt. of India (1982), Report of the Committee of Forest and Tribals in India, New Delhi: Ministry of Home Affairs, Tribal Development Division.

Kapur, M.L. (1979), A Report on Programmes for Weaning Away Shifting Cultivators of Andhra Pradesh — A Study Conducted in Visakhapatnam and East Godavari districts.

Lakshminarasimha, K. (1992), *Forest Laws in Andhra Pradesh*, Hyderabad: Asia Law House.

Sastry, V.N.V.K. (1983), Displacement of PTGs for Rehabilitation of Tiger, Paper presented at XI ICAES, Vancouver.

Sastry, V.N.V.K. (1989), *Between Gond Rebellions*, Hyderabad: Udyama Publishers.

Sastry, V.N.V.K. (1990), Chenchu Food Gatherers and Hunters of Nallamala Forests in South India: Problems of Transition, Paper presented at VI CHAGS, Alaska.

Sastry, V.N.V.K. (1991), *Evolution of Scheduled Areas and Changes in Muttadari System in Andhra Area*, Hyderabad: Tribal Cultural Research and Training Institute.

Sastry, V.N.V.K. (1992), Perpetual Land Problems and New Dimensions of Unrest in Tribal Areas of Adilabad District, Paper presented at the Workshop on Land Reforms in Andhra Pradesh, National Academy of Administration, Mussoorie.

Sharma, B.D. (n.d.), *Forests, Tribal Economy and Regional Development*, New Delhi: Ministry of Home Affairs, Govt. of India.

Singh, Bhupinder (1987), Forest Policy and Tribal Development, Paper presented at the Seminar on Forest Policy and Tribal Development, TCR & TI, Hyderabad.

Tata Consultancy Service (1992), *Forests, Tribal Economy and Regional Development*, New Delhi: Ministry of Home Affairs, Govt. of India.

13

Environment, Health and Nutrition in Tribal India

D. Hanumantha Rao

INTRODUCTION

India has about 68 million tribal population spread all over the hilly areas as per the 1991 Census. They form about 8 per cent of the total Indian population. The tribal population of the country can be broadly divided into three principal territorial zones—the North Eastern Zone, the Central Zone, and the Southern Zone. A small fourth zone consisting of Andaman and Nicobar Islands is in the Bay of Bengal.

The North Eastern Zone consists of the sub-Himalayan region and the mountainous areas of the North Eastern India, east of the Teesta valley and the Jamuna-Padma portion of the river Brahmaputra, inhabited by the tribes like Gurung, Lepcha, Aka, Dafla, Abor-Miri, Mishmi, Mikir, Garo, Khasi and Naga groups. The Central Zone consists of the plateaus and mountainous belts between the Indo-Gangetic basin to the mouth of the Krishna river in the South, populated by Santhal, Munda, Oraon, Ho,

Savara, Baiga and Bhil etc. The Southern Zone comprises of the peninsular India falling south of the river Krishna, inhabited by the tribes, Toda, Urali, Kanikkar and Chenchu etc. The small fourth zone is inhabited by the Nicobarese, Onge, Jarwa, and North Sentinelese.

However, a great majority of them inhabit the central mountainous belt formed by the Satpura and Vindhya ranges, which stretch across the state of Madhya Pradesh and the contiguous states of Orissa and Andhra Pradesh on the South East, Gujarat and Maharashtra on the West and South-West, and Uttar Pradesh on the North. There is enormous variation in the type of social organization and religious activities of these tribal groups.

The Garo and Khasi of Northern Himalayan region are matriarchal, whereas the rest are patriarchal. Most of the tribes have well-defined traditional village councils to administer justice. The literacy level is very low. Ethnologically some of the tribal groups are well studied, while groups like the Jarwa and North Sentinelese are only recently been approached by the anthropologists and development administrators. The languages spoken by these tribes could be classified into three groups — the Dravidian, Austric and Sino-Tibetan.

The ecosystems in which these tribal groups live are also varied. The patterns of settlement, the land ownership system, production of crops and their distribution, the demographic and socio-cultural aspects are also influenced by the ecological condition. All these factors, in turn, influence the health and nutritional status of the tribal groups. In this paper, an attempt has been made to review the studies conducted on the nutritional situation and their correlates by National Institute of Nutrition (NIN) among different tribal groups. The purpose was to highlight the influence of ecology on the demographic, socio-economic and cultural conditions, and their combined effect on their health and nutritional status.

Materials and Methods

The National Institute of Nutrition (NIN) had carried out nutritional surveys in some selected tribal groups. These included clinical surveys for nutritional deficiency signs by trained public health medical men (Jelliffee 1966) and anthropometric measurements as per standard preocedures (Weiner and Lourie 1969). The dietary intake studies of the whole family and individual members were carried out by 24 Hour Recall Method (intake of the previous day by oral questionnaire method). The information on ecosystem and other related factors were collected both by interviewing the local people and observation of the local situation. The studies were not carried out simultaneously. So the seasonal variations among the different tribal groups could not be taken care of.

These tribal groups could be broadly classified into four categories:

1. Typical hunter-gatherers, viz., the Onge of Little Andaman.
2. Forest dependent and subsistence agriculturists, viz., the Chenchu of the Nallamalai forest in Andhra Pradesh.
3. Subsistence agriculturists and shifting cultivators, viz., the Savara of Srikakulam district of Andhra Pradesh, the Koya Dora of East Godavari district of Andhra Pradesh.
4. Settled agriculturists and commercial horticulturists, viz., the Nicobarese of the Nicobar Islands.

Ecosystem

The Onge inhabit the Little Andaman Island in the Andaman and Nicobar Islands. Their population is around 100, spread over a 300 sq.mile area of dense forest intervened by creeks. Ethnically, they belong to the Negrito stock. The women have steatopygea. They are nomadic and have not adopted any form of agriculture or horticulture. They move in a group of 3-4 consanguineous or affinal families. Their main source of food is from hunting, fishing and gathering. The Onge term for fish is *cioghe*, which means 'food' and this indicates that fish might have been their staple long before the appearance of other animals on the Little Andaman (Swaminathan *et al* 1971).

The Chenchu are basically hunters and food gatherers like the Onge, reaping only what the nature provide them. A Mohammedan army personnel in 1694, as quoted in Ferishta's

History of Deccan recorded, 'Their common food is honey, the roots of trees, plants and the flesh of animals caught during hunting'. This is also borne out by their use of bamboo vessels and gourds for cooking and eating, and leather bags for carrying water. They lived under trees and in rock shelters. The remains of ruined towns, forts, temples, and a number of wells and tanks at certain places in the Chenchu habitat of Amarabad plateau in the Nallamalai forest indicate that some people from the plains invaded the area during the last Hindu kingdom of the Deccan (Furer-Haimendorf 1943). After the invaders had left the area, the Chenchu settled down around the areas of wells and tanks and started cultivation of Indian corn and some vegetables on small plots. They started domestication of animals purchased in exchange for large quantities of minor forest produce, collected by them and sold to the people from the plains nearby. They used the animals for transportation of minor forest produce. The Chenchu like the Chimbu of New Guinea and Cameroon Massa (de Garine 1972) do not kill these animals for food. They do not either use them as symbol of wealth to procure spouses. The animal dung served as manure for the small patches of jowar, maize and ragi fields cultivated with the help of a digging stick, and off late by plough cultivation, with the use of domestic animals. Some of them have started milking them. Now some of the Chenchu work as farm servants, night watchmen for standing crops of neighbouring non-tribal landlords, and others as forest contract labourers and Government servants. With the improvement in communication (opening up of their habitats by laying roads etc.), many non-tribal groups have made their way into the Chenchu inhabited areas. With the dwindling of the forest cover and their food resources, the Chenchu have been facing acute hardship in sustaining themselves. Immigration of non-tribal groups has compounded their problems as they cannot compete with them.

The Savara inhabit the agency tracts of Srikakulam district of Andhra Pradesh, bordering the state of Orissa. They have been traditionally shifting cultivators. Food gathering and hunting also play important roles in their economy. Most of the fertile land surrounding their villages have been taken over by the non-tribals and now they work as agricultural labourers on their own land.

The Nicobarese are traditionally settled agriculturists-commercial horticulturists. They have coconut and arecanut plantations all over the circular island, the fruits of which they market through well organized, self-managed cooperative societies. They do not cultivate any of the cereals or millets, such as, paddy or jowar. They grow pandanus (screw pine), banana, papaya (*Carica papaya*) and a variety of tubers in their plantations. They also raise pigs. As they are surrounded by the sea, they do fishing for self-consumption. They buy their requirements of rice, wheat, pulses, sugar, tea, coffee etc. and clothing from their cooperative stores, through which they also sell their plantation products. Majority of them embraced Christianity and the religious head has been from among them. He has been an effective force behind the cohesive social and economic organization of the Nicobarese.

Settlement Pattern

The Onge are nomadic and move from place to place in search of food, aş they being neither horticulturists nor agriculturists—primitive or advanced (Table 13.1). They live in circular low roofed communal huts at different places and occupy them only for certain periods depending on the availability of food. The entire group comprising of 3-4 families cook, eat and sleep in the same hut. They sleep on raised wooden or bamboo platforms arranged in a circular form inside this communal hut.

Table 13.1: Settlement Pattern of Tribal Groups

Tribe	*Settlement Types*
Onges	Communal huts occupied by 4-5 families.
Chenchus	Scattered hutments of 20-50 families, sometimes 4-5 also occupied by nuclear families.
Savaras	Barrack type/individual homes occupied by nuclear families.
Nicobarese	Individual houses in a cluster to live and a common kitchen to partake food.

The Chenchu settlements consist of 20 to 50 scattered huts. Similar settlements consisting of 4 to 5 families are also known.

The Savara settlements are of the barrack type, where upto 40 families live. Some of the Savara families occupy temporary sheds near the shifting cultivation plots. Other tribes like the Koya Dora and the Gond live in individual houses.

The Nicobarese joint family allocates the married couples with independent houses, and the unmarried live in a common hut. Food is cooked for all the members in one hearth and all of them take food from the same kitchen.

Thus, the settlement pattern of these communities is moulded by its economic system.

Land Ownership

Onges do not exercise any absolute right of land ownership as there is no dearth of land for the members of the society (Table 13.2). By convention and for convenience, different groups move along different creeks. On the other hand, Chenchus and Savaras have acquired absolute ownership on the land cultivated by them. Although among Savaras no ownership right is vested with the cultivators of *podu* fields, there is no incidence of encroachment of the fields from the neighbours. Minor Forest Produce is freely collected from the forest. However, individual families have established right over toddy palms. The right of ownership over the plantations is held by joint families among the Nicobarese; since the plantation land is held as one single piece, all the members of the joint family work on it.

Table 13.2: Land Ownership of Tribal Groups

Tribe	*Land Ownership*
Onges	No absolute ownership rights of the vast forest.
Chenchus	Individual ownership of cultivated land, territorial rights for forest produce, by convention.
Savaras	Individual ownership of cultivable land and *podu* fields, freedom for collection of forest produce.
Nicobarese	Joint family ownership.

Food Production, Procurement and Quality

Food procurement (and for that matter production) techniques play a key role in the economic organization of the simple societies (de Garine 1972). Onges do not grow or produce any food crops. Low population density in the Little Andaman

Island allows the Onge to hunt for sustenance, as in the case of Mussey of Chad and Cameroon (de Garine 1980). They catch fish and turtle in the creeks, collect roots (*Theithekroi* and *Gegi*), tubers and honey from the forest, and turtle eggs from the sea shore (Table 13.3). Thus the Onge diet consists largely of animal foods. Cereals are completely absent in their food and the roots, tubers and honey are the main sources of carbohydrates. Thus, the Onge derive the calorie mostly from flesh due to the absence of green leafy vegetables in their diet. The source of Vitamin A is only fish. Chenchus, on the other hand, grow jowar, maize and ragi in small plots owned by them, collect a variety of roots, tubers and green leafy vegetables according to their availability in different seasons. Hunting as a source of food is being discouraged due to forest laws. The freedom of movement of Chenchus is also restricted considerably by the forest regulations. Thus, the Chenchu derive their calories from jowar, millets, and green leafy vegetables are the main source of vitamins.

Table 13.3: Production and Procurement of Food

Tribe	*Food Production & Procurement*
Onges	Only hunting, fishing and food gathering.
Chenchus	Incipient cultivation of available and, food gathering and hunting.
Savaras	Cultivation — permanent and shifting.
Nicobarese	Commercial horticulture, fishing and piggery — sale and procurement through cooperative stores.

The Savara and other tribal groups of Srikakulam and East Godavari districts obtain their staple food, such as, jowar, maize, bajra, and rice from the *podu* fields and from the rainfed land cultivated with simple agricultural implements and techniques. In some villages with the facility of irrigation, the tribes have started raising paddy as a single crop. A variety of green leafy vegetables, roots and tubers, fruits, flowers of Mohua (*Bassia latifolia),* and Minor Forest Produce like Tamarind (*Tamarindus indica*), Adda (*Bauhinia vahlii*) and nuts are collected from the nearby forest for sale. Hunting is limited to small game, jungle fowls only. Protein and calorie requirements are derived primarily from cereals and millets, and vitamins from green leafy vegetables and Mohua flowers.

The Nicobarese procure cereals from the cooperative stores. A variety of roots and tubers, bananas, pandanus and papaya are grown in their plantations. Coconuts from the plantations form an important item in their diet. Pork from the pigs reared by them and fish from the sea are the sources of animal protein. Vitamin A is obtained from pandanus and papaya fruits (Satyanarayana *et al* 1974).

Family Characteristics

Although the family size is similar in all the tribal groups studied, their living habits are different. Onges live and move about in small groups of 15-20 members from 3-4 families, related by blood or marriage (Table 13.4). The group movement facilitates hunting and fishing, and provides security from wild animals. Chenchus and Savaras live in nuclear families, while the Nicobarese live in big joint families consisting of as many as 70-80 members, which provide familial labour for the plantation work.

Table 13.4: Family Characteristics in Tribal Groups

Tribe	*Family characteristics*
Onges	Live in groups.
Chenchus	Nuclear families.
Savaras	Predominantly nuclear families.
Nicobarese	Big joint families.

Culinary Practices

The Onge usually steam-cook pork for their consumption. They dig a hole in the ground and fill it with red hot stones, cover it with fresh green leaves and spread the pork over the leaves. They spread a second layer of green leaves and plaster it with mud. The pork is cooked for 3-4 hours. Now, of course, they have started cooking in Kerosene tins thrown off from the moving ships (Table 13.5). No condiments are added. Even salt and pepper are not added. They extract fat pork by prolonged cooking and use it as an additional dish while eating roots and tubers.

Chenchus cook cereals and vegetables and some meat foods by boiling in mud pots or aluminium vessels. During hunting in the forest, the Chenchu hunters roast the birds and small games for eating in the forest itself. Small quantities of Ragi (*Eleusine coracana*) flour is cooked in big mud or aluminium pots with large quantities of water for the preparation of gruel. Salt and chilly are commonly added to this gruel. Seasoning with oil is done occasionally. Similarly, the Savara cook their food with salt and pepper. Use of oil is very rare. Green leafy vegetables are cooked with cereals and millets in the form of a gruel and consumed. The Nicobarese cook a variety of dishes using oil and condiments. Steaming as a way of cooking is very common with them.

Table 13.5: Culinary Practices in Tribal Groups

Tribe	*Culinary Practices*
Onges	Simple boiling of food material without salt and condiments.
Chenchus	Cooking of all food materials with least seasoning. Gruel — Large quantities of gruel from very small amount of ragi flour, tamarind mixed with ash.
Savaras	All food materials cooked with minimum seasoning. Palm toddy and sago gruel consumed in large quantities in off season.
Nicobarese	Advanced type of cooking with a variety of dishes.

Material Culture

The level of technology acquired by a community is determined by the type of material culture it possess and this determines the success of the community in solving its food problem by harnessing its environment (de Garine 1978). The Onge material culture includes bow and arrow for hunting pigs, harpoon for fishing, canoe for catching turtles, and baskets made from wood or cane. They do not have any storage material since they do not store food. The Chenchu material culture includes a digging stick for cultivation, bow and arrow (of late, guns for hunting), basket and rope for honey collection, and a few mud or aluminium vessels for cooking and eating. Recently, they have started using plough for cultivating their land. Savaras use a stick in the *podu* (shifting cultivation) fields and a plough for cultivating the plain land. As they have some surplus food at the time of harvest, they store them in big mud pots or baskets. Better clothing and personal ornaments of aluminium and silver are acquired. The Nicobarese material culture is elaborate. They have acquired the modern gadgets. They have been able to build good houses and are well dressed. Since they harvest coconut and arecanut on commercial scale, they construct store houses. They also use storage bins for storing roots and tubers grown by them for self-consumption. All these changes have come about because of commercialization of the production of coconut and arecanut by the Nicobarese.

Uncertainty in Food Supply

In the past, Onges were not starved in normal days as evidenced by the presence of their steatopygea, which is an indication of the calorie reserve. Non-availability of food in the Little Andamans is because of cyclonic storms or heavy monsoon rains, when Onges are forced to remain indoors. It is noted that it rains for about 280 days in a year in the Andamans. As a number of non-tribals now living in the island have started hunting wild pigs with modern sophisticated weapons, the Onge find it difficult to continue with their hunting activity. In order to adapt to the changing situations, they are now exchanging pork and honey for wheat flour, tobacco etc. with the non-tribals living in the island. Because of these problems, there is some amount of uncertainty in food supply and also changing food habits among the Onge (Table 13.6). The Onge eat as much as they can when the food is available, and go about without it when food is not available. Saving and storing of food is alien to them. Unfortunately, the food they normally eat cannot be stored unlike the cereals. They have not yet taken to horticulture as they do not live in places where the government has raised coconut plantation for settling them permanently. As a result, their nutritional status may worsen in the year to come.

Food availability is restricted by the type of agriculture practiced by the Chenchu. They experience food uncertainty due to the failure of crops, lack of rain, non-availability of roots and tubers etc. Hunting is also restricted because of forest regulations. Some of them have acquired guns for hunting, but they find it difficult to maintain them when the game is scarce. They boil small quantities of ragi flour for preparing gruel and drink it. They mix burnt ash with tamarind to neutralize the acidity and consume it at the time of food scarcity.

Table 13.6: Coping Up with Uncertain Food Supply

Tribe	*Cause of food uncertainty*	*Coping up Strategy*
Onges	Cyclone, non-availability of games, non-tribal influx.	Eat as much as they can when available, storing food materials is alien to them.
Chenchus	Lack of rain, non-availability of games, roots, tubers etc.	Small quantities of ragi flour boiled in large quantities of water to make gruel to fill stomach.
Savaras	Lack of rain, non-availability of games, roots, tubers etc.	Fell sago palm trees. Cut open the trunk, take out the starchy pitch, dry it and store. Grind it to powder and cook gruel out of it. Palm toddy as food in lean seasons.
Nicobarese	Non-supply of cereals from the mainland India	Roots and tubers, pandanus and papaya fruits and pork eaten till supply is resumed.

The Savara and other tribal groups also experience food uncertainty due to crop failure and non-availability of roots and tubers. They grind sago pith into powder and cook into gruel to drink. The palm toddy (*Bassia tari*) forms a major food for them during the lean seasons and they drink upto 1500 ml. of it per day per person.

Food shortage is experienced by the Chenchu and Savara due to the alienation of land, sale of food crops at low rates to the non-tribals, and exchange of food for other non-food items. The Nicobarese, however, can still maintain themselves on pork, roots and tubers, pandanus, papaya and coconut grown by them, when cereals are not brought into the island from outside for any reason.

Nutritional Status

The pattern of deficiency among the tribes is essentially similar to that of the non-tribes (rural population) around urban centres, though the extent is different (Table 13.7). The percentage prevalence of severe forms of protein calorie malnutrition, Vitamin A and B-Complex deficiency is the highest among the Chenchu preschoolers and the least among the Nicobarese. The Vitamin A and B-Complex deficiency signs are either completely absent or negligible among the tribal groups as compared to their non-tribal counterparts in the rural pockets of India.

Table 13.7: Nutritional Deficiencies and Anthropometric Measurements among Pre-school Children

Tribe	*Nutritional Deficiency Signs (%)*				
	One or more signs of PEM	*Vit-A*	*B-complex*	*Height (cm)*	*Weight (kg)*
Onges	0	0	0	75.9	9.1
Chenchus	19.0	3.1	3.2	92.1	9.7
Savaras	10.7	0	0	83.5	9.6
Nicobarese	0	0	1.0	86.6	12.0
Non-tribal	15.0	12.7	7.7	81.3	10.2

The Nicobarese preschool children are taller and heavier compared either to other tribal or the non-tribal rural groups. The percentage of preschool children having body weight deficiency of 40 per cent or more of the American Standard (less

than 60 per cent of standard: Gomez grade III) is only 1.9 per cent among the Nicobarese, while among the Chenchu and Savara it is 16.8 per cent and 22.5 per cent respectively, as against 18.0 per cent among the non-tribal or rural preschool children (Table 13.8). According to Seoane and Letham's classification that indicates the type and duration of malnutrition, 43 per cent of the Nicobarese preschool children are normal as against 14.1 per cent in the rural area, 1.6 per cent among the Chenchu, and 2.0 per cent among the Savara (Table 13.9). The percentage of children suffering from long duration malnutrition is similar in Savaras (69.6 per cent) and Chenchus (66.4 per cent), as compared to the non-tribal groups (48.1 per cent), where as it is much less among the Nicobarese with 20.1 per cent only (Hanumantha Rao 1974). The percentage of preschool children suffering from current short duration malnutrition perhaps due to a severe epidemic of gastro-enteritis just before this survey was very high among the Savara (14.7 per cent) compared to all other tribal groups.

Table 13.8: % Distribution of Pre-school Children according to Gomez Classification

Tribe	*% of American Standard*				
	> 90	*75-90*	*60-75*	*< 60*	*Total*
Onges	*	*	*	*	
Chenchus	0	12.8	70.4	16.8	100
Savaras	0	21.6	55.9	22.5	100
Nicobarese	22.1	52.9	23.9	1.9	100
Non-tribal	3.0	14.0	65.0	18.0	100

*** Small sample size.**

The real extent of malnutrition in a population could be assessed by examining the percent prevalence of both, past chronic malnutrition and current long duration malnutrition. Based on this criterion, 94.4 per cent of Chenchus, 84.8 per cent of Nicobarese preschool children are observed to be malnourished.

The results of diet survey (Table 13.10) indicate adequacy of both calories and proteins among the Nicobarese children. The protein intake in other tribal and non-tribal groups are either deficient or marginally adequate, while the calorie intake was inadequate by about 25 to 35 per cent.

Table 13.9: Classification of Nutritional Status of Children based on Height for Age, Weight for Age and Weight for Height

Tribe	*Nutritional Status*			
	Normal (NNN)	*Current Acute Short duration malnutrition (NLL)*	*Past Chronic malnutrition (LLN)*	*Current Long duration malnutrition (LLL)*
Onges	*	*	*	*
Chenchus	1.6	4.0	28.0	66.4
Savaras	2.0	14.7	13.7	69.6
Nicobarese	43.3	1.9	31.7	20.1
Non-tribals	14.1	1.1	36.7	48.1

* Small sample size.

Note: Heights and weights above third percentile of American values were taken as normal. Weight for height 90 per cent of the standard was taken as normal.

Table 13.10: Nutrient Intake in Pre-school Children

Tribe	*Dietary Intake*	
	Protein (gm)	*Calories (Kcal)*
Onges	*	*
Chenchus	23.2	794
Savaras	18.0	752
Nicobarese	45.0	1475
Non-tribal	17.9	640

* Quantitative data not available.

The Onge adult males and females are the shortest in height (Table 13.11) among the groups discussed here. Savaras are shorter than Chenchus, and the Chenchu adults are comparable with those of the non-tribal groups. The Nicobarese adult males and females are the heaviest, while those of the Onge and the Chenchu are the lightest. Correcting for the height, the body weight for height is the highest among the Nicobarese, comparable with the people in the West and well-to-do Indian adults. The weight for height is the least among Chenchus, thus indicating that they are more severely malnourished campared to other tribal and non-tribal or rural groups.

Table 13.11: Mean Value for Height, Weight and WT/HT² X 100 of Adults of Different Groups

Tribe	Male			Female		
	Ht(cm)	*Wt(kg)*	*Wt/Ht² X 100*	*Ht(cm)*	*Wt(kg)*	*Wt/Ht² X 100*
Onges	149.8	43.2	0.193	140.4	43.0	0.218
Chenchus	160.2	43.7	0.170	149.9	40.6	0.180
Savaras	157.5	45.2	0.182	145.8	37.8	0.178
Nicobarese	158.1	56.3	0.225	149.5	47.2	0.211
Non-tribal	161.7	58.3	0.180	149.5	41.7	0.190

The Nicobarese as a cohesive group remain a relatively isolated and unexploited community. While exploiting the sea and forest resources, they capitalize on commercial crops like coconut and arecanut. They could effectively avoid commercial exploitation by the middle-men by organizing into co-operative societies. They maintain their joint family system, which is conducive to commercial horticultural activity. The economic soundness and indigenous procurement of fish, honey, roots and tubers, and pork through piggery contribute to higher consumption level among them. High rate of literacy also enables them to make the best use of the health facilities. Thus, the Nicobarese are nutritionally better compared to other tribes as well as the rural population.

The Onge, because of larger land mass available, move from place to place. They make use of the forest food available to them in abundance. Hence, they do not take up the activities of growing food either through agriculture or horticulture. The nomadic life which is characterised by group movement, mainly for protection from wild animals, never create the necessity of village settlement for the Onge. Nevertheless, command over large land mass with capacity to provide plentiful of food enable the Onge to stay nutritionally better than others.

The Savara are cultivators, following both shifting type and settled cultivation. However, neighbouring non-tribals encroach their land and perpetual exploitation reduced them to manual labourers on their own land. Poor forest resource base, unremunerative produce from *podu* cultivation, and meagre wage income fail to meet even their basic nutritional requirements, as evidenced from their poor nutritional status.

The Chenchu were traditionally food gatherers and hunters in dense forests, where they enjoyed unrestricted access to forest resources. Hence, their agricultural technology remained simple. But with the advent of forest laws, their movement and exploitative activities were restricted without commensurate earning and opportunities for wage earning. This resulted in a very poor nutritional condition of the Chenchu.

Thus, the study demonstrates the overall role of ecology in determining the socio-economic setting of the population, on which the subsistence and nutritional status depends.

REFERENCES

De Garine, I. (1972), The Socio-cultural Aspects of Nutrition, *Ecology of Food and Nutrition*, 1, 143-163.

De Garine, I. (1980), Approaches to the Study of Food and Prestige in Savannah Tribes - Massa and Mussey of Northern Cameroon and Chad, *Social Sciences Information*, 19 (1), 39-78.

Furer-Haimendorf, C.V. (1943), *The Aboriginal Tribes of Hyderabad, Vol I, The Chenchus*, London: Macmillan Co.

Hanumantha Rao, D. and K. Satyanarayana (1974), Nutritional Status of Tribal Preschool Children of Andhra Pradesh, *Ind. J. Nutr. Dietics*, 2, 328-334.

Jelliffee, D.B. (1966), *Assessment of the Nutritional Status of the Community*, WHO Technical Series No. 53, Geneva: W.H.O.

Satyanarayana, K. *et al* (1974), Nutritional Status of People of Andaman and Nicobar Islands, *Ind. J. Med. Res.*, 62, 662-671.

Swaminathan, M.C. *et al* (1971), Health Survey of the Onge Tribe of Little Andamans, *Ind. J. Med. Res.*, 59(7), 1136-1147.

Weiner, J.S. and J.A. Lourie (1969), *Human Biology — A Guide Book to Field Methods*, International Biological Programme Handbook No. 9, Oxford: Blackwell Scientific Publications.

14

Perceived Environmental Changes and Adaptive Strategies: A Micro Study in the Mica Belt of Andhra Pradesh

N. Sudhakar Rao

INTRODUCTION

The Nellore district of Andhra Pradesh has been experiencing inconsistent rainfall for the last several decades. There is almost consistent loss of income for several households pursuing agriculture as main occupation either due to floods or drought. Those agriculturists who depend on rain fed land have been suffering more from this natural calamity than their counterparts in canal irrigated areas. Furthermore, in the southern part of the district, the agricultural economy has to sustain from the onslaught of mica mining. In this background, the objective of this paper is to examine the perception of people about the changing environmental scenario. It also attempts to understand the adaptive strategies of the people to cope up with the unsteady environment due to inconsistent rainfall and mica mining.

The present study focuses on a village in the mica belt of Nellore district[1], where an intensive anthropological study was conducted during 1990-91. It is a micro study in the sense that the study focuses on a single village and depends on observations and experiences of the researcher. Nevertheless, since this village represents the region of the mica belt, generalizations made here are applicable to the southern part of the district. I shall first describe here briefly the soil types, crops grown etc., after giving a village profile. It will follow a discussion on the rainfall and establishment of mica mines in the area. Then, there will be a description of the environmental changes as perceived by the villagers. Finally, the adaptive strategies to cope up with the environment and concomitant changes that the environment has brought about are discussed.

The Village — Anthatipuram

As a typical South Indian multi-caste village, Anthatipuram, a pseudonym, is inhabited by a total population of 2211 in 1991, divided into 23 castes. About 39 per cent of the households of the village depends on mica mining, 23 per cent on agriculture, including agricultural labour, and 14 per cent lives on non-agricultural labour. More than 8 per cent of the households depends on charcoal making, a relatively new economic pursuit. Only 3 per cent of the households lives on traditional occupations, such as, hair cutting, laundry, priesthood and so on. The remaining households live on service, business and some other non-traditional occupations.

This village comes under Sydapuram Mandalam, a subdivision of the district[2] for administrative purposes. But before 1984, since when the Mandalams had replaced the Talukas, the village was under the Rapuru Taluka. It is connected by road to Sydapuram as well as Podalakuru towns.

Soil Types

The erstwhile Rapuru Taluka was surrounded by the Eastern Ghats on the west, Venkatagiri Taluka on the south, Guduru

Taluka on the east, and Podalakuru Taluka on the north. While the Eastern Ghats (locally called as Rapuru hills) with thick forest, where teak, red sandal wood and other important varieties of trees grow, used to cover some part of the Taluka, a larger portion consisted of undulated terrain with rocky red soil and hillocks. Streams that originate in the Rapuru hills flow down towards the Bay of Bengal at a distance of less than 60 km.

Similar environment exists around the village Anthatipuram. The soils of the village are brick and red soil with pebbles and stones. However, there are some patches of land where intensive cultivation has been practiced. In the native classification, lands are divided into three categories: *metta* or *eli* (dry), *thari* (watered by well), and *magani* (watered by tanks).

Crops Grown

Different varieties of crops are grown in these three categories of land. In dry land, crops like *jowar* (a kind of millets), *bajra* (a kind of millets), *minumulu* (black gram), *pesalu* (green gram), *kusumalu* (a kind of oil seeds), *ulavalu* (horse gram), *kandulu* (chick-beans), *verusanagalu* (peanut), *kothimera* (coriander) and *senagalu* (a kind of beans) are grown. In the land watered by wells, the most often grown crops are: ragi (a kind of millets), *verusenagalu*, vegetables like chilly, tomato, a variety of beans (*chikkudu, anapa, matika* etc.), a variety of gourds (*sora, beera, nethi beera, gummadi* etc.) and a variety of leafy vegetables (*gongura, thotakura, chukkaku, kambalaku* etc.). Recently, lemon and mango gardens are also developed near wells. The lands under tank irrigation are exclusively used for rice cultivation.

Irrigation

The total land under cultivation in Anthatipuram is about 3460 acres, out of which 3256 acres (or 94 per cent) is dry, and 203.26 acres (or 6 per cent) is wet land. The dry land, in fact, includes the land watered by wells also. There are about 28 wells located mostly on south and southwest directions of the village. About 21 wells are owned by the Kamma landlords and 1 by a

Reddy, which were dug some years ago. The remaining are five years old belonging to five Scheduled Caste and Scheduled Tribe households, who dug them with financial support from the state government under development schemes.

There are two reservoirs/tanks, one on the northeast, very close to the village, which is called *oora cheruvu*, and the other on the southwest, one kilometer away, called *pedda cheruvu.* These two tanks receive water from the streamlets formed by rain in the nearby hillocks and uplands. The reservoir near the village is quite large, irrigating a large area, and it always retains water which forms the water source for the Chakalis to do laundry. The other reservoir is small and gets dry in the summer.

Dependency and Perception of Rain

Agriculture primarily depends on monsoon rain, whether the cultivation is done on *metta* or *thari* or *magani* land. According to the notions of the farmers, rain is required at least in two or three spells during the period of cultivation; but not continuously and also not during the off-season. Ideally, the first shower should be in June with a break afterwards, so that the land could be ploughed well, manured and sown with seeds. Rain is needed again in August after the seeds have sprouted and grown a little. One more shower is required after a few weeks. There should not be any rain before the harvest in December or January. What is most important is timely rain, failure of which results in crop failure. Similarly, rain should be adequate, neither too much nor too little.

The cropping pattern closely follows the amount of rain received. When there is sufficient rain at the beginning, groundnut is sown. Under similar conditions, rice is grown near the reservoirs. But if the rain is insufficient, *jowar* is sown with green or black or horse gram, after sometime. In case the rain is far too less, oil seeds or *senagalu* or coriander are sown. Thus, the crop changes according to the amount of rain received. However, near the wells, crops are grown regardless of rain, which are already mentioned. But, the failure of rain affects the entire agriculture, because consecutive shortage of rain causes a lower water table in the wells. The water which springs up in them is not sufficient for the crops. If there is no rain, the reservoirs do not get filled and thus paddy cannot be grown.

Failure of Rain

Every farmer in the village lamented during the study period that agriculture has become a gamble with inconsistent rainfall for several years. Some of the villagers have reduced the extent of agriculture, and some of them have even abandoned it altogether in preference to business or mica mining[3]. The record of rainfall at Rapuru in this region supports this argument of the farmers. Table 14.1 shows very uneven rainfall in the last few years. Rain during 1984-85 and 1987-88 in Rapuru area has been excessive causing damage to the crops. However, the rainfall during 1985-86, 1986-87 and 1988-89 was inadequate. Even 1989-90 was considered to be a drought year.

The kind of erratic rainfall does not confine Rapuru area alone, but the entire district. Reddy, the District Agricultural Officer notes that the Nellore district has been experiencing either excessive or inadequate rainfall for every three or four years for the last ten years. This has caused hardship to the farmers (Reddy 1990). The average rainfall in the district used to be 1043 mm, of which 29 per cent was received during southwest monsoon from June to August, and 63 per cent during northeast monsoon from October to December. The data from 1970 onwards for the district show that the rain has been either far less or excessive (see Table 14.1). Rainfall in 1983-84 and 1985-86 seem to be more than adequate, but, in fact, it was an excessive and unseasonal shower incurring a great loss. A.P. Year Book comments on the 1983-84 rainfall, 'the district was lashed by unseasonal rains damaging crops' in the Nellore district (Anonymous 1985: 168). On the 1985-86 rains it says, 'Cyclone and floods devastated Nellore, Chittoor and Prakasam districts' (Anonymous 1988: 457). In the remaining years, the rainfall has been far below the average.

Table 14.1: Average Rainfall in Nellore District and Rapuru Region (in mm.)

Sl.No.	Year	District	Rapuru Region
1.	1901-70		1002.4
2.	1976-77	925	-
3.	1977-78	-	-
4.	1979-80	989	
5.	1981-82	-	-
6.	1982-83	735	-
7.	1983-84	1127	-
8.	1984-85	1246	1417.7
9.	1985-86	-	874.2
10.	1986-87	807	772.3
11.	1987-88	807	1185.6
12.	1988-89	899	832.0

(*Source*: Ganaka Darsini, Nellore Dist. 1988-89 and A.P. Year Book).

Inconsistent Rain and Fall of Agriculture

The effect of either excessive or shortage of rainfall can be noticed in the extent of land under cultivation. The data on actual land under cultivation for three years in the past thirty years indicates a clearly steady decline of agriculture in Anthatipuram village (see Table 14.2).

Table 14.2: Cultivation of Land in Anthatipuram (in acres)

Sl.No.	Year	Total Cultivable Land		Total Land Under Cultivation			
		Dry	Wet	Dry	%	Wet	%
1.	1970	3256	2014	2014.00	62.0	203.26	10.0
2.	1980	3256	2014	1944.27	60.0	203.36	10.0
3.	1990	3256	2014	1833.17	56.0	10.00	0.5

A reflection of this can be noted from the extent of land under cultivation in the district also. It has been decreasing or at least fluctuating, depending on the rainfall, more significantly in the case of *jowar*. Since the primary crops grown in Anthatipuram are *jowar* and *bajra*, I have noted cultivation of these crops at the district level along with rice, which is the main crop of the district. The production of rice has been growing, because basically rice is grown along canals and large tanks in the district. Production of *jowar* in the district has been steeply decreased, compared to other crops (see Tables 14.3 and 14.4). One can note the fluctuation in case of *bajra* and almost a decreasing trend with regard to *jowar*. On the whole, during the past six years period for which data are available, the dry crop agriculture in the district and in Anthatipuram has been neither constant nor on increase.

Table 14.3: Land Under Cultivation in Nellore District (in acres)

Sl.No.	*Crop*	*1983-84*	*1984-85*	*1985-86*	*1986-87*	*1987-88*	*1988-89*
1.	*Paddy*	590164	473590	519009	498969	519216	578254
2.	*Jowar*	110951	95776	81383	74155	71235	46855
3.	*Bajra*	33217	29263	18635	13635	14837	15002

The above situation has been very discouraging for the farmers in the district in general and Anthatipuram in particular. The total cultivable land or the land which was cultivated before was 3256 acres dry and 2014 acres wet in the revenue village, under which Anthatipuram is a hamlet. The percentage of land under cultivation during three years in a span of thirty years shows significant decrease in both dry and wet land cultivation. Among the Kamma landlords, who owned 55 per cent of land in the village, 12 per cent of them have given up agriculture totally. 68 per cent of them are cultivating small portions, and largely growing lemon gardens. Among the Reddys, the next main cultivating group (6.4 per cent), only half of them continue to live on agriculture. One family among the Brahmins and a few among the lower castes and untouchables still depend on agriculture. This situation is further aggravated due to mica mining in the area.

Table 14.4: Production of Main Crops in Nellore District (in Metric Tons)

Sl.No.	*Crop*	*1983-84*	*1984-85*	*1985-86*	*1986-87*	*1987-88*	*1988-89*
1.	*Paddy*	316700	366000	459000	431000	526000	557000
2.	*Jowar*	19776	17468	21763	20106	16373	14913
3.	*Bajra*	19702	15024	8545	5581	6443	10875

Mica Mines and Fall of Agriculture

Beginning from 1887 mica industry in this part of the district grew rapidly with 240 leases by 1940 (Prasad 1974; Alluri 1990: 81). Before 1990, while there were 25 mines in the vicinity of Anthatipuram village and 3 more were established later, in 1990-91 only 6 mines were functioning and one was being closed. Though the mica industry gradually fell into evil eyes since 1962 or so, it continued to affect the agriculture to some extent, as labourers always preferred to work in the mica mines because of higher wages.

Out of 25, only 4 mines are located in government land, whereas the rest are in private lands. In 3 mines, the local landlords have partnership in a marginal percentage. Only one of them is functioning now and the rest 2 are already closed down. Most of these mines are located in the north and northwest directions of the village.

An impact of the mica mines on the cultivable land can be noted from well irrigation. As mentioned earlier, most of the wells are located on south and southwest directions of the village. This is due to the fact that digging of wells becomes expensive in north and northwest directions where mica mines are located, because the wells have to go to a great depth. Since the mica mines go more than 200 feet, the water surrounding that area finds way into the mines, which is pumped out regularly. Thus, in order to touch sustainable water table, the wells have to be deep enough. This is not only capital intensive, but also the land cannot retain water in the deeper layers. Because of the mines, several acres of land surrounding the mica mines have become less productive. So, the farmers prefer digging wells away from the mica mines, i.e. mostly in the south and southwest directions of the village.

It is evident from the above description and analysis that the villagers know the changing pattern of rainfall and its consequences by experience. They are also aware of the impact of mica mines on digging wells and agricultural production. Since mica mining has been a source of income by providing value to the land and employment to the people, the problems of mines are not considered as serious in nature. So a pragmatic approach is taken by them to cope up with this predicament. Before the adaptive strategies are examined, it is also important to note the cultural aspects of rain, which direct the behaviour of the villagers.

Rituals of Rain and Production

A majority of the villagers believe that gods control the elements of the universe. It is very important for the villagers to worship female gods, who are considered responsible for rain, good crops and well being of the cattle and human populations. Thus, inconsistent rainfall and crop failure are believed to have been due to interventions of goddesses, who are not pleased with the behaviour of the villagers towards them. One goddess called Kattalamma enshrined on the bank of *oora cheruvu* is worshipped to restrain herself from flooding the village by breaking the bank of the reservoir, when it is filled with rain water. She is also prayed for the bounty of crops. Another goddess called Munindamma enshrined in the northeast area of the village, closely to the reservoir mentioned above, is worshipped annually for granting timely rain and good harvest. But these rituals have been given up in Anthatipuram since a few years, because of economic distress. Traditionally, these rituals are required to be initiated and performed by high caste landlords with the participation of the lower and untouchable castes. Since the landlords have not been able to make enough money through agriculture, they have lost interest in conducting these rituals.

In this connection, mention may be made about two incidences on possession of goddesses in June 1991. This is the time when annual village rituals appeasing the goddesses are celebrated in several villages in this area. Further, during this period, farmers eagerly wait for the rains to come and everyone guesses the prospects of good crops in the ensuing season. At this juncture, two middle low caste women were possessed separately by the village goddesses within a span of ten days. Both of them declared a prophesy that misfortunes and shortage of rainfall were bound to happen in Anthatipuram for the reason that they had been neglected by the villagers. One woman said pointing to the death of a boy in the village and there would be two more unnatural deaths, unless the villagers corrected themselves and offered worship to the goddesses. The woman tried in vain to persuade the village elders to conduct rituals and thus help getting timely rain. Thus, supernatural intervention is considered necessary for timely rainfall in the area. But village elders and educated youth were skeptical about the efficacy of these rituals. So they ignored these warnings with an apathy towards theses goddesses.

There is a practice in this part of the country to pour water on a frog, which is believed to cause rainfall. Since rain did not come even by the end of June in 1991, a few women and children of a neighbouring village visited Anthatipuram with a basket containing a small frog covered by *neem* leaves. The basket was carried to every house and songs were sung pleading the rain-god to shower. After collecting alms, the rain-god and the goddess of water, Gangamma, were worshipped at a well in the village. Several pitchersful of water was drawn from the well and poured on the frog that was sitting in the basket, as a symbolic action of downpour. Thus, the ritual actions are part of the agricultural activity which is tied up with rainfall. The villagers perceive rainfall having a relationship between humans and gods and the cause of failure of rain is in the disrupted relations.

Coping up with Inconsistent Rainfall

Along with pleasing gods and goddesses as an attempt to restore normal rainfall, the villagers also try to cope up with the harsh drought and unseasonal rain by developing a variety of adaptive strategies. While no attempt could be made to protect the crops from damaging unseasonal rain, the villagers did try to withstand the shortage of rainfall. The farmers wanted to cultivate those crops which require less water, such as, tobacco. Beginning from 1975, tobacco was cultivated in about 200 acres for five years. But this had to be given up later on as it failed, though it was successful in the first two years. Next attempt was to reduce the area of cultivation, but develop intensive cultivation in small areas. Growing lemon gardens was thought to be an appropriate strategy. Thus, since 1980, about 215 acres were brought into lemon gardens around the wells by either deepening them or by installing bore wells. Attempts were made in 1991 to grow tamarind and soap nut which can withstand drought conditions. Consistent efforts have been made by the villagers to adapt themselves to the changing environment.

Concomitant Changes

The nature seems to have its own way to vandalize, and at the same time to provide an alternate means of recourse for human sustenance. Growth of a wild thorny bush (*thumma chettu*) stands as an irony in this context. About 40 per cent of the cultivable land was left fallow in Anthatipuram during 1990-91, which became fertile for this wild growth. It could grow profusely with limited amount of rain water and did not die when there were floods or heavy rain.

Over the years, the bushes have even changed the appearance of the village itself with their thick growth. Even though the thorns are quite troublesome when they prick, but many people are not averse to these bushes because of their utility. These bushes are used as fence to the houses of the poor and to the agricultural fields. Several poor people used the dried branches of the bush as firewood. It has now become a source of income for the landlords who did not invest anything on it; a blessing in disguise while they suffer from drought. Since these bushes grow within a period of three years when cut at the trunk, there is no need for plantation. When the bushes are sufficiently grown, the landlords either auction or employ labourers to cut down and transport to their homes. The best use of this bush is to make charcoal. However, it must also be pointed out that the farmers do realize the harm done by these bushes to the agricultural land. They believe that since total uprooting of the bushes is very difficult, the land cannot be reclaimed easily, if needs arise, and favourable conditions for cultivation set it. But they are neither optimistic nor pessimistic of the future.

Similar to the landlords, poor farmers and landless agricultural labourers are benefited by this wild growth. They convert them into charcoal which has a good market in the towns. Charcoal was used to be made of entirely forest wood, but is now partially substituted by this wild growth. It is because of the fact that nearby forests are denuded, and also it is an offence to cut forest. As an alternative energy to firewood, kerosene and cooking gas, charcoal serves a good purpose. It is also widely used by washermen for ironing clothes, tea shop keepers for making tea and coffee, and blacksmiths and goldsmiths in their respective works.

As mentioned earlier, more than 8 per cent of the households in the village are engaged in charcoal making. This work provides higher wages compared to agricultural labour. The daily wage for a male agricultural labourer is Rs. 15, whereas for a charcoal labour it is Rs. 20. Further, since charcoal making is usually done on a contract basis, the labourers enjoy freedom of work. They can work whenever they want in a fixed number of days.

Those involved in charcoal making need to obtain a lease for three years from the revenue office by paying a fee of Rs. 200 per acre of land growing thorny bushes. The lease holders are usually from rich high castes who can invest money, and most of them do not belong to this village. After obtaining a contract from the landlord (for about Rs. 100 or so per annum) to cut the bushes, the entrepreneur applies for a lease from the revenue office. Then he employs three or four labourers either on daily wages or on a contract basis to cut the bushes into small pieces of one and a half or two feet size, and keep them under the sun to dry. Before the wood is completely dry, these are stacked in a heap, around which some more pieces are closely arranged in a vertical position. Some hay and cow dung cakes are spread around the heap of semi-dry wood pieces, and then a film of mud is applied over the heap. At one place, a gap is left to light the wood. After it is set on fire, the gap is closed, so that the fire does not go out. In three or four days, the wood becomes charcoal, which is lifted in sack bags and transported to the towns. The wood from one acre of land fetches around Rs. 2000 in one year, where the investment is about Rs. 500 apart from the lease amount. Thus, in three years there is an income of Rs. 4500 approximately.

The entrepreneurs in this case hail from Guduru or Podalakuru, where it is mostly marketed, but sometimes it is transported to Nellore or Chennai by train or by truck. The Kamma landlords of this village are not interested in this business, mainly because of the labour problem. They argue that it is very difficult to manage with the labourers these days. Unlike in the past, the labourers today are not sincere in their work. Most of the times, they take wages in advance, but either evade work or do not complete it on time. So, the investor has to go round the houses of the labourers requesting them to complete the work, as they cannot repay the advance back to the entrepreneur. This is something the Kamma landlords had never done before. They may even visit the labourers' houses, but cannot tolerate their impolite behaviour, which was not exhibited in the past. If the request fails, the investor either has to complain to the police or else make a physical threat or assault, which the landlords do not like to do now. This way of handling disrupts peaceful relations between the landlords and the workers, and the landlords are afraid that this will affect their support in an election for a political office. But a stranger from outside the village normally does not care for taking the labourers to task, as neither he is interested in any political office nor does he need the support of the labourers for anything. His relations are contractual and temporal. The relations of the villagers are different in the sense that there is high degree of interdependence between the landlords and the workers.

CONCLUSION

To conclude, the agriculturists in the mica belt of Nellore district in Andhra Pradesh are beset with the problems for several years due to inconsistent rainfall and establishment of mica mines. They perceive environmental changes by experience and attempt to cope with these changes by developing suitable adaptive strategies. Several villagers believe that supernatural intervention is necessary for timely rain. The frequent droughts necessitate the farmers to leave large chunks of land fallow, where wild thorny bushes grow. Though the wild growth has come as a boon for the poor, the landlords feel depressed of the land left barren. The farmers are impassive toward agriculture due to the changing environment caused by inconsistent rainfall and establishment of the mica mines.

NOTES

1. It extends from Vindyaram, 16 km south of Gudur town on the grand trunk road to Udayagiri, covering an area of 1500 sq.km.
2. There are 46 subdivisions called Mandalams for revenue as well as development purpose in the district.
3. Here it must also be mentioned that mica mines contributed to the fall of agriculture in Anthatipuram. Further, abandonment of traditional patron and client relationships between the landlords and the service castes also created disadvantage for agriculture (see Rao 1997).

REFERENCES

Alluri, R. Reddy (1990), Nellori zillalo mica ganulu (Mica Mines in Nellore district), in N. Sriramamurthy (Ed.) *Jaminraithu Diamond Jubilee Publication 1930-1990,* Nellore: Jamin Raithu Press.

Anonymous (1985), *Andhra Pradesh Year Book,* Hyderabad: Govt. of Andhra Pradesh.

Anonymous (1988), *Andhra Pradesh Year Book,* Hyderabad: Govt. of Andhra Pradesh.

Prasad, K.H. (1974), On Nellore Mica Field, in *Souvenir: Seminar on Mica Mining Industry,* Gudur: All India Convention.

Rao, N.S. (1997), Impact of Erratic Rainfall and Mica Mines in a South Indian Village, *Journal of Human Ecology,* 8 (5), 339-346.

Reddy, P. (1990), Vysvasayakanga Nellore (Nellore in Agriculture), in N. Sriramamurthy (Ed.) *Jaminraithu Diamond Jubilee Publication 1930-1990,* Nellore: Jamin Raithu Press.